Vision and Supervision

Supervision in analytical psychology is a topic that until recently has been largely neglected. *Vision and Supervision* draws on archetypal, classical and developmental post-Jungian theory to explore supervision from a variety of different avenues.

Supervision is a critical issue for therapists in many training programmes. Quality of training and of therapeutic treatment is paramount, and increasingly the therapy profession is having to devise ways of assessing and monitoring themselves and each other. In this book, Dale Mathers and his contributors emphasise a model of supervision based on parallel process, symbol formation and classical Jungian analysis rather than developmental psychology or psychoanalytic theory, to show how respect for diversity can innovate the practice of supervision. Divided into three parts, this book covers:

- the framework of supervision, its boundaries and ethical parameters
- individuation
- supervision in different contexts including working with organisations and multicultural perspectives.

Written by experienced clinicians, *Vision and Supervision* brings insights from analytical psychology to the supervisory task and encourages the supervisor to pay as much attention to what does not happen in a session as to what does. It offers a fresh perspective for analysts and psychotherapists alike, as well as other mental health professionals involved in the supervisory process.

Dale Mathers is a Jungian Analyst in private practice. He teaches analytical psychology in the UK and Europe and directed the Student Counselling Service at the London School of Economics. He is a Professional Member of the Association of Jungian Analysts.

Vision and Supervision

Jungian and post-Jungian perspectives

Edited by Dale Mathers

Routledge
Taylor & Francis Group
LONDON AND NEW YORK

First published 2009 by Routledge
27 Church Road, Hove, East Sussex BN3 2FA

Simultaneously published in the USA and Canada
by Routledge
270 Madison Avenue, New York NY 10016

Routledge is an imprint of the Taylor & Francis Group, an Informa business

Copyright © 2009 Selection and editorial matter, Dale Mathers; individual chapters, the contributors

Typeset in Times by Garfield Morgan, Swansea, West Glamorgan
Printed and bound in Great Britain by TJ International Ltd, Padstow, Cornwall
Paperback cover design by Design Deluxe

All rights reserved. No part of this book may be reprinted or reproduced or utilised in any form or by any electronic, mechanical, or other means, now known or hereafter invented, including photocopying and recording, or in any information storage or retrieval system, without permission in writing from the publishers.

British Library Cataloguing in Publication Data
A catalogue record for this book is available from the British Library

Library of Congress Cataloging-in-Publication Data
Supervision of music therapy : Jungian and post-Jungian perspectives / edited by Dale Mathers.
    p. cm.
  Includes bibliographical references and index.
 ISBN 978-0-415-41579-8 (hardback) – ISBN 978-0-415-41580-4 (pbk.)
1. Jungian psychology. I. Mathers, Dale, 1955– II. Association of Jungian Analysts.
  BF175.V547 2008
  150.19'54–dc22
                                                                                   2008014904

ISBN: 978-0-415-41579-8 (hbk)
ISBN: 978-0-415-41580-4 (pbk)

To our supervisors and supervisees

Contents

About the authors	ix
Foreword	xi
MURRAY STEIN	
Acknowledgements	xv

1	Introduction	1
	DALE MATHERS	

PART I
Strange effects at boundaries   11

2	Boundaries: separateness, merger, mutuality	13
	JEAN STOKES	

3	Ethics in supervision	31
	FIONA PALMER BARNES	

4	Difficult patients	47
	DALE MATHERS	

PART II
Individuation   65

5	Individuation	67
	MARTIN STONE	

6	The spirit of inquiry	81
	JACK BIERSCHENK	

7	'Mind the gap': the symbolic container, dreams and transformation CAROLA MATHERS	97
8	Representation, evocation and witness: reflections on clinical scenes and styles of presentation RICHARD WAINWRIGHT	113

PART III
The collective 131

9	Working with organisations JAMES BAMBER	133
10	Seeing the point of culture BEGUM MAITRA	146
11	'Spooky action at a distance': parallel processes in Jungian analysis and supervision GOTTFRIED HEUER	164
12	Afterword KEVEN HALL	183

Index 191

About the authors

James Bamber PhD Supervisor with Association of Jungian Analysts (AJA) and the Institute of Group Analysis (IGA). Works in the National Health Service (NHS). A chartered counselling psychologist, Director of the Highgate Counselling Centre; formerly a forensic educational psychologist, and Senior Lecturer in educational psychology at Queens University, Belfast.

Jack Bierschenk Past Chair of AJA. Supervisor with AJA and the International Association for Analytical Psychology (IAAP) St Petersburg, Russia Developing Group. Formerly Assistant Director of Peper Harow. Interested in the relationship between community and the individual realised through connection with the Luethi-Peterson Camps and the Ecole d'Humanité in Switzerland.

Keven Hall PhD, BD, AKC, Member of AJA, supervisor and in private practice in London Bridge. Formerly worked in the NHS in West London. Graduate in arts and sciences from the universities of Auckland, New Zealand, and King's College London, UK, where he has taught, researched and practised in human development, counselling and education.

Gottfried Heuer PhD Training Analyst and Supervisor with AJA, Neo-Reichian body psychotherapist, numerous lectures and publications on the links between analysis, radical politics, body psychotherapy and spirituality, and on the history of analysis. Graphic artist, poet and photographer. Chair of the International Otto Gross Society (IOGS).

Begum Maitra MB, BS, MRCPsych, MD. Consultant in Child and Adolescent Psychiatry. Researcher, trainer and supervisor on matters relating to culture and families and particularly as these influence legal considerations about the welfare of children. On the Board of Advisors of the Centre for Research on Nationalism, Ethnicity and Multiculturalism (University of Surrey).

Carola Mathers MB, BS, MRCPsych. Chair of the AJA Training Committee, in private practice. Formerly a member of the Society of Analytical Psychology, London, organised its supervision course in Cambridge. Training therapist and supervisor for psychosynthesis groups, member of British Association of Psychodynamic Psychotherapy Supervisors (BAPPS). Seminar leader for several psychotherapy trainings in London. Formerly Consultant Psychotherapist, St George's Mental Health NHS Trust. Artist.

Dale Mathers MB, BS, MRCPsych. Member of AJA and BAPPS, in private practice. Psychiatrist, psychologist, teaches analytical psychology in the UK and Europe. Directed the Student Counselling Service at the London School of Economics and was a Mental Health Foundation Fellow at St George's Hospital, London, researching addiction. Writer.

Fiona Palmer Barnes Supervisor with AJA. Involved in working with ethical concepts and their consequences over twenty years, writing codes of ethics and practice, and chairing ethics committees for AJA, the British Association for Counselling and Psychotherapy (BACP) and the United Kingdom Council for Psychotherapy (UKCP). Liaison to the IAAP developing group in Poland. Runs staff support groups at two London hospitals.

Jean Stokes MA Supervisor with AJA, member of BAPPS. Psychoanalytic psychotherapist member of FPC (Westminster Pastoral Foundation). Training supervisor with other London psychotherapy trainings. Extensive supervising experience in psychotherapy, counselling and previously in teaching.

Martin Stone Past Chair of AJA. Supervisor with AJA. Joint organiser and supervisor for the IAAP training programme in Moscow. Interests include the mind–body interface, synchronicity, complex theory and typology.

Richard Wainwright Member of AJA and the Foundation for Psychotherapy and Counselling (FPC). Supervises for several psychotherapy organisations. Formerly Senior Lecturer in Drama Therapy at the University of Hertfordshire. Lectures internationally on the interface of artistic and analytic practice.

Foreword

Murray Stein

Gradually, since the early 1990s, an important body of literature has been taking shape within the world of analytical psychology around the theme of supervision, a topic that had been largely neglected before this time. Two collections of essays (Kugler 1995; Wiener et al. 2003) and many journal articles with a specific or tangential focus on this topic have been published by now, and these represent only the tip of an iceberg if one thinks of all the seminars, discussions and meetings that have been held on this theme in recent years. The chapters in this volume represent one such series of seminars. Nowadays, there is little room for doubt that supervision is a 'critical issue' in therapist circles. Certainly it is a lively topic of discussion in many Jungian societies and training programmes.

Supervision is an issue that arises with ever increasing energy and urgency as the realisation of what is at stake becomes evident. Fundamentally, the key question, which demands the kind of deeply considered responses represented in the present collection, circles around the quality of therapist training and therapeutic treatment in the contemporary cultural settings where these are being conducted, and within that frame a bright light is directed to the responsibility of the therapy profession to the public for services it offers and renders. These are grave matters.

Vision and Supervision marks an advanced stage in this collective elaboration of thinking about supervising, about being supervised, and about the training of supervisors, including the supervision of supervisors. The chapters in this volume extend the parameters of the discussion by introducing reflections on nearly every conceivable facet of supervision. For instance, there is the inevitable question about veracity that nags at one whenever a student (or experienced and fully qualified therapist, for that matter) puts together 'cases' for presentation (an epistemological quagmire) to a supervisor. The contributors also consider the equally inevitable conflict between the requirement for confidentiality in therapy and the intrusion of the supervisor's presence (often noted unconsciously by the patient). Then there is the paradox that every person is different and yet similar to many other 'cases' and the ethical imperative for supervision and the ethical imperative for freedom from external authority and control in a therapist's and patient's work together, and the new entry of supervision into the collective, that is into multicultural settings and organisational work. The chapters in this volume are full of zest and imagination, and they manage at once to capture much of the urgency, the excitement and the challenge of the questions that face the therapy profession in the present multifaceted, multicultural, multidisciplinary world. They also display appropriate humility, I am happy to add.

The issue of supervision first appears in training. The training of new therapists, at least in the Jungian world, is generally managed in a complex series of stages that build upon three foundations: the personal life experience and analysis of candidates-in-training (all training programmes require many hours of personal analysis before and during training); the mastery of psychological theories and other intellectual materials from a variety of sources, which takes place in classroom seminars, through preparation for examinations, and in various additional ways; and (most importantly for this present volume) the careful, but also creative and imaginative, supervision of candidates' clinical work as they train to become therapists. The chapters in this book focus on the third of these, though they touch as well on the other two.

The entire weighty enterprise of training therapists, and then of course too of maintaining the quality of services offered by them after they graduate, must above all else be seriously and conscientiously dedicated to the vision of sound practice and social responsibility. Present-day training institutes are keenly aware of the responsibility for promoting and maintaining this vision and the standards that support it as never before due to legal and other collective pressures that have come powerfully into play in recent times worldwide. The primary rationale for the great amount of energy expended in training programmes is to ensure that the applicants who are allowed to enter and to pass through them, and eventually to become inscribed in the registers of professional societies, are well grounded in the depth psychological traditions and are, above all, competently prepared to serve their patients' best psychological, social and spiritual interests.

All the efforts put into training would be indefensible if training programmes lost their orientation to service, that is, if they were geared only to preparing students to make good incomes for themselves or to elevating their self-esteem by being able to call themselves 'analysts' or 'professional psychotherapists'. Training cannot be ethically justified if it is geared only to the personal benefit of the persons undergoing training, or to keeping the practices of their trainers filled, or to enhancing the status or viability of the training institutes in which they study and function afterwards. Training must be geared to service, that is, to providing the best possible psychotherapeutic assistance for those individuals who need and ask for it, and through that means to enhancing the benefit of patients' improved psychological functioning to the families and the societies in which they live. At bottom, healthy (enough) individuals are needed for healthy societies and healthy societies for a saner humanity in general, which is now commonly known to be at great risk of losing its footing on the planet that has given it the chance for life.

Psychotherapists work principally with individuals, it is true; but it is our conviction that these individuals can make a difference in society and in the world at large. Of course, therapists want above all to help individuals to live a better, fuller, more creative life for themselves, but the well-being of the whole of humanity also depends on a significant minority (at least) of balanced, conscious individuals making small or large, but steady and significant, contributions to the general welfare. So, as therapists we work not only for ourselves and our individual patients, but also in a limited and yet quite precise way for the whole of humankind.

The reflections on supervision contained in this volume demonstrate keen awareness and respect for the point of view that therapy and therapists must be held accountable, but they do this without becoming heavy-handed and weighed down with moralistic attitudes. This is a blessing. Supervision can so easily become superego-ism. Here the reader will find it described as anything but. Nevertheless, accountability is, necessarily, what supervision is all about. And it is pertinent not simply to the period of training. Experience and wisdom teach that good practice requires not only good training in the first instance but also ongoing learning and increasing consciousness throughout one's career as a therapist. In this, too, supervision plays a key role. Through supervision, an individual therapist finds a deep and abiding connection to community and tradition as well as to innovation and new perspectives on the work.

The book as a whole is aimed importantly as well at the newly emergent issue of training supervisors, and so at lifting up the most important considerations in the supervision of training candidates as well as graduated therapists. To be allowed or qualified to do supervision, it might be thought, is a second leg in the journey from graduate therapist to fully fledged training therapist. To become a supervising therapist in the present-day professional climate has come to require a further level of training beyond what one receives normally in the course of training to become a therapist. This additional stage of preparation and training should be counted as a sign of increasing maturity in the field. The training of supervisors and the supervision of supervisors represent a new and more acute degree of awareness and ethical responsibility among therapists actively engaged in the education of the next generations. Previously, it frequently had been considered good enough if a therapist had logged in five to seven years of experience after graduation before automatically taking up the role of supervisor of candidates-in-training. This is no longer deemed to be good enough. The training of new supervisors, conducted by other more senior and experienced supervisors, helps to secure high standards and the best of the depth psychological tradition.

Nowadays, too, it is strongly recommended and in some cases even required that qualified therapists remain in supervision, or 'intervision' with colleagues, throughout their careers. The insight behind this new development is that the complex dyadic relationship formed in deep psychotherapy poses a significant enough threat of regression and loss of professional consciousness to even the most savvy and experienced of therapists that this additional requirement in postgraduate clinical work is a reasonable prophylactic. It was naive, it is now recognised, to suppose that well-trained and experienced therapists could maintain their level of consciousness under any and all clinical conditions. Earlier, it would have been insulting to think otherwise. But the opposite has been found to be the case in too many instances for comfort, and serious misjudgements and clinical failures due to therapists' loss of professional consciousness have been noted in nearly every professional association. Therefore, establishing the principle that no one is immune to regression and loss of consciousness and therefore should remain in contact with some sort of supervisory body or with an individual supervisor seems both hygienic and sane. This recommendation also adds further substance to the generally accepted rule requiring ongoing professional education for therapists at even the most advanced stages and ages of professional life.

So it is with great pleasure that I recommend these highly instructive and imaginative chapters to anyone engaged in the training of depth psychotherapists or for that matter to anyone interested in learning about the supervisory perspective for whatever reason. The chapters are invariably challenging and bear well and with style the load of much insight and experience. They are especially a gift to the field of analytical psychology, for which I am personally very grateful.

Zurich, December 2007

References

Kugler, P. (ed.) (1995) *Jungian Perspectives on Clinical Supervision*. Einsiedeln, Switzerland: Daimon.
Wiener, J., Mizen, R. and Duckham, J. (eds) (2003) *Supervising and Being Supervised*. London: Palgrave Macmillan.

Acknowledgements

For help in reading and improving the texts: Jean Carr, Ann Casement, Johanna David, Damien Doorley, Moira Duckworth, Jennifer Forssander, Elena Hinshaw-Fischli, Birgit Heuer, Marjorie Hudson, Meenakshi Krishna, Julienne McLean, Alan Mulhern, Amelie Noack, Lynda Norton, Adam Phillips, Michele Roberts, Franziska Rymel-Nye, Claudia Salazar, Elisabeth Sutherland, Mary Travis, Ruth Windle.

For editorial help and support: Jane Harris, Kate Hawes.

Front cover illustration

'Holding the child Courage', by Lindsey Harris. Oil pastel. Lindsey Harris is a Jungian analyst, and member of the Association of Jungian Analysts. A former practising artist, she values artistic expression as a therapeutic process towards inner psychological and spiritual transformation. She has a private analytic practice in Hereford.

Permissions

Glen Baxter for generous permission to reprint his drawing on page 95. Routledge and Princeton University Press, for permission to quote from the *Collected Works of C. G. Jung* (1953–1973) ed. Sir H. Read, M. Fordham, G. Adler and W. McGuire, 20 vols. London: Routledge & Kegan Paul, © 1971 Princeton University Press (1999 renewed PUP). Reprinted by permission of Princeton University Press. For permission to use an extract from 'Intuition', © copyright 1983, the Estate of R. Buckminster Fuller.

Chapter 1

Introduction

Dale Mathers

> 'Is there any point to which you would wish to draw my attention?'
> 'To the curious incident of the dog in the night time.'
> 'The dog did nothing in the night time.'
> 'That was the curious incident,' remarked Sherlock Holmes.
> Sir Arthur Conan Doyle (1985: 250)

A vision of supervision

Supervisors and therapists can feel like detectives trying to solve impenetrable mysteries. Unlike this duo, a supervisor rarely has a 'cold, precise but admirably balanced mind' like Holmes, nor are our supervisees all warm-hearted *Boy's Own Paper* heroes, like Dr Watson. Conan Doyle based Holmes on a teacher at his medical school, Dr Joseph Bell, an Edinburgh surgeon, to whom is attributed another of Holmes' famous phrases, 'it is a capital mistake to theorise before one has data' (Conan Doyle 1985: 12). An aim of this book is to help us notice when we theorise without data and forget to pay as much attention to what does *not happen* in a session, as to what does. Supervisors use metaphors to hold and contain mysteries, until they can be solved, if they can be.

'The curious incident of the dog in the night time' is a metaphor for things significant because they are not there; of the 'not knowing' we need to 'be with' as supervisors. Conan Doyle's image helps us distinguish between showing and allowing something to be seen, or *not seen*. We need metaphor to contrast languages of knowing with languages of not knowing – that is, any 'theory of supervision' as against the real, lived and felt experience of being in a room with a colleague or colleagues describing being in a room with another human being.

This metaphor was taken up by the bestselling novelist Mark Haddon (2004) in his book of the same name, to describe 'missing affects' – a defining characteristic of his hero, Christopher Boone, a teenage boy with Asperger syndrome. One morning, Christopher finds the corpse of his neighbour's dog impaled by a pitchfork. He decides to investigate. But he gets into problems because he is often unable to put his feelings into words, using 'rational thoughts' instead – theorising, without data, particularly about the feelings and motives of others. As supervisors, we may find ourselves in a similar position; becoming, like Christopher, inarticulate or (usually, internally) aggressive when flooded with seemingly random affects, ranging from the erotic to the murderous. Our task, like detectives, is to work out to whom these fragments of feeling belong, and return them to their owners, transformed (we hope) in and by the process of perception. Our supervisees, as therapists, in their turn, may then be able to allow their patients to do the same: giving them the choice of acting with response-ability, rather than re-acting.

A primary task in therapy and its supervision is to help people give names to things; affects, complexes, transferences and countertransferences. Transference is comprised of affects compressed through time; counter-transference mirrors this both in the therapist and supervisor. An everyday encounter with transference phenomena arises when we create metaphors to help name feelings (discussed in the next section). The opposite task is as important – to recognise when affects cannot be named, or held by a metaphor; if no one is able or willing to take responsibility for them. When this occurs, it is important to recognise it, and stop trying to make sense of the senseless. There are limits to what can realistically be achieved in therapy, and in supervision.

Just as Donald Winnicott, the pioneer of analytic work with children, described the 'good-enough' mother, so there can be 'good-enough' supervision: let us hope this will be far enough away from 'perfect' to be in touch with collective reality. We hope to show how 'good-enough' supervision can be achieved, by creating and maintaining safe reflective space. We may use metaphors from alchemy to do this, such as the *Vas* – the alchemical container – or the *temenos* – from the Greek, meaning the sacred space around a temple. We also use metaphors from our experiences training therapists, such as 'beginner's mind'. In fact, each chapter could be thought of as a set of metaphors – from the metaphor of boundaries (Chapter 2) to the metaphor of parallel process (Chapter 11).

The authors are a diverse group of analysts, holding a wide range of theoretical positions. As the analytical psychologist Rosemary Gordon put it, 'Getting analysts to agree is like herding cats' (personal communication). If the unconscious really were an 'inner world', you could say each of us has explored it and come back with differing myths and maps. Suppose 'the unconscious' is itself a metaphor – neither a place, a thing or an object, but a word which is a useful shorthand for the interaction of billions of neurons? Rather like naming the constellations in the sky, our understanding of what these neurons say to each other is still at the mythological, or metaphorical, level. So, before going further, let's discuss what a metaphor is.

Meta . . . and Metta

The prefix 'meta-', from Greek, means 'after, later, with (implying change . . .) beyond, or above'. A metaphor is 'a figure of speech by which a thing is spoken of as being that which it only resembles, for example, when a fierce person is called a tiger' (Chambers Dictionary). The word comes from the Greek, metapherein, to transfer: meta- 'implying change', combined with -pherein, 'to bear'. A metaphor carries the idea of change, and may help us bear it. It is also 'above, or outside': a meta narrative, for example, might be a description of a novel's plot, or a critical commentary, above, beyond, outside the actual text. Supervision is a 'meta narrative': outside the intimate space between therapist and patient, within which a patient's story is narrated.

(And this paragraph is a meta narrative: there are all kinds of exciting political arguments and rewarding economic implications attaching to terms used for the players in 'the therapy game'. For simplification, and to avoid repetition, we chose to use 'therapist' to mean mental health professional, counsellor, therapist or analyst and 'patient' to mean mental health service user, client, patient or analysand.)

Similarly, metaphysics is the part of philosophy dealing with 'what kind of questions is philosophy able to ask'. In supervision, are our questions Aristotelian, concerned with first causes (the a priori environment) and with being *qua* being; or Kantian, accepting the a priori is unknowable, and that all we can do is make statements about the structure of our thinking about the world (Loux 2007: 1–16). Therapists tend to go pale when philosophy is mentioned, wondering 'what has this to do with patients?'

To show it does, apply these two views of metaphysics to the therapy game. Game is not a pejorative term, it means 'an amusement, played according to a system of rules'. Among the meanings of 'amuse' are 'to beguile with expectation', 'to put into a muse', 'to provoke mirth', in line with Freud's apocryphal but oft quoted remark that 'the goal of analysis is to replace hysterical misery with common unhappiness'. If so for analysis, more so for supervision.

In 'the supervision game', we play with the person receiving the story a person tells about themselves, so the storyteller can make a 'director's cut' – a version of themselves which works better for them, their society and the culture they live in, as amplified by Begum Maitra in Chapter 10. There is no implication here that anything anyone says in therapy or supervision is, or has to be, true or false: it is a story, both true and false, neither true nor false. Therapists make up stories (narratives) to tell supervisors using images drawn from a patient's a priori inner and outer environment (Covington 1995). Supervisors make up fresh narratives, construct images from images, of the therapist's view of the patient.

Supervision is a narrative about a narrative, a myth about a myth, a fable about a fable about a life; a meta narrative, an invitation to muse.

These stories are told in symbols, as discussed by Carola Mathers in Chapter 7. The stories can be descriptions of 'first causes', provided we understand the commonly used developmental and archetypal theories are also narratives told in symbols. Almost by definition, symbols are means of handling the dilemma Kant described – the unknowability of 'reality'. As Jung said, 'A symbol always presupposes that the chosen expression is the best possible description or formulation of a relatively unknown fact, *which is nonetheless known to exist or postulated as existing*' (CW6 para. 814, Jung's italics).

Supervisory stories are intuitions about the structures of the thinking and feeling of at least two other people, about *relatively unknown facts*. It is no novelty to suggest supervision is a metalanguage: a language dealing with what another language is able to say, in this case, the languages of and between a patient and a therapist, between them and a supervisor and between all of these and the collective. Like any language, this metalanguage has a grammar and a vocabulary, as well as differing registers (levels of politeness: see Fiona Palmer Barnes on ethics, Chapter 3). It has an aesthetic: does what is said in it accurately and beautifully enough convey its intended meaning, as explored by Jack Bierschenk in Chapter 6 and Richard Wainwright in Chapter 8.

The essential idea in these 'metas' is that one cannot comment on a system from within. This was described mathematically by Alfred Tarski, as t ϕ l : Σ L. 'The truth of a statement t, in language l, can only be given in a metalanguage L, the language of interpretation' (see Chapter 4). If therapists go pale when they meet philosophers, they feel faint when they meet mathematicians. This young Polish mathematician gave us a model for a language of interpretation in the 1930s. It arose from his work on topology, the mathematics of shapes: literally, a mathematics of boundaries (see Chapter 2, where Jean Stokes explores boundaries). Those who enjoy the creativity of Wilfred Bion, pioneer of group analysis (a maths teacher), find his ideas clarify the nature of being *qua* being – for example, his description of how beta elements (pre-thoughts) are transformed by being held and contained into alpha elements (thoughts). This is taken up by James Bamber, in relation to group supervision (Chapter 9). Bion, as a young soldier (a tank commander in the First World War, decorated for bravery), experienced at first hand the intense emotions involved in being under fire from two sides in 'no man's land', in liminal space, between boundaries. Supervision exists in such a space. It is a liminal activity.

In our book we borrow theory from many disciplines to enable being in the room with a colleague talking about another human being, developing a spirit of enquiry so those involved may individuate – become more of who they really are (see Martin Stone, Chapter 5). In analytical psychology, Jung suggested the structures we observe in each other are reflections of Archetypes – the a priori of the unconscious mind:

> The ground principles, the archetypoi, of the unconscious are indescribable because of their wealth of reference, although in themselves recognisable. The discriminating intellect naturally keeps on trying to establish their singleness of meaning and thus misses the essential point; for what we can above all establish as the one thing consistent in their nature is their *manifold meaning*, their almost limitless wealth of reference, which makes any unilateral formulation impossible.
>
> (CW9i para. 80)

Given that multiplicity of meaning is the 'default condition' for symbols, the language of the psyche, to read symbols will require a sustained ability to tolerate difference; to remain, like Bion in his tank, under fire in a liminal space. There isn't one English word which captures the quality required to do this – but there is a word in Pali, the language spoken by Gautama Buddha: *metta* or 'Loving-kindness' (Nyanatiloka 1952: 118) one of the four *brahma viharas* (Spiritual homes) – the other three being *karuna* (compassion), *mudita* (sympathetic joy, 'amusement') and *upekkha* (equanimity). Meta (signifying being 'above') can be achieved without being 'super' through using *metta* – loving-kindness, supported by compassion, joy and equanimity.

The alchemical metaphor

Crucial to supervision is creating a safe space in which trust can develop. Jung often described this using the Greek word *temenos*. This is the name for the sacred precinct around a temple: a place for prayer and meditation, to await the God's presence. He used this word as a metaphor for the psychically charged area surrounding a complex, guarded by the defences of the ego. Hence it has come to mean the analytic precinct, created by the setting, the room, the time, and the exchange of gold (fees). It also means the psychic space made by the transference and countertransference in which both analyst and patient (and here, supervisor) are in the presence of the unconscious. It is a numinous space, that is, one in which spiritual activity takes place.

The laboratory of a medieval alchemist was such a space, for the activity of alchemy was, as Marie-Louise von Franz (1997: 13) said, both external (playing with chemicals) and internal (playing with meaning). Another way to understand *temenos* is to think of it as the well-sealed vessel used by the alchemist (see Figure 7.1, p. 102). The vessel has to be kept at the right (emotional) temperature; too hot and it will explode, too cold and nothing happens. Inside, the ingredients combine and change. Or the vessel might be an alembic (a still) where the mixture is distilled, condensed, distilled and condensed . . . again and again and again, until the 'gold' or the 'philosopher's stone' is achieved. And whatever else is going on, the alchemist will be describing it in wonderful, flowery language, designed as much to obscure as to instruct.

Once a safe space has begun to exist, supervisees can get to know themselves as therapists – question, think, reflect, feel. They can bring mistakes and successes, strong countertransferences, both negative and positive – a few of the possible 'chemicals'. They can let themselves be open to praise, discussion, criticism and reflection – the 'transforming processes'. They can be helped to stay with discouragement, anxiety, despair and frustration – routine in alchemy. The alchemical metaphor shows there is no perfect answer and, as in alchemy, much gold may change hands. Alchemy is rich in process metaphors: the 'stone' itself was thought to be hidden in the *prima materia* (the initial muck in the vessel) and change colours from black to red, to white to gold. As any good alchemist knew, if you didn't put gold in at the beginning, how could you get gold out at the end? Alchemy reminds us that supervision is an investment.

Training metaphor

This investment is seen most clearly in the training of therapists, which we use in the book both as a literal and metaphorical image: literal, in exploring the special skills needed to use supervision as education, and metaphorical to bring the advantages of a 'beginner's mind' to the fore. Training is a process of transformation, particularly transformation of the ego. Trainees are challenged to learn how to reality test in the 'inner world', in their unconscious, as well as in the 'outer world' provided by learning how to use a therapeutic frame. Jungian ideas about the role of the ego suggest its temporary relinquishment of control is needed for the alchemical mix between patient and therapist to 'turn into gold'.

The medieval alchemist Maria Prophetissa said the secret of the transforming work lay in knowing about the hermetic vessel, and the 'mercury' it contained, mercury being a medium in which transformation takes place (CW12 paras 338–340). Training in therapy requires a well-sealed vessel, within which 'One becomes two, two becomes three, and out of the third comes the one as the hidden fourth' (the Axiom of Maria, see CW8 para. 962). There are various meanings of 'one, two and three'. It could be the trainee, their analyst and supervisor. Or it could be the trainee is one, the patient makes two, and the supervisor three, and the hidden fourth is the training institution?

However, there can be many other 'fourths' – seminar leaders, assessors and other students as well as the families, groups, societies and cultures influenced by a trainee's growth and change. The extent of this influence depends on how the ones, twos and threes construct the boundaries of the 'vessel'. Throughout the book, we will refer to triangles and triads; pointing out it is important not to be so focused on the triad (patient, therapist, supervisor) that the fourth, whatever it might be, is forgotten. Four is an important number in Jungian thinking: for him, four elements, four mental functions (sensation, intuition, feeling and thought) made the whole. Thinking about the dynamics of supervision as a four (a three-dimensional tetrahedron, rather than a two-dimensional triangle) gives a more complete picture of the dynamics.

Therapy often involves a 'journey through hell'; training to be a therapist nearly always does. It is useful to keep the symbol of Hermes in mind. He guides souls to the Land of the Dead, the kingdom of his uncle, Hades. Mercury (Hermes) is also the god of shepherds, merchants and thieves (tricksters) (see CW13 paras 239–303, *The Spirit Mercurius*). Good supervision draws on all three of his trades: we shepherd, we market theories, sometimes we 'steal' (ideas), occasionally we use tricks (such as positive connotation or paradoxical injunction). All of these allow the 'fourth' – communicating a message.

Structure of the book

This book is derived from a course for therapists organised by the Association of Jungian Analysts (AJA). In preparation for the course and the book, we researched with our colleagues. The result, we hope, is a practical introduction to the tasks involved in bringing insight from analytical psychology into supervisory space and time, creating and maintaining a reflective space. Analytical psychology values an ability to 'be with not knowing'; the opposite of 'being with knowing'; seeking to impose theoretical ideas and 'grand narratives' upon multilayered intersubjective systems. We favour staying with what the Buddhist philosopher and Zen Scholar, D. T. Suzuki (2001), calls 'beginner's mind'. Beginners more easily notice the dog that did not bark, the interpretation that was not given, the feeling that cannot be named. There is no special theory for this: there is however, a 'general theory' – supervision needs an open meaning system, and an open meaning system needs clear (not rigid) boundaries.

Definitions of boundaries in supervision vary, they are not yet theoretically established. Experienced practitioners tend to use models drawn from therapeutic boundaries: a 'two', not a 'four'. We begin with a chapter examining the history and refinement of supervision as a task distinct from analysis, exploring how distinctions between professional development through dialogue about a patient–therapist relationship differ from personal development through analysis, by exploring countertransference. This plays the role of the mercury in the vessel; countertransference being 'mercurial', like quicksilver, it is extremely hard to pin down, especially as it is more often sensed and felt, rather than 'thinkable'.

Jung said: 'theory is the very devil', and 'scientific theory has . . . less value from the point of view of psychological truth than religious dogma'

(Samuels et al. 1986: 149). Unfortunately, analytical psychology has many competing 'theories', and we offer no consensus. To position ourselves, we do not privilege a 'Holy Grail' of four or five times a week work; this lacks a good evidence base (see Stone and Duckworth 2003). We have a background in, and commitment to, economically accessible practice; all of us counsel, do therapy and analyse. Our approach, our vision, then, is closer to artists and craftsmen.

We divided the book into three parts: boundaries, individuation, and the collective. Chapters are based on seminars, the ideas were tested live, and improved by feedback from participants, who deconstructed our certainties. 'The postmodern position is one that questions fixed ideas of reality or truth as it deconstructs modernist certainties and meta narratives, and promotes a plurality of perspectives against singular views' (Hauke 2000: 236). We have not attempted to write a specifically 'postmodern' text; many of us find its language bewildering. However, as a postmodern would advise, do not assume what we say is 'true' or 'false'. It may be both true and false, neither true nor false.

Our title *Vision and Supervision* suggests supervision depends on perception: developing an ability to see things as they are (rather than whether they are true or false), to attempt to so do, and, when we can't, have the courage to admit we can't, and 'be with not knowing'. We didn't notice the dog in the night time because it didn't bark, and we didn't notice that either. As supervising (counselling, therapy, analysis) is an art, when practising it we experience what all other artists experience: whether facing a blank canvas, a blank page, or as a musician or actor beginning an improvisation. We can't use 'something we prepared earlier'. An aim of counselling, therapy and analysis is to allow people to become more whole. A sense of the beautiful, then, as likely to be as good a guide to practice as theory, for

> In reality of course we cannot have experiences, however acute and unexpected, which are bracketed from assumptions, or concepts. Experience comes already informed with meaning, because meaning is inseparable from experience.
>
> (Richard Wainwright, Chapter 8)

References

Conan Doyle, Sir A. (1985) *Sherlock Holmes: The Complete Illustrated Short Stories.* London: Chancellor.
Covington, C. (1995) 'No story, no analysis? The role of narrative in interpretation.' *Journal of Analytical Psychology* 40(3): 405–419.
Franz, M-L. von (1997) *Alchemical Active Imagination.* Boston, MA: Shambhala.

Haddon, M. (2004) *The Curious Incident of the Dog in the Night Time*. London: Ventura.
Hauke, C. (2000) *Jung and the Postmodern*. London: Routledge.
Jung, C. G. (1953–1973) *Collected Works*, ed. Sir H. Read, M. Fordham, G. Adler and W. McGuire, 20 vols. London: Routledge & Kegan Paul.
Loux, M. (2007) *Metaphysics: A Contemporary Introduction*. London: Routledge.
Nyanatiloka (1952) *Buddhist Dictionary*. Kandy, Sri Lanka: Buddhist Publication Society.
Samuels, A., Shorter, B. and Plaut, F. (1986) *A Critical Dictionary of Jungian Analysis*. London: Routledge.
Stone, M. and Duckworth, M. (2003) 'Frequency and analytic framework.' In R. Withers (ed.) *Controversies in Analytical Psychology*. London: Routledge.
Suzuki, D. T. (2001) *Zen Mind, Beginners Mind*, 3rd edn. New York: Weatherhill.

Part I

Strange effects at boundaries

Chapter 2

Boundaries
Separateness, merger, mutuality

Jean Stokes

Introduction

All relationships, if they are to work, require reciprocal respect for, and attention to, boundaries. We are often most aware of boundaries when they are challenged. Where the relationship is asymmetrical, as in analysis and supervision (and training supervision in particular) respect for boundaries is needed more. This chapter explores how the concept of boundaries evolved in psychodynamic supervision, their place in different supervisory situations and possible influences on the supervisor in making decisions about boundaries in practice. I shall not deal here with major ethical transgressions of boundaries such as sexual and financial exploitation, but focus on what can undermine and blur boundaries as related to clinical supervision.

Boundaries regulate distance between people. They involve recognising an appropriate physical or emotional proximity for the relationship, neither a defensive barrier nor an intrusion. Images associated with boundaries include: border, frontier, perimeter, barrier edge, borderline, margin, brink, verge, extremity and point of no return. Boundaries get broken, stepped over, crossed. They can also be blurred, misunderstood or allowed to collapse because they are not properly maintained. These are probably the most likely dangers present in supervision. The word 'boundary' comes from the Latin *bodina*, meaning specifically a landmark showing the limit of an estate. In ancient Greece, boundaries were marked by a *herm*, a stone with a phallus etched, carved or placed on one side. Hermes, the messenger of the gods, had a special role, and as a conductor of souls to Hades' kingdom, shepherded them over the boundary between life and death. Knowing what marks a boundary facilitates both parties moving freely within both their own area and in any shared areas where agreements about usage (temporary or permanent) may take the place of the usual boundary markers. In supervision this is the contract, which has the value of a psychological passport or visa to enter temporarily the inner world territory of the therapeutic couple.

A boundary separates and/or encloses and embodies the notion of limit or restriction. This is the idea contained in a key Jungian image, the *vas bene clausum*, the well-sealed vessel of alchemy, likened by Jung to the magic circle: 'In both cases the idea is to protect what is within from the intrusion and admixture of what is without as well as to prevent it from escaping' (CW12 para. 219).

Psychologically, boundaries regulate optimal intimacy, between self and other, and between the different inner world selves we experience. In Jungian terms, the main internal relationships are between persona (social self), Ego, Shadow, Animus/Anima (Otherness) and Self. Boundaries refer to individual identity; to edges of difference; to an ability to create, maintain and tolerate, or relinquish, separateness in the interests of mutuality and merger. A capacity for maintaining boundaries involves a flexible Ego, through which split-off psychic contents are allowed back into consciousness enriching intrapsychic and/or interpersonal dynamics. As in bodily terms the boundary of skin may be permeable, impermeable, or both, so the supervisor, open psychologically to the affects and material of the therapeutic couple, allows herself to be affected by them, then steps back to reflect. This conscious collapsing of psychic boundaries, followed by restoration, is the basis of empathic and reflective practice. Rigidity in boundaries restricts this potential for opening up new meanings in supervision; failing to maintain or restore boundaries and allow Ego back equally limits understanding.

As they involve consciousness and differentiation (both functions of the Ego) boundaries are described by Jungian analyst Hugh Gee (2003) as an 'ego-activity'. Ego, in the form of firm but flexible boundaries, creates a safe place, physical and psychological, for the supervisee to bring the darkness of their work as well as the light. The Self can then constellate, the *prima materia* can find its shape, and the unknown be faced. (*Prima materia*, also known as *massa confusa*, is an alchemical term, referring to the original elements in a state of chaos, used metaphorically by Jung to describe undifferentiated psychic contents.)

The god of boundaries is the alchemical figure of Mercurius, known in American Indian mythology as the Trickster, and to the Greeks as Hermes. Krashen (1996) suggests that the archetypal image of the Trickster holds and combines opposites, making him a deity of 'the threshold' and, as such, a god of the transitional and liminal (from the Latin *limen*, meaning threshold, doorway, entrance). Supervisors, especially training supervisors, like Janus, the god of the threshold, face two ways: towards the therapeutic couple and candidate whose professional development they have at heart, and towards the profession and institution, whose standards they represent. An uncomfortable position, a training supervisor works in the liminal space, to assist in the rite of passage to qualification.

Hermes is associated with paradox, with communication, with revelation, and with 'transformation of the meaningless into the meaningful' (CW9i para. 458) which both analysis and supervision set out to facilitate. However, Jung then describes the Trickster as a shape-shifter, demonic and divine, tortured and healing, like the Shakespearian Fool. While similar ethical codes in analysis and supervision make it possible for a well-boundaried practitioner to initially manage supervisory boundaries by transferring the understanding used in their clinical work, this alone cannot last long. Trickster makes his presence felt, often in the form of blurred boundaries and enactments. Dilemmas arise which cannot necessarily be answered in terms of psychic process in the client, the supervisee or the supervisor.

Fundamental questions for a supervisor might be the following:

- How differently do I treat supervisees from my patients?
- To what extent is the supervisory container the same as the analytic?
- What differences do we provide in the frame we offer supervisees?
- What is the reason for these differences?
- How explicit do I make the ground rules (the frame) beyond setting, time, frequency and fee?
- To what extent is it appropriate to take up projections on to the supervisor in supervision?
- How much do I actively teach?
- How much do I reveal of my own professional experience to assist learning?
- How do I move between a supervisee in training and the institution?
- Where I do not have clinical responsibility what effect does this have on the way the container is provided and maintained?
- Who needs to know what?
- How do I relate to my colleagues in respect of this supervisory task?
- Where is my support?

The supervisor will be aware of conscious and unconscious questions about boundaries in the supervisee, even one with considerable experience. Experienced supervisees may wonder how supervision outside of training functions and what the role of a non-training supervisor is, particularly when they have ended their personal therapy. For example, here are some common questions for beginners:

- If I talk about my patients with my therapist, how is that different from talking with my supervisor?
- How do I decide what to take where?
- What are the limits and how do I find out about them?
- Can I take a personal problem to my supervisor and in what circumstances is this appropriate?

- Where do I take a problem with my supervisor?
- Where do clinical seminars fit in?

Supervisory and analytic settings have much in common: both involve relationships based on trust where a great deal of intense emotion is shared in intimate detail (Gabbard and Lester 1995), yet boundaries in supervision practice are often not as clearly delineated or theoretically agreed as in analysis. The therapeutic element in supervision is a case in point, as is how the countertransference should be handled, and how discussion of a supervisee's dreams about a patient may further understanding. Being open about countertransference experiences heightens a supervisee's vulnerability. The ambiguity and diversity of attitudes to boundaries in supervision is further complicated because all supervision (including for trainees) takes place between fellow professionals and so is collegiate by nature. This fact can be made good use of, or fall into shadow, be split off and unconsciously exploited.

The first question around boundaries refers to both supervisor's and supervisee's need to know what supervision does and does not do, its extent and limits. This is expressed well by Jacobs et al. (1995):

> Supervision is an intimate situation, *but without clear and consensually agreed upon boundaries for the discourse, until the supervisory pair establishes an understanding about these*. A supervisor and supervisee may explicitly talk about ground rules for supervision, but these are often left unstated, and the dialogue is left open-ended, its direction and profundity to be discovered in process. This situation may make the supervisee feel vulnerable, for it is not clear whether the supervisor will maintain her *interest in the patient* or become interested in the experience of the supervisee.
>
> (Jacobs et al. 1995: 210, my italics)

Framing the task of supervision

Only recently has supervision come to be recognised as a craft in its own right. In the early days of analysis little distinction was made between analysis and supervision. The differentiation of the one from the other initiated thinking about the specific frames and tasks of each.

Recognising the danger of psychic infection for the analyst, Jung was the first to insist on personal analysis as part of analytic training. His emphasis on all analysts being analysed was crucial in highlighting the need for them to develop a capacity to both immerse in the work – the alchemical mix – and separate themselves from it, so avoiding a 'folie à deux'. However, analysis alone was to prove insufficient.

Where to deal with countertransference difficulties was at the heart of the debates from which supervision emerged. In 1909, caught in a collusive erotic transference to his patient Sabina Spielrein, uncontained in the therapy (Martin 2003), Jung wrote to Freud for help, 'the first request for supervision' (Kerr 1994: 122). Both Freud and Jung recognised that case discussion with colleagues could provide increased objectivity and understanding. Later, in *Memories, Dreams, Reflections*, Jung wrote:

> It often happens that the patient is exactly the right plaster for the doctor's sore spot. Because this is so difficult situations can arise for the doctor too – or rather especially for the doctor. Every therapist ought to have a control by some third person, so that he remains *open to another point of view*. Even the Pope has a confessor.
> (Jung 1963 para. 133, my italics)

These words, 'open to another point of view', highlight the benign function of supervision as a psychic health check for the therapeutic couple. In the early days of analysis such a collegial resource was sought informally – through letters, personal meetings, and international conferences. Seeking specific help with specific cases was an early recognition of the need to distinguish personal from professional development. Choosing to focus on the patient and explore blocks to the work established the task of supervision as patient-based. However, whether this was with one's personal analyst or someone else, and how this might affect any discoveries made, was not considered.

By the 1930s, ideas had changed. In psychoanalytic circles, following much controversy about where countertransference should be explored, it was agreed personal analysis should be separated from the teaching work of what was then called 'control analysis' (a direct translation from the German which, according to the American Jungian Mary Ann Mattoon (1995), includes the idea of examination and inspection as well as overseeing). In her account of the development of supervision in Jungian circles, she describes how by 1948 in both Zurich and London 'control analysis' was distinct from the personal. In London, Michael Fordham (with Gerhard Adler and Herbert Read one of the three co-editors of the collected works and a co-founder of the first London Jungian Group, the Society of Analytical Psychology) stressed the importance of treating trainees as junior colleagues (Fordham 1995). The archetype of the mentor became constellated as a blueprint for the role of the supervisor. The goal of supervision today is well described by the American Jungian August Cwik, who sees it as promoting the fullest expression of the professional self of the clinician, which for him is 'that aspect of the true self that operates through a developed persona in a therapeutic situation' (Cwik 2006: 209).

Ann Shearer, a Jungian analyst and writer, points out supervision is in itself a boundary question as it means breaking the seal on the analytic vessel, for two must become three (in group supervision the group itself becomes the third psyche). Paradoxically, it is exactly this triangulation that enables supervision to offer 'containment, a keeping of form and to task' (Shearer 2003: 208). She reminds us that three is a sacred number across time, place and cultures. Jung says the number three is not a natural expression of wholeness, 'since four represents the minimum number of determinants in a judgement' (CW12 para. 31) and cites a central tenet of alchemy, the Axiom of Maria Prophetissa: 'One becomes two, two becomes three, and out of the third comes the one as the fourth' (CW8 para. 962). As a result of the work the supervisory couple do together on the patient–therapist relationship, the fourth, new possibilities emerges. It is to be hoped that change occurs in all those involved, including the supervisory couple. In the same paragraph, Jung draws attention to the repeated oscillations between three and four. This oscillation is present in the struggle for understanding, which might occur when the supervisee feels lost or stuck, or in struggles with transference and countertransference, on which the fourth of new experience depends. Jung again: 'in principle new points of view are not as a rule discovered in territory that is already known but in out of the way places that may even be avoided because of their bad name' (CW8 para. 962).

Attitudes to the supervisee's countertransference still cause debate about boundaries between supervision and analysis. The countertransference itself has qualities of Trickster about it: a shape-changing, double-edged, mischievous quality often hard to identify and think about, requiring us to expect the unexpected. Strong differences of opinion exist as to whether and when the supervisor should suggest their supervisee take a countertransference experience to personal analysis or work with it in supervision. Is it patronising and intrusive or responsible and helpful to suggest this? What matters most is not *whether* the countertransference is interpreted but *how*. While the focus remains on the therapist–patient relationship, the supervisee also needs to feel seen and understood, without being exposed to 'wild analysis'. Making an interpretation about the inner world of the supervisee, which has to be dealt with outside the context of supervision, is breaking a boundary. Having said this, a persistently troublesome countertransference, occurring with more than one patient, needs to be sensitively brought to awareness and contextualised within professional development. When the supervisee is no longer in therapy – usually the case with experienced practitioners – then supervision has to provide a place for attention to their inner world as seen in their professional self.

Boundaries and ego-activity

Returning to the idea that boundaries are an ego-activity, I now look in more detail at Jung's ideas about the Ego, and their relationship to boundaries in supervision. In his essay on the archetype of the Self, he described the Ego as 'part of the personality but not the whole of it' (CW9ii para. 11), it is 'the complex factor to which all conscious contents are related. It always finds its limit when it comes up against the unknown' (CW9ii para. 2). Consciously or unconsciously, the supervisee brings to supervision whatever challenges their existing ideas of good practice, of setting up and maintaining the frame. The supervisor needs to provide firm holding for the supervisee to venture into the unknown with the patient. Jung further maintained that the Ego 'seems to arise in the first place from the collision between the somatic factor and the environment . . . it goes on developing from further collisions with the outer world and the inner' (CW9ii para. 6).

Collision, implying some degree of pain and shock, suggests how encounters with the Other (patient, supervisor, the experience of training, the agency or institution) play a part in the development of the therapist's professional self. For Jung, one of the main characteristics of the Ego is its individuality: 'it retains its identity up to a certain point. Its stability is relative . . . alterations need not always be pathological; they can also be developmental' (CW9ii para. 10). Here *individuality* reminds us of the importance of respect, treating the supervisee as an equal despite the asymmetrical relationship, and recognising differences, including personal style and ability. *Relative stability* implies endeavouring to maintain a consistent approach, holding the frame and ethical attitude, thus enabling divergences to be reflected upon and intense affect explored. The statement as a whole recognises supervision as a growth process on both sides.

> Ego-consciousness is differentiated i.e. separated, from the unconscious and exists in absolute space and time . . . anchored in the world of consciousness . . . fostered by a very precise adaptation. For this certain virtues like attention, conscientiousness, patience, etc. are of great value on the moral side just as accurate observation of the symptomatology of the unconscious and objective self-criticism are valuable on the intellectual side.
>
> (CW9ii paras 45–46)

'*Differentiated, separated from the unconscious*' highlights key functions of supervision: helping to hold the Ego–Self axis, fostering a re-balancing and development in the supervisee, reflecting on merger and enactment experiences through the lens of parallel process. In '*space and time*' stresses the importance of setting a clear frame, and establishing the supervisor's availability. *Attention, conscientiousness, patience, accurate observation, objective self-criticism*: all refer to the how of supervision, to the tools of reflective work.

Each of Jung's terms describes the basis of the working alliance in the supervisory team by suggesting aspects of setting and maintaining and flexing boundaries. Jung described his aim as an analyst to 'bring about a psychic state in which my patient begins to experiment with his own nature – a state of fluidity, change and growth' (CW16 para. 99). This description fits supervision, where unconscious contents in the therapist–patient relationship come into contact with ego, so enriching ego activity available to the supervisee. Jung's definitions of Ego functions imply they are used to reflect – the purpose of a supervision space is to do just this.

Within this space experience is created more than the sum of the different individuals, which includes the patient. Once understood and articulated with or on behalf of the supervisee, the new, shared understanding of process can be taken back to the therapist–patient relationship. The image of the sealed vessel (the *vas bene clausum*) mentioned earlier is central here, for supervision is often a place of intense affect – in the material, in transferences and countertransferences and the resulting dilemmas. The affects stirred in the supervisor are added to the alchemical mix. Parallel process (Chapter 11) is crucial and inevitable, but not comfortable, and needs a firm frame for the supervisory team to tolerate its storms. Then they can see it for what it is: a pattern of symbolic meaning.

Personal boundaries and the learning experience in supervision

The Swiss analyst Verena Kast echoes Jung when she talks of 'the expanding significance of personal activity, or ego activity' as we expose ourselves more or less painfully to relationships and experiences. She continues: 'Becoming oneself implies redefining the boundaries between oneself and the unconscious' (Kast 1992: 52–53), adding that a defined ego allows us to accept situations of ego-loss in the knowledge we will be able to survive and reorganise. Her description of boundaries is especially relevant when supervising trainees; mature adults with established personal and social identity, rooted in family, vocational and professional life.

Training rituals can feel fossilised and infantilising and may actually be so. Having said this, part of the experience of training is, at a deep level, to re-examine attitudes central to one's existing sense of identity. Aspects of ego-identity may be sacrificed to find a new relationship with the Self. The experience of training (in which supervision is a key feature) is intended to be a container where such change can come about. In supervision, the trainee is helped to face the challenge, inherent in clinical work, to their Ego–Self axis, developing authenticity in their professional self. Here is an example:

A new group of four supervisees on a psychodynamic training met with me as their first supervisor. A businesswoman, a teacher, an actor and a nurse, their ages ranged from 30 to 55. None had worked formally with clients psychodynamically; all had some experience of counselling. Clients were yet to be allocated. Apprehension and anticipation were high, as they had heard supervision was where learning this new craft really took place. As I began to find out about the different members of my new group, I enquired how they were feeling at the end of their first training day. One said how difficult it was to be taught after years of teaching and criticised some of the teaching styles. The actor said he felt he had to improvise. The businesswoman said talking about her feelings was irrelevant and she was here to find out how to organise the first session. The nurse was silent but eventually said he thought this training was going to be very demanding and he wondered how he was going to cope. I could see that, painfully conscious of their initiate status and feeling de-skilled, they were falling back on professional ego-identities.

Keeping boundaries and patient-based focus of supervision in mind, I encouraged them to reflect on how they might make use of this uncomfortable experience to consider how a client might feel in their first session. The tense atmosphere in the room relaxed. The group engaged in making conscious their experience of the unknown and began to play with parallel process. To consolidate this, further contain anxieties and move the group forward, we then talked about how their previous professional skills could be useful in clinical work and to the group.

The function of the frame in supervision

In supervision both parties are involved in clinical thinking about a third person – the patient. The frame is instrumental in keeping both parties to task: this collegial interaction is not social. Understanding the differences between supervision and analysis enables the practitioner to establish explicit as well as implicit models for the use of boundaries, which can then be used to consider what to do when boundaries related to contractual elements are crossed.

The frame consists of ground rules laid down by the supervisor (and possibly also an institution), aiming to manage and hold supervisees' felt experience. Ground rules enable the supervisor to maintain sufficient objectivity to help the supervisee to reflect on their work with patients:

- What sort are needed?
- Which are stated and which unstated?
- How does the supervisor decide?
- How can a container be created and maintained, respecting both the asymmetrical nature of the professional relationship and the collegial element without it becoming open to abuse on both sides?
- Is the frame imposed by the setting (which might require adaptation) or is it one both have thought through and are comfortable with?

Shortly before writing this chapter I joined a new peer supervision group. The experience of negotiating our boundaries as a group highlighted for me the ones necessary to attend to the task in hand. The reciprocal nature of peer supervision and the likelihood of a degree of at least professional intimacy, means formality in structuring the experience is crucial for the encounter to remain patient-focused. An agreed appropriate setting (comfortable, quiet, free from intrusion, a set period of time and format) all ensure that members' attention remains professional in its approach. Personal matters are kept to a friendly minimum necessary to build a rapport, except where personal experience impinges on the professional self and needs attention. Observing these details keeps the Jungian idea of a setting as a *temenos* or sacred space: a physical and symbolic place for the goddess Psyche to inhabit.

In asymmetrical supervision this same formality is in place. The difference is that a fee is involved and roles are not interchangeable. The frame is similar to a therapy session: fixed time and place, agreed length of session and fee. Frequency, setting, session length and length of commitment may be dictated by an outside agency or by the supervisor. At an emotional level, frame becomes container: the supervisor strives to offer a sustained ethical and analytic attitude to hold the affects and anxieties present. In training, this is an attitude the supervisee can gradually internalise and further strengthen when qualified.

In training, the supervisee has little control over the frame, and may not even have a choice of supervisor. Both resistance and counter-resistance can enter as a result. The same may be true when there is a long wait for training patients. Non-existent or absent patients may dominate the dynamics. The clinical needs of a training patient may conflict with the training needs of the supervisee. The supervisory team may want to alter the frame of both therapy and supervision. Such dynamics and their effect on the supervisory team need to become conscious and be explicitly addressed to allow learning to take place. The firmer the frame, the easier it is to bring divergences – in the form of actual or fantasised enactments – to awareness.

The collegial nature of supervision can confuse and blur maintenance of the frame. For example, some will regard offering tea or coffee as simple unambiguous hospitality, distinguishing between supervision and analysis. Others regard this as potentially seductive. As with any element of the frame, such as starting and finishing on time, what matters here is consistency and keeping to task, taking the frame as seriously as in analysis. Not to do so risks what Edward Martin (2002), writing about ethics, calls 'theft of the safe container'. Hermes was, after all, also a thief.

Supervision in an agency is at lunchtime and the supervisees bring food and drink. In my view, if the agency is not itself able to provide nourishment or take account of the need for this in scheduling, then it is important for supervisors to consciously recognise physical needs for themselves and their supervisees and the adverse effect on learning if ignored. In individual private supervision, which is usually shorter and at a mutually agreed time, this would be breaking a boundary.

Supervisees may act out to test unstated differences between boundaries in analysis and supervision. This is not open to interpretation as it would be with patients, and does not always prove to be an enactment reflecting parallel process. An example from private practice takes place in a liminal space:

A supervisee rings the doorbell early. When I open it the supervisee is looking embarrassed and says, 'I have forgotten my purse. Could you lend me money for parking?' I decide I can. The money is refunded the following week. In another case, the supervisee waited till the bill was due and tried to add the money to the monthly bill. I felt this was blurring a boundary and refused, saying it was a separate issue.

Another frame issue concerns missed and cancelled sessions:

A supervisor regularly takes a summer break from mid-August to mid-September and maintains the usual analytic structure of charging for all cancelled sessions. The supervisee, in training, needs to take an earlier holiday, which does not coincide. At his last session he announces he is reluctant to pay for the missed sessions, maintaining this is not analysis. Can he have replacement sessions instead? The supervisor is sympathetic to his view but feels put on the spot and controlled, as the supervisee has known her dates for some time. The two talk about the similarities and differences between analysis and supervision. It becomes clear the supervisee is struggling to differentiate between the containment offered and sought in the two relationships and feels trapped between two parental figures. Recognising this is a feature of their work with the patient, the supervisor suggests they turn their attention to how the patient is responding to the coming break. The supervisee talks about a struggle for control with his patient who wanted to have a replacement session to which he agreed but which the patient then missed. Having discussed this in terms of the patient's need for containment, the supervisor brings the discussion back to supervision, asking how the supervisee now feels it would be fair to proceed. He replies, although ideally he would still like replacement sessions, he sees he needed to have raised this earlier. He admits feeling a last minute change would be unsettling and leave him feeling his supervisor is also anxious. The supervisor for her part acknowledges this grey area in the contract and would consider one replacement session in such circumstances in future. She checked the supervisee was now feeling confident about starting with the patient again and they parted with the supervisory relationship restored and strengthened.

In an agency, this dilemma might not have arisen, as the supervisor is usually paid by the institution and supervision may be free for the therapist. However, the example does show any setting calls for clear ground rules. As in analysis, without them it is difficult to maintain sufficient objectivity to identify projections and counter-projections at work in the therapist–patient interactions and within the supervisory team. Only then can the supervisor decide how and when to flex the frame to model the thinking behind both firm adherence to boundaries and flexible, bespoke interpretations recognising individual needs and responsibilities. The supervisory team meet with a conscious wish to carry out a task: to examine the interactions with a patient and expand the supervisee's professional ability, promoting conscious awareness, differentiation and objective self-criticism. Clarity about the nature of the task is essential to a working alliance so both parties know their responsibilities.

With beginners, it obviously helps to make clear that the focus of supervision is the patient–therapist relationship and how illuminating the dynamics present in the room during each presentation can be. The supervisor may wish to indicate the format of a session, including the most useful way to present patient–therapist interactions. In training, especially in the early stages, 'verbatim' reports, including countertransferential responses of all kinds, are useful. They help the supervisor to 'be in the room' with the patient. This not only shows how the therapist works but also what pressures they find themselves under and which aspects of clinical work they need help with. At the same time, there needs to be awareness that any report on a session is, at best, a reconstruction; at worst, a defence (Chapter 8).

Ann Shearer (2003) says the term 'supervision' with its idea of 'over see' suggests a seductive knowingness untrue to the mystery of any unfolding psychic process. She points out that from the same root we also get 'oversight' and reminds us the so-called 'control analyst' is not in control. For example, unlike analysis, the supervisor can deal only with what *has* happened and what *may* happen in the therapeutic encounter, not what *is* happening. Another London Jungian, Louis Zinkin (1995), noted supervision (which suggests being able to see the actual patient being discussed) is impossible. He describes supervision as:

> a shared fantasy. The process is the result of the trainee trying to imagine what he and the patient have been doing together and the supervisor trying to imagine it too. Supervision works best if both remain aware that what they are jointly imagining is not true.
> (Zinkin 1995: 247)

Keeping in mind what these analysts say holds a boundary between fantasy and reality and helps avoid an inflated attitude. Jacobs et al. (1995: 6) remind us: 'Supervision is a process during which supervisor and supervisee are learning together – about the patient, about one another and about themselves.' This deceptively simple statement is full of complexities. It highlights the mutuality of the process yet appears to play down the inevitable differences in role and the task's fundamentally asymmetrical nature. Boundaries between setting and task often risk being blurred.

Boundaries and management issues

Trainees need help to differentiate between management and therapy. They learn to deal with practical issues (session times, fees, cancellation policy, holidays) at a non-interpretative level (Gee 2003) as well as to see their implications. Through different clients and clinical situations they develop the capacity for firm but flexible management. They have experience of the management of their own therapy yet need to discover this was an approach tailored to their needs rather than a universal. Pointing this out requires some tact. In an agency or institution the supervisee's own experience of therapy may be limited and/or different in orientation. It is important to find out early on whether or not a supervisee is in personal therapy, what experience they have of it, and their theoretical orientation. This helps anticipate and understand clinical and theoretical conflicts, consider how to approach cases brought and decide how best to intervene.

Learning to think behind the frame and boundaries helps supervisees hold the work. They are then free to explore meaning changes with the patient when the frame is distorted, misunderstood or ignored. This is essential when a supervisee is working with non-psychodynamically orientated colleagues. Wishes for psychodynamic reflection and input can be met by thinking together on how best to set up or adapt boundaries.

Experienced therapists often bring management issues involving setting or frame; moving consulting rooms, taking breaks, making changes in the room such as introducing a couch, noise, personal events which may or not may not be able to be planned for. Often at the root of this is the impact on therapist's own psychic and external reality, their anxiety about containing change. By looking at anticipated and actual responses of different patients the supervisee is helped to disentangle the neurotic from the syntonic (same feeling) countertransference.

Boundaries, triangles and the fourth

The supervisory relationship involves triangles and fours (Chapter 1). The regular triangle we work with is patient, therapist and supervisor, giving triangular interpretations through parallel process. Such manifestations are more easily identified when both parties are familiar with each other's work and style. The supervisor is then in a better position to differentiate, to stand back from the dynamics and put a boundary round a particular clinical experience, inviting reflection, for example, on an enactment.

When concerned about a trainee's progress, the supervisor will want to address this with them first. However, this is not always as easy as it sounds. It takes time to reflect on the dynamics and the triangles. Bringing in a fourth in the form of consultation can be helpful. A supervisors' group provides this function. In one instance, in consultation, I realised I was presenting more about the patient–therapist relationship than the supervisory one, as if I myself were the therapist. This made me aware of how little confidence the supervisee had and my own anxiety. When I held back more and concentrated on affirming the therapist's strengths and limiting other interventions, the supervisee began to move forward. In subsequent consultations our relationship took proper precedence.

In another case, the fourth (the training committee) acted as a father. I found myself stuck helping a candidate increase the frequency with his patient. Despite us both agreeing the patient would benefit, there seemed to be a resistance in the candidate to discussing this. The training committee's insistence on the need for both patient and trainee to have this experience successfully galvanised the trainee into upping the frequency. It was a parallel process at a different level, enabling us to reflect on the role of the paternal in the patient's experience.

There may be a dilemma as to whether to involve the fourth by seeking help from a training committee. Often this is a matter of timing. Alternatively, it may be useful to discuss a matter in confidence, informally, with someone from the training institution. The trainee should be made aware of concerns and of any official contact with the institution.

Disclosure and mutuality

In analytic practice, where facilitating the development of transference is important, it is unusual to disclose personal or professional autobiographical information beyond details essential for the real relationship or those inevitably available to the patient through setting and persona elements, such as physical appearance, style of dress, speech, including register of voice (Chapter 6). In supervision, where transferences and countertransferences between the unseen patient and the therapist are the focus, the transferences of the supervisee are likely to receive attention only if they visibly interfere. Consequently, disclosure in supervision (conscious and unconscious) has to be considered differently.

By disclosure I mean anything the supervisor opts to reveal in a boundaried way as part of their educative function. For the supervisee, particularly a beginner, it can be useful to discuss how important it is to be as conscious as possible of what one reveals and why. Setting is a simple example of both conscious and unconscious disclosure. In an agency, a third party provides the supervisory setting. It is communal and the territory neutral. The supervisor's responsibility is limited to ensuring the setting makes available the minimum requirements described earlier. In common with therapeutic work in an agency, disclosure becomes limited to persona elements. By contrast, private consulting rooms, particularly at home, are not neutral: therapists reveal more of who they are, what they like, financial and family status, aesthetic sense – more of their Self.

Newly qualified therapists, particularly those moving out of agency work, are excited and anxious about this change. Private practice offers an opportunity to discover their own personal approach as well as a threat chaos will break out without a parenting institution. In my experience much of the work in preparation for setting up and maintaining private practice is dominated by concerns about boundaries. For example, anxieties about the increased personal availability can emerge in discussing how patients will contact the therapist. The task is to help anticipate the effect of a changed setting, expanding awareness of boundary issues and their meanings into a mature independent attitude. My aims are often achieved by modelling. Willingness to reveal who we are through the nature of the consulting room is a personal disclosure. It makes supervisees think about Otherness and difference, leading to discussions about what they wish to provide and what choices may disclose:

- Where will they feel most comfortable working – at home or a rented room?
- What impact might family members, including pets, have?
- What sort of stationery including bill forms to use?
- What about books, pictures, objects?

Professional disclosure: clinical amplification

The popular suggestion that supervision is less than therapy and more than teaching portrays the essential paradox of the task. Teaching usually implies imparting knowledge and sharing experience. Therapy implies encouraging self-knowledge and relies less on imparting knowledge and experience. Both involve helping another to learn through discovery and require good relationships. Supervision has all these elements. It is closest perhaps to 'educate' in its original Latin meaning: *educere* means 'to lead out from'. Here therapy and teaching meet.

The supervisor has the task of holding the opposite ends of the spectrum and being conscious of where on the spectrum the team are or need to be. This helps decide the timing and nature of interventions, how to attend to the countertransference, when to share knowledge and when to stand back to let the supervisee make their own discoveries. A new trainee will have different needs from one reaching the end of training; a newly qualified therapist different needs from an established practitioner. What is needed in supervision will be influenced by the demands of the patient's psyche and the current state of the therapist's inner and outer worlds.

To teach effectively we use our own work with patients and offer theory to elucidate and amplify complex dynamics. When work with a patient comes clearly and persistently to my mind in supervision, I regard it as a synchronistic, meaningful response, a symbol constellating in an interactive field and, as with any other countertransference, reflect on how best to use it. For example, do I offer it raw – an explicit parallel example from a colleague? Or do I offer it implicitly, as a possible interpretation of dynamics? Either approach will have an effect on the boundaries and means thinking about the use of amplification: it opens the dyad to show another couple at work, struggling to resolve similar problems. As the therapist in the example is the supervisor, it is good modelling, showing the supervisor can also learn from experience. It reveals experiencing and reflecting processes at work and shows how long these take. For trainees in individual supervision, especially those with limited experience, it gives insight into different clinical situations and common problems.

We need to be judicious in using amplification. The aim has to be kept clear, or else it may seem to a supervisee struggling with a difficult patient that the supervisor is all-knowing, or simply showing off. Clearly, it is not advisable to crowd the room with too many patients. Misused, clinical amplification pampers a supervisor's narcissistic needs, and serves to compensate for the fairly isolated life of an analyst. These are temptations and defences against maintaining an analytic attitude.

Understanding parallel process balances the use of clinical amplification. Being aware how it comes to consciousness, helps us decide when its use will be constructive and when gratuitous, blurring a boundary. For example, I noticed I was frequently engaging in enjoyable theoretical speculation with a trainee about his patient who was often absent and brought this to his attention. He realised the patient used similar intellectual games to distract him from deeper feelings. He owned his own part in the collusion, fuelled by the fact he was in training. It showed us the paucity of emotional content due to the patient's actual and psychological absence and our need to compensate. We talked about how best to sustain moments of emotional connection in the triangle.

Personal disclosure

Personal disclosure, exchanges not directly related to clinical work, may refer to either internal or external reality. It is important to notice how often these occur, what about, whether they happen more with some supervisees than others.

Is a supervisee's regular initial comment about the traffic simply a 'settling in' remark? Sociolinguists call this feature of discourse 'phatic communion': a linguistic item in which the content is unimportant as the primary aim is to ease communication. Or is it more, perhaps also an unconscious communication about the effort involved and feelings of resistance? Does a question about where I went on holiday feel intrusive? If so, why? Alternatively, if I feel constrained to maintain a blank screen what intimacy am I resisting and why? What might a more open attitude with the supervisee bring about?

Here is an example of personal disclosure deepening a supervisory relationship:

Jan came to supervision in distress, having had a visible attack of vertigo which temporarily disrupted a session. His main concern was how to handle the matter in the next session. After an exploration in terms of the patient, his needs were only partly met. He still felt isolated. There were feelings of shame, evoking a memory of a similar difficult experience of my own. How best to use this? An experienced therapist, he was no longer in personal therapy. I decided to take the risk of sharing selected aspects of my experience with him, introducing it by saying why I had decided to do so. Mutuality and ego entered the room and with them, objectivity. Jan became more able to think how to manage the matter with the patient, including the usefulness of my experience. In the next meeting, to check he did not feel burdened by my autobiographical information, we talked briefly about the impact of my temporarily relinquishing an analytic attitude. It became clear my willingness to trust our relationship and reveal vulnerability to connect at a deeper level meant a great deal to him. The experience had been intense (an immersion in the alchemical bath leading to a new awareness: the *coniunctio* or mystical marriage). To contain the new level of intimacy there was a mutual need to reinforce the container by asserting our separateness and reinstating the usual boundaries.

References

Cwik, A. (2006) 'The art of tincture: analytical supervision.' *Journal of Analytical Psychology* 51(2): 209–225.

Fordham, M. (1995) 'Suggestions towards a theory of supervision.' In P. Kugler (ed.) *Jungian Perspectives on Clinical Supervision*. Einsiedeln, Switzerland: Daimon.

Gabbard, G. and Lester, E. (1995) *Boundaries and Boundary Violations in Psychoanalysis*. Washington, DC: American Psychiatric Publishing.

Gee, H. (2003) 'Boundaries in supervision.' In J. Wiener, R. Mizen and J. Duckham (eds) *Supervising and Being Supervised*. London: Palgrave Macmillan.

Jacobs, D., David, P. and Meyer, D. J. (1995) *The Supervisory Encounter*. New Haven, CT: Yale University Press.

Jung, C. G. (1953–1973) *Collected Works*, ed. Sir H. Read, M. Fordham, G. Adler and W. McGuire, 20 vols. London: Routledge & Kegan Paul.

—— (1963) *Memories, Dreams, Reflections*, ed. A. Jaffé. London: Routledge & Kegan Paul.

Kast, V. (1992) *The Dynamics of Symbols*. New York: Fromm Psychology.

Kerr, J. (1994) *A Most Dangerous Method*. London: Sinclair-Stevenson.

Krashen, D. (1996) *The Inner World of Trauma*. London: Routledge.

Martin, E. (2002) 'Giving, taking, stealing: the ethics of supervision.' In C. Driver and E. Martin (eds) *Supervising Psychotherapy*. London: Sage.

—— (2003) 'Problems and ethical issues in supervision.' In J. Wiener, R. Mizen and J. Duckham (eds) *Supervising and Being Supervised*. London: Palgrave Macmillan.

Mattoon, M. A. (1995) 'Historical notes.' In P. Kugler (ed.) *Jungian Perspectives on Clinical Supervision*. Einsiedeln, Switzerland: Daimon.

Shearer, A. (2003) 'Learning about supervision.' In J. Wiener, R. Mizen and J. Duckham (eds) *Supervising and Being Supervised*. London: Palgrave Macmillan.

Zinkin, L. (1995) 'Supervision: the impossible profession.' In P. Kugler (ed.) *Jungian Perspectives on Clinical Supervision*. Einsiedeln, Switzerland: Daimon.

Chapter 3

Ethics in supervision

Fiona Palmer Barnes

Introduction

> The individual has a right, indeed it is his duty, to set up and apply his standard of value. In the last resort ethics are the concern of the individual.
>
> (CW10 para. 912)

In this statement, Jung drew attention to the cardinal importance of a therapist's personal ethic in their work with patients. Nowadays, therapists and supervisors need to hold in mind tensions between their personal ethics and value systems, the demands and pressures arising from the ethos of the profession, the pressures of agencies and employers and attitudes to government legislation. Pressures also arise within the profession; principles guiding our work – codes of ethics, rules and codes of practice, the ethos of organisations and the peer pressures they exert on therapists in training or on members. Our personal ethics are informed by what we consider to be acceptable and unacceptable. As Richard Rowson (2006), an ethicist and author, points out:

> Every day we make such judgements from the perspectives of law, social convention, professional codes of conduct, religious beliefs, aesthetic taste, politics and practically. Moreover we often consider a situation from the standpoints of more than one of these.
>
> (Rowson 2006: 19)

These pressures on supervisee and supervisor inform their personal attitudes. For example, the area of confidentiality and its ethics has become increasingly complex since the mid-1990s with the intervention of legislation demanding disclosure. How supervisors understand the ethical nature of their own clinical work gives solid and clear foundations to their practice. Supervision by its nature raises ethical questions; simply discussing a patient with another potentially breaches confidentiality. Professionals have traditionally justified this, arguing that maintenance of safe practice takes precedence over close confidentiality.

In this chapter I consider how the complex relationships between supervisor and supervisee cause practical difficulties and dilemmas for them separately and together which have ethical dimensions. I will discuss: the contract and relationships; issues raised by theoretical orientations; backgrounds to requests for supervision; bona fides of a supervisee, including membership of an institution; registration and insurance; whether a supervisee is a student or qualified; the contract for supervision and who pays; and difficulties which arise from dual or overlapping relationships (belonging to the patient, supervisee, supervisee's training institution, supervisor's other patients, supervisees or colleagues or worlds beyond) affecting expectations, transferences and countertransferences.

I explore potential difficulties: with the patient (health difficulties, suicidal intent); with the supervisee (family difficulties, poor health, illness or ageing; poor or negligent practice); with the supervisor (health or personal difficulties); construing problems and difficulties as learning experiences. I look at supervision, the law and breaches of the law; the Human Rights and Data Protection Acts and ethical questions arising in planning and while doing research and in maintaining research records.

The contract and relationships

I have previously suggested that those who practise within an analytic organisation often presume their members share a common ethos (Palmer Barnes 2003: 39). This is indicated by failures to distinguish between statements of ethical principles (ideas and values are assumed to be held in common) and codes of professional practice (guidelines or rules). This failure to differentiate appears to arise from presuming an individual practitioner has thought about and understood the metaphysical and philosophical bases of their work (their ethic) and has thought about consequential dilemmas which arise. Therapists and supervisors may presume a collective ethos with their supervisees. Our personal ethic touches our sense of identity and Self as well as collective values. How far do we share these values and therefore a common ethos with others? Are our views and values similar, or similar enough, to enable us to undertake a common task?

It is necessary for supervisors to discuss their ethical and philosophical bases and ideals and to identify areas of discord and/or consensus. This provides a basis for mutual respect and toleration of difference. For example, a trainee once came to me from a humanistic psychotherapy background. After discussion, I realised we were going to have to live with a difference of ethos. We discussed this but felt we had enough in common for her to feel that she could benefit and learn.

Thinking about the contract between you

It is always worth considering the background to any request for supervision. What are the supervisee's expectations and what are yours? Why has the supervisee come to you? Have they heard of you from someone in particular, heard you speak, read something of yours? In other words, is there an active transference? How do you feel about the potential supervisee either from previous experience or from your present meeting? It is important to be clear about thoughts and expectations of how work will proceed. Before you start, it is helpful to check the bona fides of the supervisee.

- What was their training or are they still training?
- Are they appropriately registered?
- What code of ethics and practice are they working to?
- Which grievance and complaints procedure could be called into play if a complaint is made against them or their work proves unsatisfactory?
- Are they insured and with whom – do you feel this is adequate?

Personal indemnity insurance is essential for working in private practice. Insurance is required by all professional bodies in the UK and most EU countries. The supervisee may be working in an agency. The question is again whether the supervisee is adequately covered.

Whether a potential supervisee has completed training raises important questions.

- What is the standard of the training, the expectations of their training organisation, what level of obligation do you have and to whom?
- What level of reporting to the training organisation is expected?
- Will this be unpaid time and is that acceptable?

It is too late if you become resentful when lengthy reports are expected but no fee is paid. You need to know at the outset what your obligations are, otherwise you may experience surprises and ill-feeling may get into the work.

You may think together about how many patients will be supervised in the time you have. Where will they come from? Will they be from private referrals, agencies, professional organisations or from clinic work? The patient could be a friend of friends or, in possibly the most difficult cases, they could be trainees on the same counselling course but in another year of the training. That situation is most likely to become unsatisfactory. If the patient has been referred by a clinic, has an assessment been done by a psychotherapist, general practitioner (GP) or psychiatrist? Do they maintain clinical responsibility or does it rest with your supervisee? If, say, the supervisee works in the National Health Service (NHS) in the UK and is a trainee on a placement, usually a consultant psychiatrist retains clinical responsibility; or, if the supervisee is a counsellor (say in a university health service), they will probably hold clinical responsibility themselves.

If therapists work directly for agencies, or when patients are being referred from GPs, educational establishments, through employee assistance programmes, or in any way other than by personal referral, it is essential the therapist knows the terms of the contract. Increasingly, medical insurers and other agencies ask for signed contracts from those paid by them. Legislation has become increasingly complex in this area. It is understandable that employers wish to cover themselves against litigation. However, such limitations can mean confidentiality may be severely compromised. If a therapist is working for an agency which makes these demands they will need to explain the limits of confidentiality clearly to the patient. Employers or educational establishments may include clauses demanding disclosure if an individual knows of a breach of health and safely law, or if sexual abuse has taken place. These conditions may not have been written by the therapist. It may be helpful if they discuss them with their employer before there are difficulties, and, if possible, get them removed from the contract.

It is essential to establish where you both think clinical responsibility lies, as more and more registering bodies are seeing supervisors as holding some. This needs clarity. Who pays for sessions is also important. It is about investment in the process, both conscious and unconscious, as well as about responsibility. Who owns the process, the supervisee or their agency? You are establishing ethical and clinical responsibility through asking such questions.

Finally, the number of patients relates to the intensity of supervision. You need to think together about what feels appropriate. Some supervisors are willing to take on responsibility for the whole clinical load of a supervisee. Others want to work in depth with one or perhaps two patients only. The intensity of supervision needs to be comfortable to both.

The main ethical question for a supervisor is whether a supervisee seems to have the potential to work with them, to grow and improve their practice. It presumes they can develop their inner reflective processes and way of being with patients, that they are and will remain in good enough mental health to withstand the hurdles and rigours of practice without splitting and disintegrating or finding self-doubts develop into self-destruction. Have they the flexibility and creativity to manage their work with patients and the process you experience together? The same criteria apply to practising counsellors, psychotherapists or analysts: is there enough flexibility to manage a variety of patients, are they motivated to increase their skills and knowledge? For a supervisee, choosing you will depend on the above and whether they feel they will be able to learn and be stimulated.

The complexity of therapeutic relationships

I now discuss some of the taxing issues where an ethical attitude is most needed. These often result from and in shadow issues which can cause considerable difficulties. Jung describes the shadow as follows: 'The shadow is a moral problem . . . To become conscious of it involves recognising the dark aspects of the personality as present and real' (CW9ii para. 13) and 'they have an emotional nature, a kind of autonomy, and accordingly an obsessive, or, better, possessive quality' (CW9ii para. 15). I will now look at the complexity of relationships involved in supervision; when the supervision work is part of the assessment process and the complexity of social relationships within the context of the Shadow.

The multiple relationships in therapeutic organisations are enormously complex. From Figure 3.1, you will see some of these possible connections; I am sure there are other connections too. (I have developed this diagram used by Renos Papodopoulos and Shayne Spitzer for supervision seminars held at AJA.)

In Figure 3.1, the inner circle represents collective archetypal issues, complexes and projections. The arrows in and out represent the candidate in training, the analyst, the supervisors, training patients and training and assessment committees. Arrows represent the vectors of relationships,

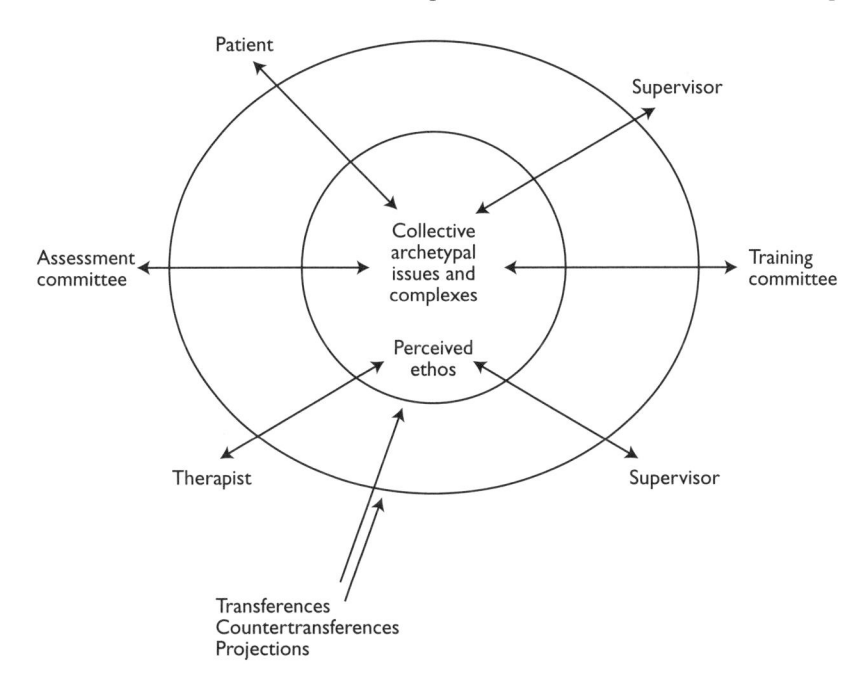

Figure 3.1

conscious and unconscious. Within therapeutic organisations there are potential connections between supervisees, their analysts, trainers, supervisors and assessors. There may also be potential overlaps between training patients and colleagues, for example, between

- supervisees and supervisor as supervisor and, possibly, as trainer
- supervisor and analyst
- training patients and supervisors and trainers in seminars
- supervisors and assessors.

All these relationships carry conscious and unconscious projections, transferences and countertransferences. The potentials for conscious and unconscious competition give rise to complex field interactions which may challenge ethical standards. Supervisors need to ask themselves whether other connections than those belonging to their work are prejudicing them.

Figure 3.1 shows some patterns of loyalties and differences in an organisation, which, in their turn, affect collective and organisational attitudes towards supervisees. Most organisations have tried to exclude certain connections; for instance, that the training analyst has access to the assessment of the candidate or is consulted about final assessment for qualification. However, questions sometimes are raised in assessment: 'Am I prejudiced against this candidate because I know something of his private life?' The smaller the organisation and the more relationships are inclined to extend beyond the task of supervision, the greater the hazards.

Assessment

Organisations where we 'therapise', train and supervise candidates carry incestuous dimensions which are at their most problematic during assessment. Therapists have positive and negative, loving and hating views about each other. We hear comments like: 'Candidate Y will be all right with Mr W for supervision, he will sort out her difficulty regarding the father complex', or 'Candidate P will be OK because he is in analysis with Dr X', the inference being Mr W or Dr X have the innate capacity to sort out the particular imagined difficulties. Negative views of colleagues are also heard: 'It's a pity Candidate B is with Mrs A, they have the same anima problem' or 'Candidate C goes to Mr D for supervision and narcissism is his blind spot too'.

Connections between individuals involve patterns of projections, transferences and countertransferences. These can be caring and creative and also problematic and difficult to wrestle with ethically. In his article 'Thirty methods to destroy the creativity of psychoanalytic candidates', Kernberg (1996) explores how formal aspects of psychoanalytic training inhibit creativity in candidates. He mentions repetitive and unquestioning teaching of key papers by theoretical founders, hierarchical structures and relationships among colleagues; each causing systematic slowing down of a candidate's progress. His article opens up discussion about the purpose and way of supervising, the experiences we give supervisees and how much our envy and desire for possession or wish to enact the role of parent or guru may cause us to raise and raise again the hurdles we expect trainees to jump. We need to remind ourselves it is important for any trainee to get the best resources available. Their investment has been, and is, emotionally and financially high. Organisations need to continuously examine collectively their procedures to ensure they are respectful and ethical, not infantilising.

Socially

Outside our professional world there can be potential or actual problems when there is a possibility of social overlap with a supervisee or their patient. Again we only have to think about the incestuous relationships within therapy organisations. Some organisations provide many of the training and supervising staff for another organisation. The therapy world is so small that overlap may arise from colleagues sharing similar interests.

In a rural area, like the one I live in, Herefordshire, there are 180,000 people (the population of Islington, a London borough) and 40 doctors. The land area is 40 miles by 40 miles. The potential for professional and social overlap is considerable. Meeting colleagues, patients, supervisees and supervisees' patients in the most unexpected places is always possible. Both are likely to be at any training event and one may meet patients and supervisees at social gatherings.

On one occasion I was at a swimming pool and after my early morning swim went to shower. There were many women in there and clearly those of us using the shower were in the habit of stripping off. I decided to join them only to realise when fully in the buff that my new supervisee had just come in on her way into the pool. This was a level of exposure I had not reckoned on! Therapists need to think about how such situations will be managed and what their reaction needs to be. It may be there are occasions where the event or the nature of the connection warrants leaving.

Situations can arise where you hear from a colleague about a lunch party where a particular discussion took place. Then, you may hear the outcome of the same discussion which affected the patient of a supervisee. Or, you can go out to dinner and realise you are sitting with the estranged husband of your supervisee's patient or having coffee and hear all about a supervisee or their patient from a friend you thought had no connection with your professional world. The need for good and clear boundaries on all occasions, particularly under provocation, is essential. It is hard to hear a supervisee or patient being unjustly criticised and be unable to say anything.

Difficulties arising in supervision

In the supervisee's work

Ethical issues arise in various ways. A patient may have health problems and need to attend hospital appointments or have surgery. Work needs to be done to decide whether there is avoidance or denial within the patient: does the contract need variation? What happens about fees? What about visiting the patient in hospital or using telephone sessions? It is important to point out ethical questions and the need to consider the consequences of action or non-action arising within the supervisory space. Illegal or liminal actions of the patient also need to be considered transferentially and symbolically.

A patient may be at risk of committing suicide or they present a risk to others, or to the state.

A supervisee presents a new patient, Joe, whom she saw as an emergency in the student counselling service. Joe's closest friend killed himself last week and Joe has not slept since. His tutor had sent him. Joe tells your supervisee he feels suicidal. She does not feel this is so and believes the student is overtired and displaying a histrionic reaction to his friend's death. Supervisor and therapist need to weigh up the probabilities. Here, the supervisor might suggest Joe either goes immediately to his GP or to the Accident and Emergency Department of the local hospital for medication and then continue with future sessions. Ethically, an assessment of suicide risk always benefits from a second opinion.

There is other UK legislation (Children Acts, terrorism legislation and health and safety laws) which needs to be held in mind and responded to as necessary.

Bill was presented on a regular basis. In a twice-weekly analytic therapy, his initial problem was anxiety about his behaviour in his new family. He is in his mid-forties and until recently lived with ageing parents, for whom he cared. His mother died and his father, with Alzheimer's, was in residential care. Bill, a teacher, had a number of long relationships with women and married for the first time six months before starting therapy. His wife had a 14-year-old daughter and 12-year-old son. The couple were careful to try to make a smooth transfer to a joint household. Bill is concerned about his relationship with his stepfamily. He finds his stepdaughter's clothing and behaviour sexually arousing. He talks about his difficulties over the years with provocative behaviour by young girls at school and how impotent he feels in disciplining them. There are similarities to the hero in Vladimir Nabokov's classic novel *Lolita* or the emotions expressed in the song 'Don't stand so close to me' by the Police. His dreams are erotic and violent. He finds it desperately difficult when girls pass him in a crowded corridor and their breasts push against him.

Bill's anxiety has grown over recent weeks and this topic now dominates sessions. He is relieved to speak about this 'hidden subject'. The supervisee is anxious because reality and fantasy are hard to separate. In the last two sessions he talked about all he sees in the bathroom, his anxiety about doing the family laundry and having caught his stepdaughter as she fell and finding himself holding her by the crotch and her arm. The therapist is doing her best to interpret and help with symbolic understanding. In the second session that week he spoke about having time alone in the house and going into his stepdaughter's bedroom and masturbating. The therapist is filled with panic and anxiety and a wish to inform social services that the daughter is at risk.

Clearly this situation needs calming. It feels as though the patient is involved in a spiralling anxiety and growing tension. It is essential the supervisor provides containment so the situation can be explored and the countertransference of the supervisee analysed. It is necessary to explore with the supervisee her desire to breach confidentiality; is there a real risk or has Bill's anxiety provoked a punitive reaction in the therapist? The supervisor and supervisee need to keep in mind their obligations under the Children Act, to report actual or potential sexual abuse of children, and balance these with the need for therapeutic containment and thorough clinical assessment. Sadly Bill's therapist did contact social services during the supervisor's holiday and Bill was questioned. Though no charge was ever made against Bill, both the therapy and his new family were destroyed. Trust was never re-established between Bill and his wife, social services having told her about his fantasies.

With the supervisee

Supervisees may experience life changes which affect their work. There may be family difficulties, a divorce or deaths, causing considerable disruption. Such circumstances can normally be negotiated, particularly if the supervisee is open and talks about their difficulties. Additional support in the form of therapy or extra supervision can be arranged.

Intent is important in any supervisee's actions, and the supervisor is there to act in a supportive, mediatory and, if necessary, challenging way. The supervisor tries to model best practice themselves; this can act as a standard. Where practice falls short this needs to be addressed and reasons given. If the supervisee repeatedly shows poor practice and is neither improving nor learning, it may be that the only way forward is to report them to their employer or professional body for breaches of their code of good practice. The therapist who is persistently late for sessions and takes holidays with little warning may be an example of such poor practice. A therapist who does not tell patients they are taking a break and leaves vulnerable patients coming to an empty consulting room for a week shows bad practice. Each of these could happen accidentally but, if repeated, are inexcusable.

With supervisee and supervisor

However, there are more serious challenges when a therapist shows slow deterioration of their health through illness or age. Many therapists work on with limited but chronic conditions, which may not affect their work in any material way for a long time. However, some conditions, by their nature, deteriorate. Ageing brings its own difficulties with loss of function and memory. It can be tough to tell someone to take a break or consider retirement. Some organisations within the British Psychoanalytic Confederation now have an upper age limit of 70, for taking on training patients. Older practitioners need to think about how long the therapy with any individual may take and whether they will live long enough to be useful.

There is an ethical responsibility to think about permanent health insurance and pensions for there may well become a time when practice becomes poor or threatens to be become unsound and unsafe yet the practitioner feels they must continue because they need the money. For example, a newly qualified analyst presents an assessment of a new case.

Joan is in her forties and is angry and upset. She is an only child brought up in a remote community. Her mother is American and her father was old when she was born: she has a half-brother thirty years her senior. The patient wonders about her sexuality. She did well at school. The family visited the United States, when she was aged 18 months, 7, 8 and 12 years old. On each trip she believed she was emigrating to the United States until her family finally returned to England when she was 13. Joan did well at school and decided to train as a nurse in London. After completing training, she worked in a premature baby unit where she became a Sister. Her upset at children's deaths brought her into therapy and she wanted to train as a counsellor or psychotherapist. She applied to a psychotherapy association and was offered the opportunity of being a training patient. The analysis was three times weekly for six years.

During this time the therapist qualified and decided to move from London. She told Joan that therapy would have to end. However, the therapist had problems selling her home and therapy was extended on an ad-hoc basis. Joan found out she was moving to Devon, drove there at weekends, eventually discovering where the psychotherapist had bought a home. Joan called and was invited to tea. There was then considerable confusion between cups of tea, therapy sessions in London and therapy sessions in Devon. Therapy ended before the full-time move to Devon. Joan also moved there, and began work for a private nursing agency. She socialised more and more with her former therapist and often became distressed. They fell out from time to time and Joan would then bolt to relatives in the United States.

The therapist decided to breed ponies and Joan became involved, being present at the births of foals, and looking after the therapist's home when she went to shows or on holiday. On these occasions Joan lived in the therapist's home. She now wanted to work out whether she should make a complaint against her former therapist.

There are clearly unresolved transference issues here. The first therapist failed to be aware of this and the subsequent acting out by both parties. The supervisee could be encouraged to see the material as symbolic of relationships in the patient's life. This might be a constructive way forward for Joan as there is a real impasse. However, this leaves thought-provoking question of what both supervisor and supervisee might feel they need to do about the therapist concerned. In his article, 'Perversions in the temenos', Steven Galipeau (2001), an American Jungian analyst, concerned with perversions in the transference relationship, argues:

> I seek to formulate the scope of such analytic perversions to include destructive interactions that are not sexually enacted but are equally, and maybe even more insidiously, injurious to the patient . . . A numinosity or fascination exists that, though not necessarily sexual, clouds the objectivity of the analyst and allows patient and analyst to become gripped by a state of unconscious union that is covered by primitive affects.
> (Galipeau 2001: 5)

Clearly something of this sort occurred here.

In Joan's case, therapist and supervisor were able to contain the work. They agreed that since the previous therapist was no longer working, they would act on the information and formalise the complaint themselves. This may or may not be acceptable in itself to a professional organisation. They decided the important thing was to help Joan understand the predicament she found herself in and what her part was in it. The therapy lasted for four years, during which Joan resolved her transference relationship with her previous therapist and stopped obsessing about her; she was able to nurse her dying mother and to have a real and compassionate relationship with her in her last days. Joan found a new occupation and was able to move to another part of the UK and make a life there.

Supervision and the law

This section is about the relationship between codes of practice and ethics and the law. This often causes considerable anxiety, not least because the reality is complex. There are tensions between a practitioner's 'duty of care' towards patients. Keeping their work of a standard considered good practice within the profession affects how they treat their patients, how they keep records, maintain confidentiality, and manage a confidential space. They also have legal responsibilities under, in the UK, the Children Acts 1989 and 2004 or Children (Scotland) Act 1995, Data Protection Act 1998, Human Rights Act 1998, Mental Health Act 1983 and anti-terrorism legislation.

A supervisee says in supervision that a patient she saw last week reported he knew there were banned chemicals in the basement of his school. He was so upset he had left the session prematurely. The supervisee feared he would not turn up for his next appointment. She says that under her contract she feels bound to report this to the relevant authority. The balance for the supervisor and therapist is whether the therapist can get the patient back into the room to help him to report his discovery to the relevant authorities while discussing why he had not reported the chemicals himself and why he needed to come to see the therapist and tell her. This must be balanced with any possible risk to the safety of others.

How records are kept is, in the UK, influenced by the Data Protection Act 1998. This requires all records to be kept securely, with the client's knowledge, and exist no longer than for the purpose for which they are required. Files may need to be restricted. Enough information should be kept so a professional colleague who needs to get in touch with a patient in a crisis can do so. Pip Garvey (2003), when Ethics Chair of the British Confederation of Psycho-Analysis, argued we should keep two kinds of files – records and notes. *Records* include information your executor might need in the event of death or illness. She advises that to these simple records of name and contact details you might wish to add letters from general practitioners, psychiatrists, possibly also a diagnosis and the potential for suicide or psychotic breakdown. *Notes* are the personal process notes of the psychotherapist. This was the view of a number of organisations, though some have revised their opinion. If patient details are not totally removed from such notes, they clearly have connection to the patient. Supervisors need to be aware that all records and notes are subject to the patient's or supervisee's desire to see them. This is their legal right under the Data Protection Act. Records and notes need to be kept with respect for the patient being fully observed. If records are well kept there will be a suitable file for the patient to see should they ask to do so.

Garvey (2003) also points out:

> Courts are able to order the disclosure of notes, jottings, memorabilia etc. under a court order. For this reason (it has been suggested) that therapists . . . keep no notes or they recommend that notes are destroyed once they have served the purpose for which they are being kept.
> (Garvey 2003: 147)

Another view, proposed by British Association for Counselling and Psychotherapy, is to keep records and notes for a period within which the professional body might receive a complaint. Time limitations vary and rise if the complaint is of a serious nature. It is normally suggested that records and notes are retained for seven years.

Counselling and psychotherapy records are classed as 'sensitive personal data' under the Data Protection Act 1998. This covers data relating to them, opinions about them and intentions towards them. Even if records are kept apart from names, or records apart from notes, if, by putting them together, there is any chance the patient might be identified, the notes and records are considered to be 'highly structured' by the commissioner, and there is a duty to notify and register with the data commissioner. It is unlikely any process notes could be suitably anonymised. It is important to note that this UK law applies to handwritten notes as well as computer records.

Supervisors need to think about how much information they hold in notes about supervisees and whether these records would be identifiable if the patient were to unexpectedly have access to them. The Data Protection Act is about record keeping, but it is also about confidentiality and secrecy. Confidentiality, Christopher Bollas (2000: 173) argues, 'is held by our profession – not by our patients so that we may discuss our patients with colleagues, clear in our minds that in so doing we are not referring our patients to the criminal justice system'.

Such an attitude requires a commitment to the highest ethical standards. Bollas is talking about containment. The more we can contain in the consulting room, the more we can understand about the patient, help them to understand and control themselves and their actions. This is the attitude of many psychotherapeutic and analytic organisations, yet we may not be supervising individuals who come from similar backgrounds. There may be other legal and professional pressures upon them to consider the limits of confidentiality in other ways.

Confidentiality usually remains between patient and practitioner but, as we have said, supervision immediately enlarges the circle to three. Some practitioners recognise this, and may refer to it by saying to patients something like 'from time to time I discuss clinical material with a colleague, I do not give the name of the individual'. Increasingly such a statement may be understood by the patient as a reference to professional supervision.

As those who work in agencies will know, confidentiality may be 'to the agency' as the files are kept by them and assessment teams and supervision groups may be parties to the extended confidential group. There can be breaches of confidentiality which are unintentional, as in doctors' surgeries, where openly held confidentiality can, from time to time, become lax. Or breaches may occur if an employer or agency demand information be divulged for managers or others to assure themselves the law has not been broken. Increasingly, employee assistance programmes and educational establishments insist that practitioners report to them if certain subjects are discussed in sessions. An example might be where health and safety issues are discussed and others could be at risk, or where a patient declares they have been abused. In usual practice, therapists would hope to encourage the patient to report such matters to an employer, or for abuse to be tackled in person by the patient with the therapist's support. However, agencies are increasingly asking for reporting when therapists are doing short-term work, leaving the therapist in a difficult position, where the authority and autonomy of the patient are removed or the therapist is left vulnerable.

Ethical and legal questions can be problematic in planning and while doing research and in maintaining research records. Here, both the UK Human Rights and Data Protection Acts apply. In 1998, Jane Polden, an analytic psychotherapist, saw the therapist as first and foremost the custodian of the patient's rights including confidentially, giving self-determination to determine the dissemination of the story of their own life (Polden 1998: 339). She, like Bollas, has concerns about the ability of obtaining fully informed consent from any patient, when dependencies and transferences are necessarily part of the process. The patient may not be able to fully comprehend what publication may mean. Therapist and supervisor hold the confidentiality of the patient, know its limitations and if these are reached, need to explain them. That is part of the psychotherapist's duty of care.

Conclusion

In supervising, we are helping our supervisee learn to make judgements and are making judgements ourselves. It ultimately involves giving our *imprimatur* to a supervisee's work. For all practical matters discussed here, much of what goes on is about the professional attitude of the people in the room and the work they are doing. Ethics is a matter of profound personal judgement. Jung reminds us in his foreword to Neumann's *Depth Psychology and a New Ethic* about the complexity of the formulation of ethical rules:

> The formulation of ethical rules is not only difficult but actually impossible because one can hardly think of a single rule that would not have to be reversed under certain conditions . . . The solution, in my

experience, is always individual and is only subjectively valid. Despite their subjective nature, they cannot very well be formulated except as collective concepts.

(CW18 para. 1413)

He reminded us in *Memories, Dreams, Reflections* that:

> once we know how uncertain the foundation is, ethical decision becomes a subjective creative act. We can convince ourselves of its validity only *deo concedente* – that is, there must be a spontaneous and decisive impulse on the part of the unconscious. Ethic itself, the decision between good and evil, is not affected by this impulse, only made more difficult for us. Nothing can spare us the torment of the ethical decision.
>
> (Jung 1963: 361)

Once we know the rules and the law we need to suspend or contain both of these and think about what is wanted and needed in relation to the patient in the room. Creating a reflective space requires a reflective ethical stance, as promoted by Sells (1994), a Jungian analyst, who speaks of 'soul-based ethics'; the afterthoughts of ethical reflection being laws, codes and procedures. These become surrogates for the soul's innate ethical genius. Soul-based ethics give us an opportunity for ethical creativity. Both the British Psychological Society and British Association of Counselling and Psychotherapy have written an 'ethical framework' rather than 'codes of practice'. They encourage reflection and discussion to promote choices between principles, rather than legalistic codes of practice which stand as requirements against which therapists will be judged. Ethical attitudes in supervision reflect responsibility, purposefulness, mindfulness, confidentiality and impartiality. They require open-mindedness and flexibility to help supervisees think about a common task, that of working with patients on their individuation process.

References

Bollas, C. (2000) 'Confidentiality and professionalism in psychoanalysis.' *British Journal of Psychotherapy* 20(2): 157–176.

Galipeau, S. (2001) 'Perversions in the temenos.' *Journal of Jungian Theory and Practice* 3(2): 5–18.

Garvey, P. (2003) 'Setting the scene II: the BCP Working Group on Confidentiality.' *British Journal of Psychotherapy* 20(2): 141–149.

Jung C. G. (1953–1973) *Collected Works*, ed. Sir H. Read, M. Fordham, G. Adler and W. McGuire, 20 vols. London: Routledge & Kegan Paul.

—— (1963) *Memories, Dreams, Reflections*. London: Fontana.

Kernberg, O. F. (1996) 'Thirty methods to destroy the creativity of psychoanalytic candidates.' *International Journal of Psycho-Analysis* 77: 1031–1040.

Palmer Barnes, F. (2003) 'Ethics in practice.' In H. Solomon and M. Twyman (ed.) *The Ethical Attitude in Analytic Practice*. London: Free Association.

Polden, J. (1998) 'Publish and be damned.' *British Journal of Psychotherapy* 14(3): 337–347.

Rowson, R. (2006) *Working Ethics*. London: Jessica Kingsley.

Sells, B. (1994) 'Ethics after the fall.' *Spring* 56: 53–64.

Chapter 4

Difficult patients

Dale Mathers

Introduction

> In addition to the inherent duality of Universe
> there is also and always
> an inherent threefoldedness and fourfoldedness
> of initial consciousness
> and of all experience.
> For in addition to (1) action, (2) reaction, (3) resultant,
> there is always (4) the a priori environment,
> within which the event occurs,
> i.e., the at-first-nothingness around us
> of the child graduated from the womb
> within which seeming nothingness (fourthness)
> the inherently threefold local event took place.
> Richard Buckminster Fuller, *Intuition* (1983: 26)

Buckminster Fuller's description of consciousness as three- and fourfold can help open up the meaning of 'difficult'. Supervision gives a privileged view of an intimate relationship. How can we create a safe space, like a ring for diamonds, for an intimate relationship which is threefold (patient, therapist and supervisor) and fourfold (patient, therapist, supervisor and collective)? Who creates the idea of difficult? Does it mean predicament? Predicaments in therapy may evoke negative judgements; they ask for discernment, for time and space within which meanings can clarify. Maybe difficult means hard to discern? The commonest causes are being in a hurry, having guilty attachments to 'theory', having a goal in mind, and imagining we are supposed to know what is going on.

Therapeutic work concerns becoming more of one's Self, individuation (Chapter 5). We need others with whom to do this, and an intersubjective space in which to do it. Jung said individuation 'is the process by which individual beings are formed and differentiated; in particular, it is the development of the psychological individual as a being distinct from the general, collective psychology' (CW6 para. 757). Individuation is not possible apart from the collective: we cannot separate unless we are attached; we cannot be apart from, until we have been a part of. To feel cut off from everyone else is *anomie* (from the Greek, *a* = not, and *nomos* = name). The word was used by the French sociologist Emile Durkheim to describe profound alienation. An anomic person has no name and does not exist. A key task in supervision and therapy is naming: 'You're Jim, not your father', 'This feeling is called humiliation', 'That feeling is called hope'. Naming an experience that Jim has as difficult, rather than saying 'Jim is difficult', offers liberation rather than limitation. An aim of supervision is to create a reflective space within which naming can occur. This space invites intuition, trusting the unconscious – the a priori environment.

Thoughts, feelings and sensations create mindful awareness. Using awareness involves intuition. Into supervisory space come descriptions of actions, reactions and resultants. The space depends on the unconscious, on holding unknowns and unknowables. An unknown is something we could know, given time (the name of Jim's father). An unknowable is something we can never know (the names of his ancestors a thousand generations ago). Intuition gives a sense of possibility and a future perspective. It is a mental process allowing the formation and use of symbols (Chapter 8), which hold unknowable – as metaphysical operators. Often, we cannot discover other than with symbols and intuition within whom a difficulty is located. Unfortunately, intuition is right about half the time. As we never know which half that is, using intuition requires learning to *be with not knowing*, which is what this chapter is about.

What does difficult mean?

When teaching this topic, I asked the students to describe 'difficult patients'. They characterised one group as hostile, defensive and dismissive; vulnerable and fragile narcissists, with egos like eggshells. Another group were liminal, unconnected and dissociated; borderline, in whom primitive defences of the Self operate strongly (splitting, projective identification and denial). Most difficult were those raising concerns about physical safety (theirs or others, including the therapists). 'Difficult' was felt when observations did not fit theories or preconceptions, worst when unresolved core complexes were activated anywhere in the supervisory triangle. The students' examples were all people with histories of serious abuse and neglect; none described patients with 'formal' psychotic disorders, schizophrenia or bipolar affective disorder. They are not 'difficult': they may create major management problems, but supportive analytically informed counselling can relieve some suffering.

'Difficult' meant having a marked personality disorder. Suppose 'difficult' is an intuition supervisors can have about the personalities involved in a therapy? Intuition is not a wish-fulfilment, it is a predictive psychic function mediated by its Shadow, the known. The Shadow, an Archetype, can be defined as 'the thing a person has no wish to be' (Jung, CW16 para. 470; CW9i paras 13–19). It does not mean 'bad', or as in George Lucas's *Star Wars* films, 'touched by the Dark Side of the Force'; simply, 'what we have no wish to be . . .'. If I have no wish to be a policeman, my 'policeman-like' qualities – say, judgement – are in my Shadow. Intuition involves perceiving the not-known, the Shadow.

Working with personality disorders – whether present in ourselves as supervisors, or in patients, supervisees and training organisations – requires tolerating large amounts of uncertainty, the Shadow of knowing. This might be thought of as a mindfulness of the Opposite of Self. 'Self' here is a verb, not a noun. It names an action, the capacity to show 'the four invariants of self – coherence, continuity, agency and affective relational patterns [which] shape a particular ego-complex to function more or less in maintaining the unity of the subject over time' (Young-Eisendrath 2005: 208). Coherence is ownership of our history, continuity is a sense of our development, agency is our ability to make autonomous choice, and affective relating means sharing feelings, empathy.

When difficulties with some of these invariants appear in any part of the system (patient, therapist, supervisor, collective), the system loses its ability for self-determination, becoming problematic. If all four invariants are lost, it is 'difficult'. We find ourselves reacting, rather than acting. We get preoccupied with results (outcome) rather than attending to the a priori environment, the Unconscious (process). We start feeling we must do something, usually *something to someone else* to 'make them better'. For supervisors, this may emerge as an overwhelming urge to teach, rescue, advise, or just rescue. Which can mean turning the supervisory triangle into a 'victim–persecutor–rescuer' triangle.

A guiding medical principle is *primum, non nocere* – first, do no harm. Physicians call this 'masterly inactivity'. When we truly do not know, it harms us to pretend we do. We need patience or we lose dignity, that is, mutual respect, vital to a working therapeutic alliance. Often, this means holding an anguish till we find to whom it belongs. With a 'difficult patient', everyone shares the suffering, especially in training settings when such a patient may also be 'a difficult trainee'.

Suppose 'difficult' comes in flavours? Suppose sets of not-knowing exist? The first might be nominative, 'difficult for whom?' Who says a patient, supervisee, supervisor or training organisation is difficult? The second set might be called spatio-temporal, 'difficult how, when, where?' The third set, metaphysical: 'difficult – why?' is usually unknowable. 'Why' questions do badly in therapy, perhaps as the answers are often historical, political, philosophical, spiritual or religious rather than pragmatic? It is hard to find a boundary for a 'why' question.

A common sign of 'difficulty' in a supervisory system is a sudden rise to prominence in the narrative of global history, world politics, philosophising, mythologising, spirituality or religiosity at the expense of being with the transference and countertransference. This is a 'transcendent defence', or 'mandalisation'. The clinical signs are an acute intoxication with images, myths, fairy stories and grandiose amplifications of the mandala-like archetypal patterns which are always present. It is exciting, appears to give dazzling insights but usually goes nowhere. The opposite defence is 'infantilisation' – interpreting anything and everything in terms of early child development, using the symbol of the 'good-enough mother' and the baby at her breast to the exclusion of any other.

Asking, 'What does this *mean*?' allows 'I don't know' as a valid answer; as are 'I don't know yet' or 'I can never know'. Take 'difficult' as a description of a thought or felt experience for each person in a supervisory meaning-system. This gives it validity independent of theory, whether social, medical, mythical, psychiatric or psychodynamic. This is why I am not giving lists of diagnoses or managements. They are as easy to write as a repeat prescription. Intuitively, what is needed in difficult supervisory situations is the Shadow of prescriptive thinking – open-system thinking, in which the postmodern 'both–and' is used, rather than the modernist 'either–or'.

Imagine object-relations theory is like Newtonian physics. It clearly explains many things happening at a macromolecular level. It is valuably different to a quantum perspective, in touch with the ordinary realities of life. However, a quantum-time concept, synchronicity, underpins the idea of parallel process, another means by which 'difficult' can be decoded (Chapter 11). An object-relations based understanding of difficult might ask 'amongst this person's internal objects, which is difficult for whom?' and 'who names the difficulty?'

Jim, a handsome young man, ebulliently conducted our initial interview, skilfully interviewing me, till suddenly he bowed his head, whispered 'I'm gay . . .', then continued as if nothing had happened. My internal supervisor intuited naming what had happened 'shame' at such an early point would make me a difficult therapist. If someone names you 'difficult', will this prove fatal? For Jim, it almost had. He'd been self-destructive and was now actively suicidal. Waiting till our working alliance was secure let him know he'd been held in my mind, rather than judged. When I later mentioned what happened, he took nominative power, naming his feeling 'humiliation'. Leaving time and space for him to name this himself meant doing so was not a further humiliation. He then made an interpretation, contrasting my patience with his hot-tempered, violent, alcoholic, sexually abusive father.

The hardest patient to supervise is the one never brought, who cannot be held in mind as they are not special or interesting; they are too easy, or embarrassingly difficult. Such hidden patients carry a Shadow, as Jim carried the shadow of his father's homoerotic, incestuous desire. This unfortunately made Jim 'special'. Is there a difference between 'difficult' and 'special'? The psychoanalyst Tom Main (1957) pointed out in 'The Ailment' how a 'special patient' can wreak havoc on an in-patient psychiatric unit, as carers fall over themselves trying to be the best rescuer (persecuting each other in the process).

Using archetypal theory, I could say 'difficult' means not enough psychic space exists to allow the humanisation of archetypes. Using developmental theory, 'difficult' might mean acting out makes it impossible to explore developmental delays and arrests. In subject relations theory, it means someone has seized nominative power: 'Jim, who says "gay" is something to be ashamed of? Who gets to unsay it?' Supervision may be difficult as a result of a patient's internal objects or archetypal patterns or lack of nominative power; when their aesthetics of meaning gives rise to problems in the collective which reappear between therapist and supervisor.

Theory: a language of interpretation?

A theory is 'an explanatory system, a set of hypotheses arrived at by abstract reasoning' (Chambers Dictionary). A theory, according to Jung, is 'less value from the point of view of psychological truth than religious dogma' (Samuels et al. 1986: 149). They suggest that Jung held 'the analyst should not practice on the basis of ideas which are foreign to him or with which he has no experiential contact'. In supervision, this, however, is common. Supervisors attempt to observe complexes in a given patient which constellate with complexes in the therapist, supervisor, and the collectives they inhabit (Chapters 9 and 10).

Imagine this pattern is a hologram. Using laser light, if a picture is taken of an object onto a glass plate, when the plate is smashed, the picture can be recreated from any fragment, all is encoded in any part. Now, different parts in a collective name the elements in a complex differently. Suppose: I call it being gay, you call it an obscene offence against the Lord – which is 'true?' As participant-observers in a supervising system, we could recognise 'truths' are as relative as analytic theories. They are, philosophically, examples of contextuality; the truth of a discourse is true only within its context:

> Discourses make it possible for us to see the world in a certain way. They produce our knowledge of the world. If we think of knowledge as one possible account of events, one that has received the stamp of truth, then to the extent that this version brings with it particular possibilities for acting in the world then it has power implications.
> (Burr 2003: 79)

A theory is a system of nomination – a pattern by which names are given to things or events. They are described thus by, amongst others, the French semiotician, Ferdinand Saussure, the American philosopher of language, Noam Chomsky, and the French philosopher, Jacques Derrida. With an emphasis on deconstruction and the primacy of narrative, postmodernism uses linguistic theory to see through collective mazes. What would this look like in supervision? Maybe like this:

$$t \phi l : \Sigma L$$

This is Tarski's theorem, named for the young Polish mathematician who created it while researching topology (shape) in the 1930s: t means a truth function, ϕ means 'within', l means 'a language', (:) means 'such that', Σ means 'sum of', and L means 'metalanguage'; so, in words, 'the truth of a statement t, in language l, can only be given in a metalanguage L, the language of interpretation' (Tarski 1983).

If I say 'gay' and you say 'offence against the Lord', which cultural system provides metalanguage (L) here, the small one of homophobic religious fundamentalism or the larger one of a multicultural world? If a patient says 'you are a difficult therapist' are they saying 'you are a bad breast', 'you are a naughty mummy', 'you are a terrible witch-mother' or are they simply telling the truth? Curiously, it does not especially matter which theories are used in any part of a supervisory system, nor whether they are coherent within themselves, or to each other. Frequently analytic theories are everything except coherent. The question is, as supervisor, can one find a 'participant-observer position'? Can one argue for the process (rather than for patient or therapist) using a metalanguage, a language of interpretation? If so, what might that language be?

Suppose it is a language of symbols (Chapters 6 and 8)? A symbol is a (sign + {x}), where {x} is an unknowable; not an unknown which might be known, but an unknowable: {x} stands for 'not-knowing'. We can be with {x}, using a metalanguage for interpretation. Take supervision as a semiotic task, seeking to find where meaning has got stuck. We can imagine: 'Everything this person is telling me is both true and false, neither true nor false' and 'Everything can be treated for analytic purposes in the same way as the symbols in a dream, including my responses.' Symbols are *not* signs. This was a major contention between Freud and Jung, who said:

> those conscious contents which give us a clue to the unconscious background are incorrectly called symbols by Freud. They are not true symbols, however, since according to his theory, they have merely the role of signs or symptoms of the subliminal processes. The true symbol differs essentially from this, and should be understood as an intuitive idea that cannot yet be formulated in any other or better way.
>
> (CW15 para. 105)

Jung's view is postmodern. A symbol is an intuition, a metaphysical operator. As Buckminster Fuller (1983: 27) put it:

> God gave humans a faculty
> beyond that of their and other creatures
> magnificent physical brains –
> and that unique faculty
> is the metaphysically operative mind.

Difficult for the supervisor

Supervision creates a system at its simplest:

Patient

Therapist   Supervisor

Within the triangle, each in turn may be actor, reactor, or respond as resultant. Each operates within an a priori environment. But therapy actually occurs in a therapeutic tetrahedron (Chapters 1 and 2): for in addition to (1) action, (2) reaction, (3) resultant, there is always (4) the a priori environment.

Patient

Therapist   Supervisor

A priori environment

The a priori environment includes all the familial, social and cultural settings holding the participants, and the collective unconscious. For example, supervising an experienced colleague in student counselling, we discussed Amy, who had failed her first year law exams.

Amy had had to re-sit. The college felt that Amy had no chance of passing, as she seemed to have done no work, and suggested she saw the counsellor. Amy got straight As at her convent boarding school and was 'Captain of Everything'. She felt flooded by the conflicting demands of student life – an open collective, in contrast to her closed, strongly religious home and school. Early experiences of rejection and stern discipline had given her low self-esteem. To use the collective for support (to learn with other students, and discuss problems) did not occur to her. Yet she said she'd 'always wanted' this career. Free-associating, I'd 'always wanted' to be a doctor. I recalled playing 'Doctors and Nurses'. Equally, I loved being a shirtless 'Red

Indian', playing 'Cowboys and Indians'. I flushed mentioning this – it felt childish. However, as I shared memory and affect, the supervisee recognised shame as the feeling they'd had when sharing an insight with Amy, based on a 'childhood dream' they'd 'always wanted'. Perhaps Amy didn't want her childhood dream? It emerged she'd opted for law as it was the same career as her parents. Choosing to be the same, she hoped to gain their much-sought approval.

Our difficulty lay in recognising the depth of shame, and its snake-eyed hold. My colleague and I did not know, as any kind of fact, whether the collective (parents, students, colleagues, church) had actually shamed Amy, whether shame really was part of her a priori environment. Our intuition, and embodied responses, suggested this was the case, as did this, her shaming, first-ever failure.

It is often assumed that 'playful' means the opposite of 'taking things seriously'. As children, we know there is nothing as serious as play: patients and therapists having 'difficulties' easily forget this. Frequently, difficulties resolve on recognising subtle projections and projective identifications. I have no shameful memories of playing 'Doctor' or 'Red Indian'. But I felt shame mentioning play in this setting; having an internalised notion we cannot be as playful as children in supervision, perhaps? Free association means freedom to play – with symbols, in a 'Glass Bead Game' (Hesse 1969). The greatest difficulty for a supervisor is the illusion of parental authority they are given ('super' as in 'Superman' perhaps?).

Difficult for the therapist

Play is an open-meaning system by which imaginal acts install symbol formation. As a boy, 'playing doctor' I listened to teddy bears with a toy stethoscope; 'playing Indian', I enjoyed play-fights. Suppose the first symbolises 'healer', the second 'warrior'? Difficulties in therapy and supervision arise if we prematurely close on the meaning in one of a pair of opposites, rather than holding both. Or if we forget 'the importance of spontaneity in addition to intellectual control' (Klauber 1986: 109). If too much spontaneity, boundaries skew; if too much intellectual control, therapy becomes a mind-game, an intellectual defence (see Chapter 2).

Jung named the to-and-fro movement between opposites enantiodromia, a Greek word meaning 'to run contrariwise' (CW6 para. 708): everything, given time, turns into its opposite. Therapists privilege healer, rather than warrior – preferring to be 'wait and see' physicians rather than surgeons 'putting the knife in'. But if we taboo 'a surgical approach', it falls into Shadow (that which we have no wish to be), and appears in enactments: 'it' acts us out. This can appear in unexpectedly hostile countertransferences.

Discussing a 'difficult' patient, Sam, I raged at my supervisor. Yes, I could see how clever his insights were, how annoyingly wise, but it made no difference. At that moment, I hated him. And Sam, for whom I'm the third analyst in his long career as an analysand but 'You are all useless!' I began to enjoy 'warrior' anger. My joy in raging let us see how much Sam enjoyed his rage. He'd little wish to give it up, gaining perverse pleasure from playing a game of 'Oh, you're not as good as my last analyst', enviously spoiling our work. 'My own insights are far better,' he said, 'you ought to be the one on the couch'. But, if everyone is better than Dale, we realised (parallel process), everyone is better than Sam. I hadn't comprehended the depth of Sam's low self-esteem. Resolving our difficulty required a 'surgical' interpretation, naming his game.

A little hostile countertransference goes a long way. Boys often have a good scrap with a friend, to clear the air. We go on playing afterwards, staying friends. Boys play-fight in symbolic trials of strength, to build mutual respect, to maintain dignity: useful later.

A refined woman patient could not stop cursing and swearing at me like a drunken sailor. One day, spontaneously, I sharply said, 'Stop being so f***ing rude.' She stopped. Was that containing or retaliatory; is it permitted or forbidden? My supervisor's task, when we discussed this, was to discern which possibility operated – healer or warrior – and examine how useful it was, rather than taboo this act of analytic freedom (Symington 1983).

Aggressive, hostile impulses arise toward the unknown and unknowable. These impulses are best seen. Like a Native American warrior's tomahawk, they have symbolic value. Young Braves counted coup on each other, getting close enough to kill, but not doing so – 'I could kill you', being better for the lads and their tribes than 'I kill you'. Therapists often have difficulties using masculine aggression (Animus) creatively. We become bitchy instead (Anima possessed). Or obsessed by images of mother and baby, as if that were a scene free from aggression. Or mandalised. Aggressive countertransferences help keep a balance between participating and observing, between openness and closedness. And if they arise from envy, so much the better, as a function of envy is to create 'twoness' (see the case of the twins Jed and Jake, below).

Supervising a newly qualified developmentally trained Jungian colleague, we noticed that she could not stop theorising about a disturbed patient as 'repeating early infant experiences of rejection by her mother'. This blinded her to the problem her patient had in dealing with men, masculinity and Animus functions of thinking, planning, wisely using aggression and peer-bonding. When supervising a newly qualified archetypally trained Jungian colleague, he persistently attempted to interpret his own animosity to a borderline patient as 'being in the service of the patient's Hero' rather than as simple hatred. These examples may appear caricatures, but they happened while writing this, in one session after another.

Fortunately, my colleagues recognised their pseudo-interpretative remarks as 'trivial truths', applicable to anyone. They are also syllogisms: if A then B, if B then C, therefore A *causes* C. All babies drink milk, all criminals were babies, *therefore* milk causes crime. To be 'tough on crime, tough on the causes of crime' all babies must stop drinking milk! Tough on babies. Do tough experiences in infancy create psychopathology?

If you reread this, you will see that I have played with a syllogism to discredit a theory (early development causes adult neurosis). The argument is nonsense; but, on first glance, it *looks* all right. I put it here, as it is what we do when we create our worst difficulties as therapists and supervisors. We tie ourselves up in the patient's knots. We become unable to make our own sense, and start taking nonsense. Here, the newly trained therapists struggled with parental complexes, trying to keep safe by hugging 'mummy and daddy's' theories. This is what patients do too, it being safer to cling to a bad object (believing somehow its badness is our fault, then we can make it better), than to have no object at all. The Scots analyst, Ronald Fairbairn (1952: 68–70), first described this use of guilt as a defence against the release of bad objects. Supervisors can help therapists escape from guilty attachments to theory so they can get on with practising as themselves.

When we catch ourselves behaving like caricature therapists in a *New Yorker* magazine cartoon, it is likely we are caught in a complex. Jung coined this term to describe a repetition compulsion, made from delayed and/or arrested developmental patterns as well as improperly humanised archetypal patterns. For example, European cultures still demonise those with darker skins, Chinese people refer to westerners as 'ghosts', pale southern Ghanaians still refer to dark northerners as 'slaves' (they once caught them to sell). These are Shadow projections, arising from difficulties knowing what to do with the unknown and the unknowable. Theory has its Shadow, and turns into its opposite, dogma. A paradox in supervision, mentioned earlier, is that patients who are always talked about, no matter how problematic, are far easier to supervise than ones who are never talked about, Shadow patients. Intuition is useful in sniffing them out.

A supervisee, Basil, mentioned casually at the end of a session how disgusted he'd felt by Jed, a scruffy kid who sobbed behind his long blond hair, dripping tears all down his torn T-shirt. Basil didn't notice how far his response was from his usual compassion.

'Has Jed just been bereaved?' I intuitively asked, sinking inside, as if I'd swallowed the distress of this 18 year old.

'No,' he replied, 'But his twin has gone hitch-hiking across America. Why?'

It was the first time these identical twins had separated. Jed, in his first year at college, was the left-handed, introverted, academic, 'good boy'; Jake, his brother, was the right-handed, extraverted, sporty 'bad boy'. I didn't know why Basil 'missed' this. Later, we worked out he'd had his own experience of upsetting sibling rivalry. He admitted that envious feelings towards me (a big brother?) had kept Jed marginal. No surprise, Jed was second-born, fed second . . . he wanted to be a travelling Hero, as his much-loved brother Jake wanted to be an A student. Basil helped Jed discover 'Jake-like' qualities in himself by providing a metalanguage – in this case, object-relations. He helped Jed see that both twins were afraid of each other's envy and of separation. Envy, being an awareness of two-ness, is essential for separation. To individuate, they had to separate. Jake spent the summer teaching Jed to surf; Jed helped Jake to study, and win a place at (a different) college.

Difficult for the collective

Therapeutic interactions occur in relation to a collective. This may support inquiry into unconscious process – as in those legendary tribes anthropologists always seem to find, who share dreams together in the mornings. Or a society may be murderously hostile to such inquiry, made up of dangerous fundamentalists, like Neo-Con Americans. This illustrates a 'theorem' in nominative relations theory:

$Np = 1/NK$.

The nominative power (Np) of an individual is inversely proportional to number of nominators (N), and the nominative power of the group (K). Nominative power means an ability to name things our way (like Jim, in the first example choosing to call himself gay rather than a dirty queer). If maths upsets some readers, here is a worked example:

Growing up on a small island in the Hebrides, the number of people (n) on Iona in the winter of 1959 was about forty. The island had a nominative power (K) of one over Christmas. It became a closed system as strong south-westerly gales cut us off from Mull (our neighbouring island) and the mainland. I had a nominative power of 1/40th; at least, that's how it felt. Doing my part felt as important as everyone else doing theirs. My job was looking after the candles: we had no electricity. In the community of worldwide analytical psychology, I have a nominative power of about 1/2500th. As a UK citizen, I have a nominative power in elections of 1/46 million (voters in the UK).

As nominative power decreases, anomie (alienation) increases, to the limit state of mass psychosis (during war). At the same time, in large systems we more easily see that 'everyone has the same value as everyone else', rarely the case in closed systems. As a boy, I felt that the island's harbour master had most power. He 'kept the boundary', deciding when it was safe for the jetty to open or close. If everyone has similar nominative power, and is recognised as equal in value, and the social system is open, all have dignity. People with personality disorders tend to believe they have little or no nominative power, behave in undignified ways and evoke disparaging judgements throughout a supervisory system. This infects the supervisory system, disempowering everyone in it.

Without a sense of intrinsic value we are easily subject to the psychotic pressures which tyrannise groups; poignantly seen amongst fundamentalists, whether Christian, Muslim or Jewish; Animist or Buddhist; Fascist, Marxist – or analytic. When groups become closed systems, they function like complexes. In fundamentalism, nominative power is surrendered to some individual (A Great Leader), or, worse, to some 'ideal' or 'truth'; often symbolised by a 'Holy Book', 'Our Flag' or 'Our Glorious Dead'. A group can be 'working', or fall into closed patterns. The soldier, mathematician, doctor and analyst Wilfred Bion (1961) describes such systems. He named them the Church, the Royal Family and the Army. The first wait for salvation, the second produce a miraculous saviour-King, the third unite to fight. Supervisory systems can display these qualities (see Chapter 9).

People who are over-identified with a theory (in the grip of a fundamentalism) rarely come to therapy. They do so only when their belief-system is compromised: a religious vocation dies, 'the party' doesn't listen, a beloved job give them notice, their partner finds someone else. Similarly, therapists and supervisors who are over-identified with a 'pet theory' rarely learn: hence the need for 'supervision of supervision', regularly working with a metalanguage to stand outside our practice. The commonest metalanguage is ethics (Chapter 3).

As important as the degree of openness or closedness of a system is its rate and direction of change. For example, in alcoholism, the meaning system increasingly closes as 'first the man takes a drink, then the drink takes a drink, then the drink takes the man'. Premature closure is usually ugly.

The aesthetics of meaning

We could understand 'difficult' to mean 'aesthetically challenged'. In the 1960s, American radio broadcast the anarchic comedy group, 'Firesign Theatre'. In one sketch ('The further adventures of Nick Danger', July 1969) two bohemian artists are stopped by the cops, with an incriminating photo. They ask, 'Is this you?' The artists say, 'Hmm. Yeah, an interesting approach. But it's not *US*.'

This is called reframing. The artists seize nominative power. The cops signify the photo as a 'mug shot' to catch criminals. The artists signify it as an opportunity to comment on aesthetics. Firesign Theatre apply Tarski's theorem: $t \phi 1 : \Sigma L$. Aesthetics is the artists' metalanguage (L); for cops, (L) is justice. Juxtaposing meaning systems, metalanguages, creates humour. Freud recognised humour as a wonderful by-product of analysis. Life cannot be so solemn (closed) afterwards.

Therapy and analysis, like other arts and crafts, can be practised beautifully, lightly, and with humour. When examining the aesthetics of supervision, we could ask, 'Is it beautifully done?', rather than 'Is it right?', 'Is it true?' or even 'Is this furthering the soul's healing journey?'

Aesthetics is part of our a priori environment. Difficulties are aesthetic challenges if we see our work as enabling people to live beautifully. Difficult could mean 'This work is ugly'. With difficult patients, that they don't get worse, or that they learn to live with their own suffering instead of inflicting it on others, is progress. With difficult supervisees, discovering ethical and aesthetic action is far more important than 'getting the interpretation right'.

Difficult for family and friends

In strategic family therapy, a useful technique is positive connotation; encouraging a stuck family system to 'do it more'; that is, prescribing the symptom. For example, a family cannot function as they get up in the middle of the night to play with a frightened child. By positively connoting this as an expression of concern, and suggesting the family get up *every night*, their behaviour changes. The same is the basis of Masters and Johnson's sex therapy, 'Just don't do it' soon becomes 'We can't stop doing it'. Supervisors can use the same technique.

Adam is a mixed-race young professional footballer. He came to therapy actively suicidal, and self-harming with a switch-blade. He'd be late, early or come at the wrong time, fight about the bill, rage 'You're not helping' and, once, slashed his wrists in the therapist's toilet. My supervisee, Charlie, was concerned for his safety, as Adam would play with his knife in sessions. Charlie felt murderous at this threat. I suggested he felt pressure to make Adam better, but might try suggesting he 'do it more'. Charlie suddenly found himself letting Adam 'murder' one of the cuddly toys they used to symbolise the warring parts of a fragmented psyche. Adam stabbed to death 'Black Teddy', representing his heroin-using Jamaican mother. He felt she failed to protect him from the 'White Fathers' in the Irish children's home he'd been dumped in after his father died of an overdose. The first stabs were violent: then

Adam dropped the knife, sobbed and, for the first time, trusted Charlie enough to tell him of brutal sexual abuse. Up till then, we'd intuited this had happened. Now, we knew.

Using such a technique depends on compassion in the supervisory system. As I trusted Charlie's wisdom, and he trusted his unconscious, he could trust Adam. None of us planned the teddy bear's murder. Difficult people kill their social networks. Adam's career was in danger after too many fights in matches, too many red cards and too much time on the bench. He fought with team mates. He could not abide rules, having been beaten too often as a child for breaking rules he didn't understand.

Next, Charlie and I used a semiotic trick: suggesting a new metalanguage to Adam, based on the difference between a rule (a language, l) and a recommendation (a metalanguage of morality, L) which Charlie taught him through his consistent and clear boundary keeping. Adam began to see his (Irish) manager as separate from 'Irish fathers'. Adam began to have a coherent story about his troubled life. With coherence came continuity, agency and affective relating: the four invariants of Self. He stopped getting red cards and started having friends.

Difficult for themselves

Patients come to therapy as they have difficulty with themselves. Their lives are ugly in some way. If, after a period, nothing seems to be working, a supervisor needs to consider the 'aesthetics' of the therapy. This list is not definitive, but, by working through it with the therapist, who can mirror the process by working it through with their patient, clarity can be re-established, even if it does not resolve the difficulty. Sometimes, difficulties are irresolvable. If they are we could stop trying to resolve them.

- What's the matter? (reconsider the diagnosis)
- What boundary disturbances are there?
- What is the emotional age of the patient?
- Are there obvious developmental delays or arrests?
- What archetypal patterns are constellating?
- How good are the therapist and patient at symbol formation?
- What is in the countertransference?

Of these, the last two are the most useful. With Sam and Adam, the problem was expressing hatred. The therapists had difficulty symbolising their wish to be warriors, and fight back. We're supposed to be healers? No; we are paid to assist a person's individuation. This is not the same. It means accepting some things can never be resolved. Adam will never have the parents or childhood he wanted. But he might benefit from a chance to humanise his own innate archetypal parenting abilities, and thus form new internal objects. Adam may still experience himself as problematic, but not 'difficult'.

Difficult for internal objects and archetypal patterns

Difficulties have a common core, the formation and use of symbols (Chapter 7). Primitive defences of the Self (splitting, denial and projective identification) stop us using unknowables {x}, as internal objects. And an internal object is itself a symbol of an unfolding archetypal pattern. Adam's mother might form the internal object 'absent unprotecting mother', a subset of 'terrible witch mother', a subset of 'the Great Mother'. But telling a young footballer like Adam a folksy fairytale would not have worked. Nor would saying 'it's your mother'. He dissociated as a defence against symbol formation. He enacted his inner conflict by cutting and fighting. Murderous enactments, explored repeatedly, became a vehicle for his own interpretation of himself. The American psychiatrist and analyst Karl Menninger said:

> Interpretation is a rather presumptuous term, loosely applied by some analysts to every voluntary verbal participation made by the analyst in the psychoanalytic treatment process. I dislike the word because it gives a young analyst the wrong idea about their main function. They need to be reminded that they are not oracles, not wizards, not linguists, not detectives, not great wise men, who like Joseph and Daniel, 'interpret' dreams but quiet observers, listeners and occasionally commentators. Their participation in a two party process is predominantly passive . . . Their occasional active participation is better called intervention. It may or may not 'interpret' something. It may or may not be an interruption. But whenever the analyst speaks he contributes to a process.
> (Menninger 1958; cited in Sandler et al. 1973: 105)

The more difficult a situation, the less urgency there is to contribute to an already overactive process. Sometimes we need a warrior's courage to be with the unknowable: as in 'what would have happened if Adam hadn't use the knife to stab the black teddy, but . . .'

A useful metaphor comes from jazz. In jazz, as in a Bach fugue, the music comes from repetition, and from, in addition, giving space for the unknowable, improvised, notes. Therapy can be compared to jazz. At its best, it is elegant, respectful to the aesthetics of meaning, referring both to itself and to the bigger picture of the outside world. It is grounded, as jazz is in Gospel music, in collective . . .

Spiritual values

The Buddhist scholar, Shunryu Suzuki, writing in *Zen Mind, Beginners Mind* (Suzuki 2001: 21) said, 'In the mind of the beginner there are many possibilities, in the mind of the expert, there are few.' In Japanese, 'beginner's mind' is called *shoshin*. Working with the unknown and the unknowable, we need *shoshin*. Like diamonds, we are all made from Star Dust. Diamonds take millions of years to grow. So did we. Most difficulties in therapy and supervision are caused by being in a hurry. For instance, an interpretation may be correct, a 'brilliant cut', but if it is given before the patient is ready? Errors in timing are the hardest to avoid, as we all get impatient for change. Then resent it when we get it, especially when it is a change for the better.

To revisit the beginning of the chapter, successful supervision of a difficult patient is like making a ring for two diamonds. Between the facets is a holographic field, the sparkle in the participant's eyes – the play of light and dark between each other's facets (complexes). The ring is the 'gold' of the supervisor's experience; the box holding it, the setting in the collective unconscious. The jeweller's shop is everyone engaging in similar processes. But who is the jeweller? The Self?

> For in addition to (1) action, (2) reaction, (3) resultant, there is always (4) the a priori environment, within which the event occurs.

The jeweller is the a priori environment – an Archetype with many names. Difficulty is a symbolic communication of an unknowable, best met playfully. The jeweller is Hermes.

Conclusion

I explore 'difficult' in depth to permit its deconstruction. The word symbolises a serious challenge to a meaning system, asking it to exercise greater wisdom and compassion to its parts, threefold (patient, therapist and supervisor) and fourfold (patient, therapist and supervisor, and the collective). 'Difficult' happens if we experience too many challenges to our theories; if there are too many unknowns and unknowables for any view to be privileged as 'true'; if, even when we make a coherent narrative from a history, we cannot give it back to the therapist or their patient. Asking 'difficult for whom' comes before asking 'what does this difficulty signify'. I suggest we can look at how meaning is *not* being made within the supervisory system using a metalanguage, the language of symbols.

References

Bion, W. (1961) *Experiences in Groups*. London: Tavistock.
Burr, V. (2003) *Social Constructionism*. London: Routledge.
Fairbairn, R. (1952) *Psychoanalytic Studies of the Personality*. London: Routledge.
Firesign Theatre (1969) 'The further adventures of Nick Danger.' From *How Can You Be in Two Places at once When You're not Anywhere at all?* Ontario, Canada: CBS.
Fuller, R. B. (1983) *Intuition*. San Louis Obispo, CA: Impact.
Hesse, H. (1969) *The Glass Bead Game*, trans. R. Winston and C. Winston. New York: Holt, Rinehart & Winston.
Jung, C. G. (1953–1973) *Collected Works*, ed. Sir H. Read, M. Fordham, G. Adler and W. McGuire, 20 vols. London: Routledge & Kegan Paul.
Klauber, J. (1986) *Difficulties in the Analytic Encounter*. London: Free Association Books and the Maresfield Library.
Main, T. (1957) 'The Ailment.' *British Journal of Medical Psychology* 30(3): 129–145.
Menninger, K. (1958) *Theory of Psychoanalytic Technique*. New York: Basic Books.
Samuels, A., Shorter, B. and Plaut, F. (1986) *A Critical Dictionary of Jungian Analysis*. London: Routledge & Kegan Paul.
Sandler, J., Dare, C. and Holder, A. (1973) *The Patient and the Analyst*. London: Karnac.
Suzuki, S. (2001) *Zen Mind, Beginners Mind: Informal Talks on Zen Mediation and Practice*, 3rd edn. New York: Weatherhill.
Symington, N. (1983) 'The analyst's act of freedom as an agent of therapeutic change.' *International Journal of Psychoanalysis* 10: 283–291.
Tarski, A. (1983) *Logic, Semantics and Mathematics*. Indianapolis, IN: University of Indianapolis Press.
Young-Eisendrath, P. (2005) *Subject to Change*. London: Routledge.

Part II
Individuation

Chapter 5

Individuation

Martin Stone

Introduction

One of the issues facing supervisors, especially in training institutes, is for whose primary benefit is the supervision: the patient, the therapist, the institute – or even the supervisor? A case can be made for each, as each has needs – whether for love, knowledge, power or money. These are all legitimate needs, and each raises problems and questions. I want to move beyond these questions to think about supervision in the context of individuation. Two concepts central to my thinking about this are *individuation* and the *dialectic process*.

The concept of individuation is central to the process of analysis in Jungian theory, as it leads to psychological differentiation and inner development of the individual personality. In Jung's words: 'The goal of the individuation process is the synthesis of the self' (CW9i para. 278). He is clear that: 'The goal is important only as an idea; the essential thing is the *opus* which leads to the goal: *that* is the goal of a lifetime' (CW16 para. 400, Jung's italics).

Jung developed a model of psychological change through the tension of holding together opposing attitudes or views, whether conscious or unconscious. The term he used for this was the transcendent function, as an expression of the symbol, or metaphor, which arises in dreams and fantasies, and which transcends the opposites and facilitates movement from one attitude to another. Jung's concept of the transcendent function is derived from the German Romantic philosopher Hegel's notion of dialectic change (Solomon 1994: 77). Hegel's model is about the development of self-consciousness, as Jung's is about the development of the individual. For Hegel, this was through the creative tension held between thesis and antithesis which leads to a creative synthesis: the dialectic process.

Jung followed this model, noting a dynamic tension inherently exists between unconscious and consciousness. Out of this emerges the transcendent function: 'a natural process, a manifestation of the energy that springs from the tension of opposites, and it consists in a series of fantasy-occurrences which appear spontaneously in dreams and visions' (CW8 para. 121). It allows a way through internal conflict leading to the growth and establishment of a new position. In this way it can bridge the gap between conscious and unconscious, between ego and self, between rational and irrational. This, in Jung's view, leads through symbolic transformation towards individuation.

Individuation

Individuation lies at the other end of the spectrum from individualism with its narcissistic overtones. The aim is to be free of a superficial persona, and of the emotional power of the collective, the archetypal layer of the unconscious (CW7 para. 269). In his *C. G. Jung Lexicon*, Sharp (1991) paraphrases Jung when he writes:

> The aim is not to overcome one's personal psychology, to become perfect, but to become familiar with it. Thus individuation involves an increasing awareness of one's unique psychological reality, including personal strengths and limitations, and at the same time a deeper appreciation of humanity in general.
>
> (Sharp 1991: 68)

Samuels et al. (1986: 76) in the *Critical Dictionary of Jungian Analysis* describe individuation as 'the key concept in Jung's contribution to the theories of personality development' and 'inextricably interwoven with others, particularly self, ego and archetype as well as with the synthesis of consciousness and unconscious elements'. I would add to this, Jung's concept of typology, quoting again from Samuels et al. (1986: 155): 'Jung speculated that in maturation and individuation the various typological opposites merge so that a person's conscious attitudes, and, hence, a great part of his experience of himself, will become richer and more variegated.' Jung himself wrote:

> I would not for anything dispense with this compass on my psychological voyages of discovery . . . I value the type theory for the objective reason that it provides a system of comparison and orientation which makes possible something that has long been lacking, a critical psychology.
>
> (CW6 para. 959)

In this sense, individuation may be thought of as the primary goal of analysis, focusing on the development of the ego in relation to the self, and in developing aspects of ego consciousness previously unknown or repressed. Through this lifelong work, new ego positions and attitudes come about through differentiation and increasing conscious awareness. The aim is not to become better, but more whole. The repressed, inferior or shadow aspects of our personality may be acknowledged and enacted, rather than acted out: acting after we have digested and reflected, as distinct from acting impulsively and without conscious thought or awareness. Traditionally, Jungians saw the work of individuation as something occurring in the second half of life, but I do not subscribe to this. While it is true in our younger years that we generally build on our strengths, on the more conscious parts of our personality (our superior functions and attitude), we may focus more on the less known, auxiliary and inferior functions as we grow older. I see the work of individuation as starting at birth, a lifelong struggle to integrate the different confused parts of our personality, to come to terms with our natural instincts, and to meet the demands of parents and society. The second concept central to this chapter, as mentioned earlier, is the dialectic process.

The dialectic process

Jung views the two-way interaction in the relationship between analyst and patient as a dialectic process, in which both mutually affect each other. In 'The therapeutic value of abreaction' (CW16 para. 289) he writes of the 'person-to-person relationship . . . where the patient confronts the doctor upon equal terms, and with the same ruthless criticism that he must inevitably learn from the doctor in the course of treatment'. This is a flexible attitude towards analysis, and typifies an open as opposed to a closed-system approach (Mathers 2001: 20, 181). I want to extend the concept of the dialectic process from the therapist–patient relationship to include supervisor–therapist and supervisor–patient relationships, and explore how the individuation process is woven into the analytic encounter, to show how this may be seen in supervision in all three participants in the supervisory triangle.

Areas of tension and potential conflict during training

There are inevitably tensions and potential conflicts between the demands of individuation and the demands of the collective during training, as well as afterwards. Examples are:

- the therapist's need to keep a training patient in analysis, in order to qualify, even if the therapy is not progressing, or turns out to be contra-indicated
- the frequency required for training may be greater, or less, than might be thought most beneficial to the patient in other circumstances
- the supervisee's need to write a clinical paper on the work

- the requirement to work in a particular way to satisfy the training body, or indeed the supervisor.

I will present clinical examples which focus on two areas where problems can often arise.

Getting the patient you need and not the one you want

A frequently expressed notion is therapists get the patients they need, rather than the ones they want. This particularly applies to trainees. In the words of the Rolling Stones (1969), 'You can't always get what you want but . . . sometimes you . . . get what you need'. I think this often happens more during the learning process of training, just as babies learn more in the first year of their lives than at any other time. I should like to extend the idea, and suggest that supervisors also get the supervisees they need, and vice versa. Fundamental to a Jungian approach to analysis is that both analyst and patient are in the process together and can be equally changed by the work. This does not mean we change in the same way, as we are different from one another and come into the relationship from different places and with different needs. For an analysis to work, the couple engage like two dancers, moving sometimes this way and sometimes that, closer or further apart, faster or slower, always in touch and mutually effecting each other to an equal extent. Getting what we need in an analysis or supervision applies to both parties, and is an integral part of each individuation process. The question of where the primary focus of supervision should be then moves from either/or to both/and: it is not either for patient, therapist, institute or supervisor, but is for all of them.

Discussion of the countertransference

When discussing a trainee supervisee's countertransference, a potential conflict may arise between the roles of their analyst and the supervisor. An understanding of what a trainee is experiencing in the countertransference is essential for effective work. On the other hand, it is not the supervisor's job to intrude into personal areas which are being explored and worked on elsewhere. If, instead of focusing just on the therapist, we focus on individuation, then it is a duty of the supervisor to address countertransference feelings which arise between therapist and patient, and between supervisor and therapist, including neurotic countertransferences. This takes it out of the personal into the impersonal realm, rendering it less persecutory. We are dealing with a universal situation, for the process of individuation is collective, common to all, which distinguishes it from the individualistic. As we look at the case material following, we can think about the individuation process in all those involved from the perspective of increased ego consciousness, through the differentiation of ego function and attitude, by focusing on where those concerned are more conscious and where they are relatively unconscious.

One way of thinking about and measuring change is through consideration of the typologies of those involved. Jung developed his theory of psychological types to account for differences between people in character or personality, based on his observations of temperament and emotional behaviour. He noted some people orient themselves in the world by looking outwards (he called these extraverted), and others by looking inwards (whom he called introverted). When our attitude is extraverted, energy is directed outwards, we look for answers through our relationship with other people and the external world. For introverts, attention is focused inwards to the individual. The subjective response, in terms of what is thought or felt about someone or something, is more important than external events; the world of ideas, thoughts and images, counts for more than outer relationships.

As well as focusing our energy, or attention, in a particular direction (inward or outward), Jung also noted we employ different functions, or modes of orientation while doing this. We tend to rely more on one function than another. We may, for example, rely on our perceptions – using our senses or intuition, or on our judgement – thinking about things, or using our feelings (as distinct from emotions) – to evaluate what we like and what we don't. The perceptive, or irrational functions, may be based on the five senses, or on intuition. He named these functions sensation and intuition. The judging functions, thinking and feeling, are both rational, by which Jung means we use them in a rational way to evaluate the world, inner and outer. Thinking does not mean being intellectual, but refers to the way we habitually approach problems or questions, by thinking about them rationally. Feeling on the other hand is used in his terminology to describe what we do when we apply our feelings to making judgements: for example, 'I like this painting, but not that one', because I like the artist's use of colour, or form, or whatever. It is to be distinguished from emotion or affect. We *have* feelings about something or someone, but emotions *have us*.

Thus, Jung's system on typology distinguishes two attitudes – introversion and extraversion – and four functions – thinking, feeling, sensation and intuition – each of which may be either introverted or extraverted. This gives eight basic 'character types', describing the functions most developed. When we describe someone as being a certain 'type' we mean they have a tendency to function in a particular way with a particular attitude, for example, being extraverted and habitually relying more on their thinking in a given situation. This is their 'primary function', the predominant way of behaving which comes most naturally. To illustrate what these functions mean in everyday behaviour, someone with strong sensation, operating through the five senses, tends to rely on concrete, measurable qualities, and will be at ease when there is a sound, tangible connection to reality. An intuitive type will pick up unconscious signals, and be concerned with future possibilities and relationships between people and events. They are more interested in what is round the corner, out of sight, than what can be seen and measured. Thinking types use their thinking to assess rationally whether something is valid and correct, and can be quite impersonal and analytical in their assessments. Feeling types are more concerned with relative importance and value, when dealing with people and situations (Quenk and Quenk 1982: 160).

Jung observed individuals with strong sensation have much less developed intuition, and those who use their thinking most have the poorest relationship to their feeling. Thus a model is built with sensation and intuition opposing each other, and thinking and feeling likewise: the stronger and more developed the one, the weaker and less conscious the other.

Although we tend towards one function, the primary function, we do of course use all four functions, and our energy can be oriented inwards or outwards according to the situation (with good friends we may be quite extraverted, but in large groups we may retreat into a corner). The next strongest function after the primary function is known as the 'auxiliary' function, and the least well developed as the 'inferior' function. If the primary function is rational (or judging), the auxiliary function will be irrational (or perceiving), and the inferior function rational (the opposite to the primary function). If the primary attitude is extraverted, the auxiliary will be introverted. In this way the model is complemented by considering how much we use our functions, and we can build a 'type profile' (Beebe 1984: 151), listing the functions in order from most developed to least conscious, each with its corresponding attitude.

Assessing an individual's type is a matter of experience, observation and judgement, and a number of tests have been developed over the years to measure typology. These have been widely used in the world of management consultancy and human resources. Jung recognised the difficulty in accurately assessing typology when he wrote:

> Whether a function is differentiated or not can easily be recognised from its strength, stability, consistency, reliability, and adaptedness. But inferiority in a function is often not so easy to recognise or to describe. An essential criterion is its lack of self-sufficiency and consequent dependence on people and circumstances, its disposing us to moods and crotchetiness, its unreliable use, its suggestive and labile character. The inferior function always puts us at a disadvantage because we cannot direct it, but are rather its victims.
>
> (CW6 para. 956)

As for the auxiliary functions, he makes no mention, hence the value of objective tests. Among the best known are the Myers-Briggs Type Indicator

Test (MBTI), the Gray-Wheelwright Test and the Singer-Loomis Inventory of Personality. These all attempt to measure the relative strengths of the attitudes and functions, and the degree of perceiving and judging, as tools for understanding how individuals will perform in different situations, and how they are likely to get on with each other, in achieving their goals.

I attempt to apply the same criteria in thinking about the typologies of supervisor, therapist and patient in my clinical examples, and use the concept of the type profile developed by John Beebe, a Jungian analyst from San Francisco. He has written and lectured widely on the subject of typology, and how it can help individuals understand their relationships, and their roles within organisations. In a type profile the individual's functions are listed in order, from most to least conscious, each function with its corresponding attitude. For example my own type based on the MBTI came out (in MBTI shorthand) as INFJ – Introverted-iNtuitive-Feeling-Judgemental. According to the scoring, I am measured as distinctly intuitive, moderately feeling, slightly introverted and slightly judging. Thus my 'type profile' is in theory:

- introverted intuition   (primary function)
- extraverted feeling   (auxiliary function)
- introverted thinking   (tertiary function)
- extraverted sensation   (inferior function)

This roughly corresponds to the way I would describe myself. There is no doubt my feeling function is extraverted, and my inferior sensation function fascinates but constantly lets me down. Attention needs to be given to the development of the auxiliary as well as to the inferior functions. When the 'fit' between therapist and patient is more difficult, there are greater challenges. Keep the concept of type profile in mind as we come to the clinical examples.

Getting the patient you need, rather than the one you want

John was a bright, imaginative, academically minded psychotherapy trainee in his late thirties. He was a gifted secondary school teacher who taught English and drama. He put on school plays, took pupils to drama festivals, and always had some new creative project on hand. His relationships were less satisfactory, never lasting more than a year or two at the longest. This aspect of his life initially led him into analysis. A part-time counselling course developed his interest in Jungian psychology. I liked him, and found his enthusiasm and intellectual engagement stimulating and challenging.

The patient John brought to supervision was a man in his mid-twenties, married with two small children. He worked as a bookkeeper for a publishing company, and his wife, a hairdresser, made home visits to her clients while the children were at school. John's patient, Harry, was hardworking and intelligent but not academic or intellectual. He was good at figures, but not imaginative. He had come for therapy as he had problems at work and missed an expected promotion; money problems caused difficulties at home, though otherwise the marriage seemed good.

John's irritation with his patient soon became apparent. In one session, Harry was telling John how crushed he felt by his boss's criticism for not being quick enough, and John's felt response was sympathy with the boss. He too found Harry slow and ponderous. John told me he was frustrated by Harry's inability to engage with and take in interpretations and insights, however accurate they might be. He wanted to move Harry on, just as his boss wanted to speed him up.

In supervision, I felt irritated and critical of John's lack of empathy and understanding. The more he wanted to rush on, the more I wanted to slow him down. I felt my envy of John's quick intellect, but knew he was missing discovering real connections to his patient and, without more empathic understanding, there was a danger the patient might leave. This would be a loss for the patient in need of help, and for John, whose training would be delayed – which he was trying hard to avoid. I wondered at one point if John might not benefit from losing the patient, in order to learn to slow down, accept frustration, and adopt a more empathic, analytic attitude.

I felt there were fundamental differences between their personalities, seen from an archetypal and typological perspective. There were probably issues in John's past which made it hard for him to get beyond his complexes, contributing to what I experienced as a neurotic countertransferential response towards Harry. Looked at from an archetypal perspective, we might see John and Harry as at opposite ends of the *puer–senex* polarity, the youth and the old man, each either threatened or irritated by the other. Harry (*senex*) would feel constantly criticised and undervalued for his efforts, and John (*puer*) could not see the value in a solid hardworking approach unless it immediately bore fruit, nor in the committed feeling relationship Harry had with his wife (although he may have felt unconsciously jealous of it). Typologically, John, Harry and I were all very different.

Type profiles for myself, John and Harry

Martin	John	Harry
introverted intuition	extraverted thinking	introverted sensation
extraverted feeling	introverted intuition	extraverted feeling
introverted thinking	extraverted sensation	introverted thinking
extraverted sensation	introverted feeling	extraverted intuition

Whereas John was more extraverted in his superior thinking, with auxiliary introverted intuition, my superior function is introverted intuition with auxiliary extraverted feeling, the opposite. On the other hand, Harry was probably an introverted sensation type, with auxiliary extraverted feeling, similar to my typology.

I conveyed some of this to John, suggesting he think about how possible typological differences between him and his parents might have caused difficulties in childhood, which he could work on in his analysis. His fear of losing Harry and having to begin again with a new patient spurred him to face things he might not otherwise have been able to do. He rose to the challenge, growing from *puer*, the eternal boy, to hero.

The outcome benefited the process of individuation in all of us. John learnt respect for Harry's different outlook, and began to see value in his good feeling function which contributed to the warm relationship Harry had with his wife. Through his empathic response to Harry he experienced a growing professional and personal warmth which had not been there previously. He learnt that Harry's father had always wanted him to have a safe, solid job, and a secure salary. Although Harry had trained to be a bookkeeper, to which he was well suited, he rebelled against his rather overbearing father and became fascinated by the intuitive approach of the creative management in the publishing house (representing his inferior function). As Harry accepted who and what he was, he could let go of his idealistic fantasy to be a high-flying, creative accountant, and he moved to a job with a High Street bank; secure, equally well-paid, and which valued his meticulous approach.

John's approach also changed. For the first time, he agreed to do detailed process recording of his twice-weekly sessions, something he had previously resisted or evaded. He came to value this, as well as what it allowed us to see in supervision. A more grounded attitude in the work gave him more depth and solidity. I learnt later that around this time he started a new relationship, which didn't end abruptly, like so many previous ones. As for me, the supervisor, I learnt how easily I could be dazzled by intellectual brilliance, and how easily crushed I could feel when undervalued. I learnt to assess my abilities more accurately, to try to value my thinking for what it is, rather than for what I'd like it to be.

Dealing with countertransference in supervision

Lucy was in her early fifties when she came for supervision. She was in the second part of her psychotherapy training and about to embark on three times weekly work with a training patient. Her patient Carol was in her mid-thirties and worked as an 'alternative therapist'. Carol was on the one hand confident, controlling, demanding, critical and contemptuous; on the other, she dressed like a little girl in a short skirt with a fluffy-animal knapsack, and sat cross-legged on the floor. Her personal life and marriage were a mess but she couldn't bear to acknowledge this. Overtly she considered herself Lucy's equal as a therapist, but in reality she looked down on Lucy as being dull, boring and unimaginative. She shared all the details of the therapy sessions with her practice partner, who was her lover, and said she was doing Lucy a favour bringing his comments back to her.

In fact Lucy is an artistic, imaginative person, herself working through ending a difficult relationship, which left her vulnerable to criticism and contempt. She was intelligent but not intellectual. When she first came I experienced her as out of touch with her feelings. Her response to Carol's lax boundaries, inability to come or leave on time, was to let sessions overrun. She was afraid of rejecting Carol and making her angry. She became increasingly anxious her patient would either attack her with withering contempt, or quit if she tried to address this problem of time keeping. Lucy's anxiety had the effect of cutting her further off from feeling. She appeared to retreat into a frozen shell and tell me what she thought was happening. I was left holding feelings and emotions which were aroused in the intermediate space between Carol and Lucy, frustrated by my inability to do anything for either of them.

The work began with Carol asking intrusive personal questions about Lucy, who resisted answering with difficulty. The more Lucy remained firm and reserved, but squirming inwardly, the more Carol criticised her 'detachment', in contrast to her own boundaryless 'therapeutic' methods. She would explain her own marvellous healing practices in a patronising way, succeeding in getting Lucy to envy her apparently successful, and full, practice. She told Lucy about her special spiritual powers, and her beliefs in reincarnation and spiritualism. In countertransference, Lucy felt dismissive, uninterested and judgemental about what seemed to her unusual and strange ideas. She was unable to see the lost little girl seeking to magically create meaningful answers in a chaotic and meaningless life. This is illustrated by a vignette from early in the therapy. Carol asked what Lucy had done before training to become a therapist:

> C: I mean, it's not a big thing for you to tell me. Were you a rubbish collector or something?
> L (defensively): I don't see how it would help you to know what I did before becoming a therapist.
> C: Well it matters to me. I'm wanting you to help me, and you won't even tell me what you can do!

I asked Lucy what she felt when Carol asked if she'd been a rubbish collector.

> L: I thought it was kind of jokey.
> M: But what did you feel?
> L: I thought . . .

I felt Lucy was using her thinking function to protect herself against feeling hurt and angry. I said so, and the effect it had on me, which was to make me feel angry with both Carol and Lucy. I suggested she discuss in her analysis what had happened both in her session with Carol, and in supervision. We realised part of Lucy's defence was fear of her own strong angry feelings when under attack. She thought she shouldn't feel something if it's 'bad' or 'unhelpful', like being angry, critical or judgemental – and was overwhelmed by these inadmissible affects. Through discussion in supervision we came to see:

- Carol felt the same towards herself, but was unconscious of it, and projected this into Lucy.
- Lucy's victim side, reinforced by her current personal situation, made her more vulnerable to Carol's attacks.
- It was so uncomfortable, and Lucy felt so guilty about feeling sadistic, that she denied feeling anything and retreated into her primary thinking function.

Lucy courageously faced these painful issues in her analysis, and explored their origins in childhood and later relationships. She began to acknowledge to her analyst and herself how she had real difficulties engaging with the feelings of others. She was herself judgemental and contemptuous without realising it. She tried to hide her lack of sympathy or empathy towards her patients by intellectual rationalisation.

I had felt cautious about going too deeply into her countertransference feelings for fear of intruding into areas belonging to her analysis. I held back and encouraged Lucy to take anything which came up around discussion of countertransference in supervision back to analysis. We agreed a one-way flow: anything her analyst said was not for discussion in supervision. Although I knew her analyst and we occasionally met, neither of us discussed the fact that we shared someone in training. In this way, we tried to keep clear boundaries and give value to a viewpoint respecting the whole person and their right to individuation.

Both Lucy and I moved on in our paths of individuating as therapist and supervisor. Carol may also have benefited, as she came to admit she was still searching for meaning in her spiritual life and for genuine relationships in her personal one. Yet she could not let go of her contemptuous defences or recognise the need for clearer boundaries. In her parting letter to Lucy, she thanked her for the therapy, then dismissed what she'd got from it, suggesting Lucy might one day come to her to experience what she could offer as an alternative therapist. Lucy saw this for what it was, an envious attack. To her credit, she acknowledged maybe there was value in the work Carol did.

The real change in Lucy was she could value her feelings for what they were and accept them as valid, even when they were uncomfortable and not what she ideally wanted them to be (feeling hurt, angry, dismissive or judgemental). She came to see such feelings as unconscious shadow aspects of herself, projected into her patient, in a desperate attempt to preserve her self-righteous image of herself as good and correct. She became aware of her need for a greater spiritual dimension to her life, and for a less judgemental attitude towards men. She was able to revalue both her feeling and intuitive functions and restore them to places in her psyche where they could be respected and used.

For my part, I became aware how I too can lapse into an intellectual teaching mode when made to feel inadequate, just as Lucy did when put on the spot, and how my own rather obstinate defences are quite similar to hers. When we feel threatened or pushed into a corner, we fall back on our primary function. This is not a fault but an understandable human habit, to rely on what we know works well when in difficulty. What we need to do is recognise we have done it, and try and be more aware in future.

Conclusion

I would like to end with a contribution by Gustav Dreifuss. He is a Jungian analyst living in Israel, who worked for many years with Holocaust victims and has written widely on analytical psychology. I find it easy to identify with his viewpoint as his typology is evidently similar to mine. In a symposium entitled 'How do I assess progress in supervision?' (Dreifuss 1982) writes:

> The evaluation of supervision is as much a highly individual action as is evaluation of analysis. There are of course objective criteria for the profession of an analyst, like integrity and empathy, but the evaluation of their relative importance is dependent on the personality of the analyst or the supervisor respectively. A feeling type, for instance, might consider empathy as the most important assessment for the profession while a thinking type might consider insight (consciousness) of paramount importance. An intuitive type might overvalue the capacity for imagination of the supervisee, while a sensation type might overestimate adaptation to reality . . . Typology is helpful. Because of my typology and my experience as analyst and supervisor I consider empathy as one of the most important factors for a therapist. If the supervisee has a natural gift of empathy I shall, in the course of supervision, point to the problem of too much empathy whenever it occurs and bring the supervisee to the realisation of the shadow of empathy, namely the danger of *participation mystique* and lack of conscious evaluation of the analytic situation.
>
> (Dreifuss 1982: 108)

Dreifuss reflects well what I feel about the use of typology in supervision. But my reason for quoting his comments is because the difficulty I had with both of the above supervisee therapists was not the one mentioned by him. Where two people have similar profiles there is a real danger of over-identification or even collusion. This can occur between therapist and patient, supervisor and therapist, or between supervisor and patient with the therapist squeezed between them. A more challenging relationship, with manageable differences and difficulties, can lead to greater development and change. In this situation, the supervisor is required to stand back from the material presented, and from the relationship, to reflect on them. The auxiliary functions are engaged and through use they become increasingly conscious. Then the process may be said to further the individuation of both, or ideally, all three people: patient, therapist and supervisor.

As Quenk and Quenk (1982) succinctly put it when discussing the use of 'psychological typology in analysis:

> Individuation is not necessarily a goal, but a process through which the individual integrates the contents of the unconscious, leading to adaptation to the world and to the Self, in a highly individual manner. The psychology of types becomes the means through which the unconscious is manifested.
>
> (Quenk and Quenk 1982: 171)

Much of what has been said and written about supervision points to the importance of focusing on the dynamic between therapist and patient, and between supervisor and therapist, the parallel process (see Chapter 11). I am suggesting that if you concentrate only on those dynamics you may miss an important dimension, which is the whole person of therapist, patient and supervisor. Focusing additionally on these may indeed inform the supervisor on a particular direction which needs to be taken in supervision.

References

Beebe, J. (1984) 'Psychological types in transference, countertransference, and the therapeutic interaction.' In N. Schwartz-Salant (ed.) *Transference/Countertransference*. Wilmette, IL: Chiron.

Dreifuss, G. (1982) 'How do I assess progress in supervision?' *Journal of Analytical Psychology* 27: 107–110.

Jung, C. G. (1953–1973) *Collected Works*, ed. Sir H. Read, M. Fordham, G. Adler and W. McGuire, 20 vols. London: Routledge & Kegan Paul.

Mathers, D. (2001) *An Introduction to Meaning and Purpose in Analytical Psychology*. London: Routledge.

Quenk, A. T. and Quenk, N. L. (1982) 'The use of psychological typology in analysis.' In M. Stein (ed.) *Jungian Analysis*. Boston, MA: Shambhala.

Rolling Stones (1969) Album *Let it Bleed*. London: Decca.

Samuels, A., Shorter, B. and Plaut, F. (1986) *A Critical Dictionary of Jungian Analysis*. London: Routledge & Kegan Paul.

Sharp, D. (1991) *C. G. Jung Lexicon: A Primer of Terms and Concepts*. Toronto: Inner City Books.

Solomon, H. (1994) 'The transcendent function and Hegel's dialectical vision'. *Journal of Analytical Psychology* 39: 77–100.

Chapter 6

The spirit of inquiry

Jack Bierschenk

> I am not a teacher, but a fellow traveller of whom you have asked the way.
>
> Attributed to George Bernard Shaw

Introduction

In this chapter I explore transference and countertransference as phenomena taken to as well as arising in a supervisory discourse, to show how they may be creatively engaged with in the context of professional development and training. This may involve a training body, a trainee therapist (student), and a patient who may be seen through a training organisation's clinic. A student's supervisor will be an experienced professional usually chosen by them, or assigned by the training.

A training supervisor's task is to oversee the student's work and write reports. This arrangement can create difficulties, experienced as distressing by students due to the power dynamics involved when the person offering supervision is also an assessor. Such a relationship reminds us of dualities like being a child with a parent who both rewards and punishes, or a learner whose teacher can determine a passing grade or a failure. My aim is to raise awareness of infantilising habits created by institutionalised trainings so this dynamic can be held and contained, letting a student establish roots in the soil of broadly based development.

Facilitations and demons

I differentiate attitudes facilitating the development of a student's potential and individual style from dogmas arising in historical psychotherapeutic conventions, emphasising standard techniques. Consequently, I take the relationship between a student and a patient as it is encountered, rather than as a fact. Our discourse has two primary tasks: first, in regard to the therapeutic interests of the patient; second, to help the student mature as a therapist. I will describe the phenomenon of 'de-facilitation': prevailing attitudes and modes of practice creating difficulties both for the trainee therapist and the supervisor. These can be questioned and consequently deconstructed. In contrast, an attitude of facilitation is explored illustrating aspects of discourse promoting dialogue, encouraging the spirit of inquiry, and enabling the emergence of a student's professional attitude and personal style. But first, a small detour.

Engaging with psyche

Carl Jung wrote in his essay 'Principles of practical psychotherapy', 'A person is a psychic system which, when it affects another person, enters into a reciprocal reaction with another psychic system' (CW16 para. 1). In 'Psychology of the transference', he described the therapeutic encounter as a 'dialectical process' between two persons in which the therapist 'participates just as much as the patient' (CW16 para. 239). Jung believed the outcome of an analytic experience, whatever it might be, is the product of mutual influences arising from the personality of the analyst as well as the analysand, affecting both. The intimacy of a living encounter is recognised. This cannot be transposed to an alternate location without simultaneously affecting the communication and understanding of its content.

Further, when such experiences are talked about, as in supervision, the ensuing dialogue is not straightforward. The supervisee is simultaneously narrator and part of the psychic system being discussed. Several subjective psychological dimensions are visited concurrently. The London analytical psychologist Michael Fordham said of this endeavour:

> The analyst will know that every single statement he makes is an account of the state of his psyche, whether it be a fragment of understanding, an emotion, or an intellectual insight; all techniques and all learning how to analyse are built on this principle. It is thus part of the analyst's training experience to realise that he is often going to learn, sometimes more, sometimes less, from each patient, and that in consequence he himself is going to change.
>
> (Fordham 1957: 69)

Psychotherapists recognise the fragile and complex nature of the phenomenon known as psyche, which alludes to life energy and the mind. Mythologically, Psyche can be thought of as a beautiful princess loved by Eros (Johnson 1977). Other meanings include, for example, breath, butterfly (representing periods or stages of development), life and the personification of the soul. All these meanings arise from the classical roots of the Greek word, *psykhe*, and the Latin, *psyche*. Jung in later life increasingly understood the psyche not as a place comprised of content and structure, but as a dynamic phenomenon based on a system of 'readiness' (von Franz 1992, cited in Zabriskie 1997: 29).

These amplifications help us feel our way into the sensitive and affect-laden territory we enter regarding all kinds of transferences, wherever they are encountered. In supervision, we are invited into a private location, namely the dialogue of a therapeutic relationship between two people in a consulting room, itself a multidimensional and intimate place known through the metaphor of the alchemical *vas*, the sealed retort, the boundaried space, the analytic frame which serves both to contain its occupants as well as reflecting aspects of each to the other: now I return to the theme.

Engaging with transference and countertransference

Sigmund Freud expanded the concept of transference in his essay, 'Dynamics of the transference' (1912, SE 12). He coined the word *Übertragung*, from the German, meaning something 'carried over', to describe clinically those experiences arising in the consulting room where qualities of a previous relationship with a significant person are sometimes more, sometimes less, unconsciously projected onto the therapist. These reduce down to an 'infantile wish for mothering or fathering' (Peters 1991: 87). Psychoanalysis suggests a straightforward view: referring to a dictionary, *The Language of Psycho-analysis*,

> transference becomes the terrain upon which the patient's unique set of problems is played out with an ineluctable immediacy, the area where the subject finds himself face to face with the existence, the permanence and the force of his unconscious wishes and fantasies.
> (Laplanche and Pontalis 1983: 458)

Expanding, the French analytic lexicographers add an additional statement from Freud:

> It is on that field that the victory must be won . . . it cannot be disputed that controlling the phenomena of transference presents the psychoanalyst with the greatest difficulties.
> (Laplanche and Pontalis 1983: 458)

Notice the use of military terms. These have served as metaphors for many authors describing depth psychology. For example, in the 'Introductory lectures on psychoanalysis' Freud (1917) describes aspects of the father transference of a patient he was analysing as 'the battlefield on which we gained control of his libido . . . a battlefield need not necessarily coincide with one of the enemy's key fortresses' (SE 16: 456).

The *Critical Dictionary of Analytical Psychology* uses disarming metaphors to describe the transference. You are referred to articles on analyst and patient, as well as alchemy, compensation, *coniunctio*, hermaphrodite, mana personalities, and opposites (Samuels et al. 1986: 151). Transference, like alchemy, is part of the transformation of lead into gold, or of the change of suffering into compassion, wisdom and empathy. Jung approached the subject of transference using alchemical metaphor in *Psychology of the Transference* (CW16). He emphasised the struggle for understanding and learning as it arises through the therapist's receptivity to the patient's psychic reality. This, he argued, can be facilitated in the transference dynamics and through a real relationship between patient and therapist.

A therapeutic alliance acknowledges the landscape of a new psychological territory which the participants enter due to the teleological nature of psyche: in analytical psychology, this mean interpreting the phenomena of psyche in terms of purpose, rather than cause. But in practice, how useful are alchemical metaphors when the containers contain holes (Cwick 2006), or if the personality of the supervisor is placed above the student?

Transference phenomena are an aspect of projection, a specific form of communication which is universal and part of every individual's ordinary life. The New York analytical psychologist and professor of religion Ann Ulanov (1985) defines it as an event which

> occurs when one person becomes the carrier for an unconscious content activated in another person. That content carries into the present moment conflicting and unassimilated feelings about figures in the past that distort perception of the present person or situation.
>
> (Ulanov 1985: 68)

Countertransference is a phenomenon with a broad range of definition. Traditionally, it is understood as a similar process to transference but flowing in the opposite direction.

Paula Heimann (a Kleinian analyst) illustrated the humanity contained in the analytic relationship:

> The aim of the analyst's own analysis is not to turn him into a mechanical brain which can produce interpretations on the basis of a purely intellectual procedure, but to enable him to sustain his feelings as opposed to discharging them like the patient.
>
> (Heimann 1960: 9–10)

A contemporary view, represented by psychoanalyst Donna M. Orange, conceives the countertransference as the 'whole of the analyst's experience of the analytic relationship' (Orange 1993: 247). Such a view may imply countertransference is a projection of the therapist's unconscious contents onto the patient. Undoubtedly this happens.

In raw terms, countertransference is a response to, and ultimately an engagement with, reactions to everything presented to a therapist by a patient's complexes. Often, as my examples illustrate, this confronts the therapist with the unexpected. Jung proposed an objective approach to understanding transference based on archetypal constructs, the bigger picture of life, onto which our smaller, personal stories are framed and constellated. In this domain myths, theatre, art and literature illustrate such interactions.

For example, James (a patient discussed later), experienced uprooting and impermanence in childhood and found particular affinity with films or stories portraying 'the wanderer' and people who have been displaced. He experienced the alienation and separation suffered by the leading characters in Johanna Spyri's novel *Heidi* in a personal way, and identified with the soulful relationship portrayed by Philip Pullman in the novel *Northern Lights* between Lyra Belacqua and her 'dæmon'. These illustrations of archetypal images are not static metaphors, locating us in particular points of history, but rather 'nodal points of psychic energy', by which human imagination is able to apprehend all sorts of possible relationships arising from the psyche (von Franz 1992, in Zabriskie 1997: 29).

Another everyday encounter with transference phenomena arises in metaphors. They are a communication tool defined in the *American Heritage Dictionary* as 'a figure of speech in which a term is transferred from the object it ordinarily designates to an object it may designate only by implicit comparison or analogy' (Morris 1971: 1363). The word comes from the Greek, *metapherein*, to transfer: *meta* involving change, combined with *pherein* to bear. Like a painting comprised of colours, brush strokes, nuance, perspective and relief, metaphors are portrayed in words out of which energising images emerge. These illustrate ideas and experiences in ways that words alone cannot adequately describe. The experience of psychotherapy is also a metaphor of a personal engagement and synthesis which cannot be achieved in ordinary life as it rests on a framework in which transference phenomena occur as well as offering the possibility for them to be interpreted.

In clinical work, we recognise the layers of energy involved in the expression of an idealised transference arising from a patient who experiences their therapist as a person in whom there can be no failings or weaknesses, who can interpret any dream perfectly, and who can heal them from their awful affliction. A similarly minded patient may elevate the therapist as a hero, highly valued and esteemed in a positive, unrealistic way thereby disguising an additional transference, lurking underneath, denied or repressed, in which the therapist is thought of and perhaps experienced as a ruthless oppressor intent on dominating them.

The healer and the hero are archetypal figures and the transferences which arise from such ideas, following Jung's principle of *enantiodromia* (everything turns into its opposite), inevitably, become their opposites, the destroyer and the thief. Sometimes dreams provide glimpses of such an alternative point of view.

A man whom I analysed believed for years, in a one-sided way, that I was a kind and caring father. In a particularly strong idealised transference and contrary to his childhood experience, he felt I listened to him without criticism, he did not have to fit into my expectations, and I could do no harm. He assumed the camping van parked on the street in front of my house belonged to me and this promoted an additional idealised image, I was ecologically minded and loved being in nature.

Once, when he drove past my house on Christmas Eve, he noted a light burning in the garage and thought I was making wooden toys to be given to homeless children on the following day. This idyllic transferential state heralded a long, arduous trek into a different reality. In a dream he saw me hitting children just as he recalled being physically punished in school as a boy. Even more shocking to him was a subsequent dream in which he observed me carelessly littering a nature trail with scraps of paper. He experienced such behaviour as an archetypal assault on Mother Earth.

In the consulting room transference is not always a clear-cut phenomenon identifiable by a single label. In practice, particularly in matters relating to training, a tendency to classify and objectify for educational reasons is common to help students process unconscious material arising from multiple sources. Therapists who are analytically minded will be keen to tease apart, isolate and discover the roots of their psychological encounters. Some may explain them in terms of object relations, complexes and instincts; others may emphasise the religious and spiritual dimensions of the psyche. Therapists who are creatively engaged with their patients and critically attuned to their work expand their understandings through reflection, research, imagination and amplification. These are means by which clinicians become aware of themselves and their patients, and how in turn patients are enabled to broaden and enrich their own psychological domain.

The psyche is a continuously moving and interactive system, susceptible to the irrational, impossible to comprehend in isolation. Transference is comprised of affects compressed through time. Arising out of internally based dimensions and external experience it appears by degrees. Sometimes no transference is apparent, sometimes it appears in an overwhelming eruption of emotion so powerful therapist and patient may remain disturbed for long after, or become anxious about it days in advance. Here is an example of an encounter with the unknown and the subsequent experience of supervision which fostered understanding of unexpected events:

James was separated from his mother at infancy by social workers who feared for his physical safety, as his drug-addicted mother had tried at various times to self-abort him prior to birth. He grew up with foster parents and in children's homes and was physically abused and neglected. Experiences of attachment and love amounted to a few precious moments accidentally provided by well-meaning, unconnected carers. In childhood James experienced no consistency. In adult life he lived with feelings of uncertainty about his identity. As our work began, I became aware of his fear of non-being, of being hated, and feeling self-hate and self-loathing. This depth of his feelings was not familiar from my own life. James was extremely sensitive to intrusive events arising outside the consulting room: a noise in the hallway, a door slammed in the distance, or the sound of the mail falling to the floor were provoking and caused disturbed affect. These I interpreted as metaphors of memories of being taken away. I worked hard to manage intrusion and, where possible, prevent them. Alternatively, if, while maintaining my undivided focus on him, a stranger rang the doorbell and I chose not to answer, James would identify with the caller and experience this as an expression of my not being attentive.

As I became familiar with the meaning that intrusion had for him I, too, became more aware and sensitive of countertransference enactments in relation to the minutiae of sense-objects present in my room. Before he arrived, I placed extra emphasis on making sure movables such as chairs, cushions and lamps had their usual appearance and position. New objects intended for the room were generally avoided. Flowers sometimes presented difficulties especially when they began to decline and wilt. An unreplaced broken light bulb signified for him he was worthless; a bookmarker observed in a dictionary on the bookshelf suggested I'd be writing reports on him; a pencil left on the tabletop conformed this suspicion. He placed similar attention on me. A glance directed at something other than himself at the moment he observed it, a slight reticence in responding, or not indicating in the moment I did not understand something he'd said would bring about intense, incremental, unremitting rage and projectively identified hatred.

One day, after a particularly aggressive session in which he felt intensely rejected and eventually threatened to leave, I heard my own words moments after I had spoken. What I'd said was, 'I also feel our work is worthless, and you may as well consider ending this analysis.' The words came from an unfamiliar part of my psyche, an unknown other, a sense of my self I did not recognise. Of this Jung wrote: '[the therapist] quite literally "takes over" the sufferings of his patient and shares them with him' (CW16 para. 358). When I brought this to supervision I recall the difficulty experienced in conveying the intensity of the experience and dealing with my feeling of being vulnerable and judged. I was anxious about exposing newly revealed aspects of my neurotic countertransference and became protective of the syntonic (same feeling toned) ones.

My experience of non-judgemental supervision fostered a sensitive attunement to unforeseeable events and the sometimes unknowable realm of the psyche. In this regard, I do not agree that rigid separation in supervision must be drawn between the personal dimensions of the therapist and his or her professional role, or between personal therapy and what belongs to supervision. Others hold a similar view (Beebe 1995; Knight 2003). In supervision 'the central training modality [is] the [supervisor's] capacity to assimilate the candidate's suffering in an analytic way and thereby to sustain belief in the student analyst's capacity to survive in the analytic field' (Beebe 1995: 101).

With patients like James, an inevitable link arises which Jung identified as a 'bond . . . of such intensity that we could almost speak of a "combination". When two chemical substances combine, both are altered' (CW16 para. 358). Non-judgemental collaboration facilitates an introspective attitude which in turn leads to the possibly of understanding the source of fusions and amalgamations arising in altered states of consciousness. While in training, such attitudes influence how a future therapist experiences formative holding, which, when internalised, establishes the possibility of redemption in the face of immense irrationality.

At other times, an apparent lack of transference may be noted. This could a defence, or a resistance against therapy. But a supervisor can broaden the horizon by helping the student examine other possibilities: a patient's affective transference might actually be placed upon another person, a partner, or the boss at work. For example, in therapy with an adolescent living at home with parents, psychic energy may be completely cathected to them (Peters 1991). A variety of transference intensity may also be related to temperament and personality type (Chapter 5). Some people, who live their lives passionately through others, may form strong transferences, whereas a cool and contained introvert may be less likely to do so. If the relative paucity of transference creates a conundrum, another of Jung's observations can help the therapist understand he

> will infallibly run into things that thwart and 'cross' him: first, the thing he has no wish to be (the shadow); second, the thing he is not (the 'other', the individual reality of the 'You'); and third, his psychic non-ego (the collective unconscious).
>
> (CW16 para. 470)

The notion of mutuality is reflected in the work of London psychoanalysts Anthony Bateman and Peter Fonagy, who describe transference as 'the emergence of latent meanings and beliefs, organised around and evoked by the intensity of the therapeutic relationship' (Bateman and Fonagy 2004: 207). The dynamics of the here and now are emphasised as these factors arise through the 'interplay between the patient and the therapist' by means of the transference as the 'medium through which the individual's internal drama is "played-out" in treatment' (Bateman and Fonagy 2004: 207). This intersubjective position further emphasises the interplay between the subjective reality of the therapist and the patient who together 'form an indissoluble psychological system . . . that constitutes the empirical domain of psychoanalytic inquiry' (Atwood and Stolorow 1984: 64).

Ancestors, frames and consulting rooms

Does one infer transference is a component, or a stimulus, originating primarily from the patient upon which the therapist's countertransference is predicated? What about the external dimensions of the frame, the physical surroundings of the room? Might not the presence of soft furnishings, a warm sofa to snuggle into, a patterned Afghan rug to imagine into, a fire burning in the hearth on cold winter nights in turn transfer onto a future patient, one who has yet to pass through the door, something of the therapist's expectation within the countertransference? 'Ah,' the therapist might imagine of the yet non-existent patient, 'here is a place where I can regress, where I will be warm and looked after.'

Has this particular therapist, who appears needy of acceptance by the patient, noticed with similar perspicacity how the wooden floors squeak when they are walked upon by patients as they pass by, or eye one another, while sitting together in the communal waiting room? Is there awareness of the waste paper basket, located in a corner of the consulting room, full to the brim with the tissues of another's misery? And why does the therapist not realise the hygienic plastic couch-cover actually produces real, not imagined, physical discomfort to the patient on hot, humid, sweat-creating sultry summer days? Such thoughts draw on the practical considerations involved in supervision of the transference in regard to the therapist's subjective influence on the frame, the container, and significant physical, and, by implication, psychological surroundings.

For the future practitioner this is a fundamental aspect of professional attitude as well as requirements pertaining to the rules, codes and ethics of contemporary practice. Psychoanalyst Merton M. Gill drew attention to the interactional reality of intra-psychic experience by emphasising 'all aspects of the analytic situation are contributed to by both parties' (Gill 1984: 176, in Stolorow et al. 1994: 9). In his vision of psychoanalysis and psychotherapy, Gill described the analyst's role as co-determining the transference and urged the analyst should 'first focus on his contribution to the patient's experience of the relationship in the patient's response both to interventions and to the features of the analytic setting' (Gill 1984: 167).

The physical location of a therapeutic encounter is more than 'just a room'. It comprises a soulful environment. An illustrated study of contemporary German psychoanalytic consulting rooms by Claudia Guderian

(2004) reveals the minutiae of intention in the sensate design and arrangements of such rooms representing an influential image-forming extension of the psychological setting. Not attending to this environment with professional care and sensitivity may amount to neglect or abuse, thereby giving rise to a sense of violation in the patient.

A supervisee, Susan, reported being challenged on a matter by a patient, with whom after several years of analysis she had formed a positive relationship. However, the patient felt, and also observed, that at certain times Susan seemed to express herself, or make an interpretation of the patient's material with a tinge of aggression, or speak with a disapproving tone. No satisfactory resolution was found.

One day, I uncharacteristically forgot to remove the portable telephone from my consulting room. It rang during our session. I got up, turned the ringer off, and on returning to my chair noted Susan had an angry frown. I apologised for the intrusion, but as I became aware how angry she remained, I asked if we ought to explore the matter. During the intervening moments I began to feel irrationally I had spoilt our entire session. Susan became tearful and recalled, in a state of upset and sadness, during her training analysis she had never, because of fear of retribution, confronted her analyst about answering the telephone in her sessions. Susan rationalised this over the years of her analysis by recognising the calls seemed to be important and her analyst actually kept the conversations brief. However, Susan remained angry at this profound intrusion into what she felt was her personal space. Expanding, Susan recalled 'ridiculous feelings of rivalry' aroused in her by this object, which 'sat like a pet' on the table next to the analyst's chair while she, the patient, was seated some distance away. Susan's metaphors portrayed feelings of being intruded upon by the analyst's private life thereby violating a fundamental belief her interests were being respected in a professional manner.

Her analyst was a prominent individual whose authority and wisdom Susan felt could not be challenged without fear of drawing negative criticism. As a result, this matter remained parcelled away in Susan's mind during subsequent years, although the negative experience was corrected in her own practice. Susan's telephone is outside the consulting room; when it rings it can be faintly heard. But she kept in the background of her consciousness a lingering unresolved anger and resentment arising from an experience of abused intimacy.

In supervision, we speculated whether a faint ringing of her telephone, which Susan is probably more sensitive to than any of her patients, stimulated a neurotic countertransference which, when enacted, manifested as irritation. The patient became subject to Susan's unconscious expression arising from an unresolved complex containing a damaged aspect of her training experience.

Susan's feeling of resentment can be understood in terms of *Nachträglichkeit*, a word and concept originally coined by Freud to describe such phenomenon and reformulated by Arnold Modell, psychoanalyst and professor of clinical psychiatry at Harvard, who expanded classical theory by including the analytic relationship itself as a factor in the dynamics of transference.

The German verb *nachtragen* taken in context can mean to carry after, to add, as well as to bear a grudge; the adjective *nachträglich*, means subsequent, belated, with hindsight or by way of addition; and the adjective *nachträgerisch* means being resentful, or unforgiving. These definitions illustrate the complex nuances comprising the concept of *Nachträglichkeit*, which describes how an event from the past may be carried over into the present and experienced there without conscious reference to its origin; when an event recalls a trauma, the affect from which arises in the present. Modell, quoting Freud, brings forward the notion of retranscription, by which 'the material present [in the mind] in the form of memory traces [is] subjected from time to time to a *rearrangement* in accordance with fresh circumstances'. Of this Freud said: 'Thus what is essentially new about my theory is the thesis that memory is present not once but several times over' (Modell 1990: 16, quoting Masson 1985: 207).

This illustrates the ambiguous nature of the psyche. In life, and in therapy, psyche may be understood as an evolving process involving an internal and an external dialogue in relation to new experience. What Freud intended to convey by means of *Nachträglichkeit*, Modell (1990: 4) highlights, 'is that memory is retranscribed as a result of subsequent experience'.

An intersubjective field is present in relationships and affects all members of an interest group; be it a couple, a family, a psychotherapy training body, a corporation, or a nation. Such perspectives are difficult to tease apart and examine from within. Particular types of transference may be recognised as fuelled by forces of coercion, influence and propaganda enabling a specific point of view, dogma, or personality to maintain power and authority. As the previous example shows, students are particularly susceptible to the destructive consequences of institutional intersubjectivity. Individually they are on the lower rungs of the 'ladder of becoming' erected by an organisation. Where there are hierarchies there will inevitably be parallel processes. In the example, the roots of Susan's countertransference contained personal components, sometimes mentioned in supervision, such as her feelings of inferiority and her experience of being dominated by a stern, autocratic mother. But other aspects are unmistakably collective, such as the absolute and inarguable objectivity of dogma, the standardised techniques, the 'musts' and 'have-tos', or the unquestionable powers of historical convention, all of which require differentiation on the part of the student, but not necessarily with the blessing of the training body.

Recognition of transference is like post through a letterbox; it arrives, it happens. How the recipient, the therapist, engages with and becomes engaged by it is subjective and personal. Here we have a story which both is, and already has been, potentially in the making. Taken to supervision, further letters arrive, as, like the post, there is now a wider story about an event taking place in the reposting. But in supervision, the original letter is never brought, it cannot be. Instead, there is an account of the experience of receiving it. Such experiences, like letters, get subjected to all sorts of treatment: sometimes they are squashed, bent or torn, maybe lost; perhaps delivered to the wrong address and opened by people whose name is not indicated; sometimes they are rubbished, denigrated or judged in terms of good or bad, right and wrong.

Recalling our own experience of training can help us reorient ourselves to what it feels like to be supervised. Many students enter psychotherapy trainings with enthusiasm and creative expectations arising out of good experiences in personal therapy. But soon exclusion, hierarchy, and institutional imperatives produce demons. Students are constantly scrutinised, and assessed on written work and oral presentations in seminars, and by interviews. The student's demons readily include issues such as how to deal with and report on 'making mistakes', how truthfully open to be about events arising in the consulting room without evoking displeasure of the supervisor, feeling guilt, needing to please, fearing retaliation due to departure from established ideology arising from their creative or inspired thought, fearing loss of a clinic patient prior to completion of the minimal period of contract, and experiencing boundary violations arising from cracks of the therapeutic container (Cwick 2006). Narcissistic wounding and attacks upon students' morale (Beebe 1995: 99) are familiar scars of 'battle', not necessarily arising from the unconscious per se, but from engaging with the beast of training.

For the supervisor, the feeling of achieving 'good work' with the student is therefore concurrently informed by its shadow, of which the supervisor holds the greater share. This is because the latter is in a dual relationship: both an instrument of a training body with allegiances and responsibilities to the school and an employee of the student. The extreme degree to which this balance can skew has been described in Otto Kernberg's (1996) essay of poignant irony describing thirty ways through which institutions may hinder the student's capacity and natural inclination for creative learning.

Facilitation

Trees planted in a forest compete for light and growing space. A solitary oak, nurtured in an unobstructed open field, may be encouraged to branch out above the ground and concurrently develop 'rootedness' below, achieving an aesthetic and powerful structural balance as well as optimal ecological survival. A Jungian colleague knowledgeable about trees told me that an oak refers mythologically to wisdom and strength, however, in its early years it needs considerable shaping. Unlike the conifer it does not have a natural leader branch and therefore can branch out all over the place. Really tall oaks have been considerably helped by shaping for many decades. In fact, if you want a really tall oak, then you must shape it when young. Wild oaks tend to spread out much lower and in a haphazard fashion. Now that is an interesting and rather traditional metaphor for a trainee and the institution.

(Alan Mulhern, personal communication 2007)

The image of the freely growing oak stands for the fulfilled creative potential arising in an open system, rather than restrictive pruning and constraint of a closed system. Closed supervisory experiences resemble propagation in nurseries.

Facilitation in supervision is not easy. The etymology of the word facilitate, from the Latin, *facilis* (*Oxford English Dictionary* 1973) refers the reader to its opposite, *debilitare*, to render weak, to enfeeble. Facilitation means to promote, to help forward, hinting at the teleological sense of collaborative supervision which depends on mutuality and opposition. Both participants occupy interchangeable positions – doing and being done to; speaking and being heard; conceptualising and trying out; struggling and being contained; experimenting and drawing upon experience. Both participants start from different locations, one from being with a patient, the other from not being with a patient. Each brings a different form of energy to the encounter, giving rise to the imaginal. Like a tree, one participant may draw upon the energy contained in the daylight captured by the leaves, in the sense of new insights and knowledge; the other may draw nutrients from the darkness, from acquired wisdom and the roots of past experience.

But transference dynamics may be compromised by encroachment of the forest, the elements of de-facilitation: too much pruning, or the supervisor's taking the moral high ground, can readily spoil the vulnerable young oak taking root in an open field. The trunk of this tree alludes to the strength arising out of collaborative relationship. How can such a structure be encouraged?

Conclusion

The supervisor is invited to 'observe' an intimate relationship from a privileged position. Only one of the two members of this intimate relationship is consciously present, the other, 'a patient' participates as an image. This image is framed and held by shared aims. What are they? The psychoanalyst Donald Winnicott thought of them as keeping himself alive, well and awake. He wrote: 'I aim at being myself and behaving myself.

Having begun an analysis I expect to continue with it, to survive it, and to end it' (Winnicott 1962: 166). Let us look at each of these.

Keeping alive

Where Winnicott referred to keeping himself alive, the aim of supervision would include keeping the student aware so as not to annihilate the patient, for example in not denying the patient's true identity; by helping the student avoid making the patient fit a picture of their own making based on illusions, theories, and constructs. Students are bathed in theories and constantly challenged to demonstrate their use. This experience, when coupled with institutions and schools of thought, tends to create categories, and from categories '-isms' arise, such as 'narciss-isms', and '-ologies', which package, regulate, and ossify: 'the -ology, that parasitical suffix that sucks the psyche dry' (Hillman 2006: 33). The shadow of categorisation might be recognised as the loss of individuality. Wholesome supervision arises from working together rather than from a position of superiority. Wholesomeness, unlike fusion, or identification, requires a drawing together of affects rather than holding them apart.

Keeping well

Supervision involves a soulful connection to the student. In stressful interactions all of us rely on positively introjected good objects; these include meaningful persons such as one's therapist and teachers, and meaningful experiences with peers and colleagues. The supervisor also requires reflective facilities such as the supervision of supervision. I am in a peer group, which meets regularly for this purpose. Clinical nourishment is sensitively balanced with a good meal on a Friday evening of 'supper-vision'.

Keeping awake

Stimulating the spirit of inquiry encourages divergence and strengthens a student's enjoyment of the art and science of psychotherapy. The art is the individual's clinical style, their own voice for example, and their sense of timing. The science is a means with which traditional as well as innovative theoretical insights can be validated, allowing the development of the art of therapy.

Supervision gives students an opportunity to discover the depth and complexity of countertransference, a fragile and boundary-permeable organ. The capacity to sit and wait, to work with silence and emptiness, the capacity to be with not-knowing, to tolerate uncertainty, the multilayers of reality and the irrational require mindfulness and awaken us to the collective and the collaborative.

"MISTER... JES KEEP YOUR JUNGIAN ANALYSIS TO YO'SELF... YOU HEAR?" GROWLED MRS. BOTHAM

Figure 6.1

'A person is a psychic system which, when it affects another person, enters into a reciprocal reaction with another psychic system' (CW16 para. 1, *Principles of Practical Psychotherapy*).

References

Atwood, G. and Stolorow, R. (1984) *Structure of Subjectivity: Explorations in Psychoanalytic Phenomenology*. Hillsdale, NJ: Analytic Press.
Bateman, A. and Fonagy, P. (2004) *Psychotherapy for Borderline Personality Disorder: Mentalization Based Treatment*. Oxford: Oxford University Press.
Beebe, J. (1995) 'Sustaining the potential analyst's morale.' In. P. Kugler (ed.) *Jungian Perspectives on Clinical Supervision*. Einsiedeln, Switzerland: Daimon.
Cwick, G. (2006) 'The art of the tincture: analytical supervision.' *Journal of Analytical Psychology* 51(2): 209–226.
Fordham, M. (1957) 'Notes on the transference.' In M. Fordham, *New Developments in Analytical Psychology*. London: Routledge & Kegan Paul.
Franz, M-L. von (1992) 'Some reflections on synchronicity.' In M-L. von Franz, *Psyche and Matter*. Boston, MA: Shambhala.
Freud, S. (1912) 'Dynamics of the transference.' *The Standard Edition of the*

Complete Psychological Works of Sigmund Freud, vol. 12, trans. J. Strachey. London: Hogarth Press.
—— (1917) 'Introductory lectures on psychoanalysis'. *The Standard Edition of the Complete Psychological Works of Sigmund Freud*, vol. 16, trans. J. Strachey. London: Hogarth Press.
Gill, M. (1984) 'Psychoanalysis and psychotherapy: a revision.' *International Review of Psychoanalysis* 11: 161–179.
Guderian, C. (2004) *Magie der Couch*. Stuttgart: R. Kohlhammer.
Heimann, P. (1960) 'Counter-transference.' *British Journal of Medical Psychology* 33: 9–15.
Hillman, J. (2006) 'The Azure Vault: Caelum as experience.' In L. Cowan (ed.) *Barcelona 2004 Edges of Experience: Memory and Emergence. Proceedings of the Sixteenth International Conference for Analytical Psychology*. Einsiedeln, Switzerland: Daimon.
Johnson, R. A. (1977) *She: Understanding Feminine Psychology*. New York: Harper & Row.
Jung, C. G. (1953–1973) *Collected Works*, ed. Sir H. Read, M. Fordham, G. Adler and W. McGuire, 20 vols. London: Routledge & Kegan Paul.
Kernberg, O. (1996) 'Thirty methods to destroy the creativity of psychoanalytical candidates.' *International Journal of Psychoanalysis* 77: 1031–1040.
Knight, J. (2003) 'Reflections on the therapist–supervisor relationship.' In J. Wiener, R. Mizen and J. Duckham (eds) *Supervising and Being Supervised: A Practice in Search of a Theory*. London: Palgrave Macmillan.
Laplanche, J. and Pontalis, J. B. (1983) *The Language of Psycho-analysis*. London: Hogarth Press.
Masson, J. (trans. and ed.) (1985) *The Complete Letters of Sigmund Freud to Wilhelm Fleiss*. Cambridge, MA: Harvard University Press.
Modell, A. (1990) *Other Times, Other Realities: Toward a Theory of Psychoanalytic Treatment*. Cambridge, MA: Harvard University Press.
Morris, W. (ed.) (1971) *The American Heritage Dictionary of the English Language*. Boston, MA: American Heritage and Houghton Mifflin.
Orange, D. M. (1993) 'Counter-transference, empathy and the hermeneutical circle.' In A. Goldberg (ed.) *The Widening Scope of Self Psychology*. New York: Academic Press.
Peters, R. (1991) 'The therapist's expectation of the transference.' *Journal of Analytical Psychology* 36: 77–92.
Pullman, P. (1995) *Northern Lights*. London: Scholastic.
Samuels, A., Shorter, B. and Plaut, F. (1986) *A Critical Dictionary of Jungian Analysis*. London: Routledge & Kegan Paul.
Spyri, J. (1995) *Heidi*. London: Penguin.
Stolorow, R., Atwood, G. and Brandchaft, B. (eds) (1994) *The Intersubjective Perspective*. Lanham, MD: Rowman & Littlefield.
Ulanov, A. B. (1985) 'Transference/countertransference: a Jungian perspective.' In M. Stein (ed.) *Jungian Analysis*. Boston, MA: Shambhala.
Winnicott, D. W. (1962) 'The aims of psycho-analytic treatment.' In D. W. Winnicott, *The Maturational Processes and the Facilitating Environment*. London: Hogarth.
Zabriskie, B. D. (1997) 'Thawing the "frozen accidents": the archetypal view in countertransference.' *Journal of Analytical Psychology* 42(1): 25–40.

Chapter 7

'Mind the gap'

The symbolic container, dreams and transformation

Carola Mathers

Introduction

Why do people go to supervision? I suggest therapists welcome supervision as a symbolic container holding therapeutic work with patients. This container, at best, provides a space for exploring theory and practice, emotions, confusions, mistakes; facilitates working through transference and countertransference, positive and negative; mourns failures and celebrates success. In this chapter I discuss symbols, dreams and transformation. I reflect on supervision as a symbolic container: how it is formed, succeeds or fails; how it transforms the work of therapy and the supervisory couple. The work of therapy is conceived as a symbolic process even though many times it may seem to be stuck in concrete thinking of patient, therapist and supervisor.

What is a symbol?

A symbol is primarily an unknown. It expresses the unknown in the most meaningful way possible at that particular time. A symbol is intimately connected with meaning. It manifests as an image mediated by one or more of the four functions: intuition, feeling, sensation, thinking. Jung links symbols to the activity of archetypes. He notes the vital difference between semiotic and symbolic:

> Every view which interprets the symbolic expression as an analogue or an abbreviated designation for a *known* thing is *semiotic*. A view which interprets the symbolic expression as the best possible formulation of a relatively *unknown* thing, which for that reason cannot be more clearly or characteristically represented, is *symbolic*.
>
> (CW6 para. 815, Jung's italics)

Further, Jung distinguishes between a living symbol and one which is dead because the meaning has been thoroughly explored:

So long as a symbol is a living thing, it is an expression for something that cannot be characterized in any other or better way. The symbol is alive only so long as it is pregnant with meaning. But once its meaning has been born out of it, once the expression is found which formulates the thing sought, expected or divined even better than the hitherto accepted symbol, then the symbol is *dead*, i.e. it possesses only an historical significance.

(CW6 para. 816)

The aliveness or deadness of a symbol is an important aspect which supervisors take note of, as it tells them about the patient's defensive structures and presence or absence of creativity. It also tells them whether the therapist has noticed the quality of the symbol.

Jung's colleague Erich Neumann (1989: 5–6) describes a symbol as a primordial, mythological image. Joe Redfearn (1978), a training analyst of the Society of Analytical Psychology, London, refers to a synthesis of opposites, a *coniunctio* of conscious and unconscious processes. For Neumann, symbols exist in the collective unconscious and manifest in myths and fairytales, there to be discovered, as it were. For Redfearn, these processes occur in an individual: two psychic elements come together, bringing a new, third, entity into being. This is an activity of a non-ego centre, the Self. Symbols arise through the clash of warring opposites (opposing archetypal activities), a potentially explosive process which may be creative or destructive. Clinically, the opposites are considered to be intrapsychic (in patient, therapist and supervisor) and extrapsychic (between therapist and patient and between therapist and supervisor).

Christopher Hauke (2000), a London Jungian analyst, presents a postmodern view of the symbol. He says the concepts 'image, symbol and meaning' are key to psychoanalysis and analytical psychology: 'postmodern concern with signs, symbols and representation provide a context in which to read Jung's psychology as a text which . . . contributes to the discussion of the subject and his or her location in postmodern culture' (Hauke 2000: 192). Jungian psychology works within a paradigm of not knowing: this according to Hauke places it squarely within the postmodern. This contrasts with psychoanalysis which maintains 'that the unconscious, like any "object of science" can be known and talked about descriptively, analytically and deductively, using a wide variety of truth statements' (Hauke 2000: 201). A symbol is by definition something which cannot be known fully. Hauke (2000: 193) points out in postmodern language the meaning of 'symbolic' and 'semiotic' has reversed. The Symbolic as used by Lacan refers to what is known: the collective and cultural; the semiotic as used by Kristeva is more like a symbol in its unknown, shadowy nature.

A vital element in considering symbols is the individual's capacity to make use of the symbol creatively. Jung (CW6 para. 819) calls this the 'symbolic attitude' of the observing consciousness. It is an attitude which 'assigns meaning to events'. I consider it the same as 'psychological mindedness'. Redfearn (1978: 232–233) writes: 'the symbolic attitude is normally dependent upon the introjection of the mother's holding capacity. It may have to be learned from the therapist . . . *by example*'. Symbols may arrive in the patient's consciousness, in a dream or waking fantasy, showing the patient is capable of symbolising, yet the patient may not be able to utilise them at all. Such a patient may bring dreams or fantasies, expecting the therapist to decode them, contributing little or nothing to any exploration of their meaning. In this case, therapist and supervisor ponder possible meanings. Symbols arising in the supervisory discussion may allow a transformation in the therapy.

'The gap'

In the London Underground network 'MIND – THE – GAP' is announced on stations where platform and train are a distance apart. As a child, I was fascinated by this and wondered what was in this 'Gap' which had to be 'Minded'. The gap is a liminal place in which the unexpected may appear: the imaginal world may break into consciousness and symbols may form. They begin as tiny events which may easily be overlooked, such as parapraxes (see the case of Helen, below). London Jungian analyst Warren Colman discusses the idea of the 'third' in psychoanalytic and Jungian thinking, in 'Symbolic conceptions: the idea of the third' (Colman 2007: 566). He writes about a 'third (area or position)' which 'may be described as a representational space for the occurrence of emergent meaning'. This space relates to what I call the 'gap'. He continues, 'the emergence of the third could also be described as the development of a capacity for symbolic imagination or simply *imaginal capacity*' (Colman 2007: 566). 'Imaginal capacity' is the symbolic attitude, the ability to make meaning from symbols, which may begin with attention to and exploration of what occurs in the gap.

Attention to the gap requires the therapist respectfully waiting for unconscious processes to become conscious through images, dreams and active imagination. The gap is potentially present at the beginning of every therapy and supervisory session. It is an anxious moment when something may happen. The psychoanalyst Wilfred Bion (1974: 13) described it beautifully: in a session there should be 'two rather frightened people; the patient and the psychoanalyst. If there are not, one wonders why they are bothering to find out what everyone knows'. Some patients obliterate this gap or prevent its appearance by starting as soon as the consulting room door opens, or fill it by speaking as soon as they come in, sit or lie down. Some feel angry the therapist has not helped them over it. Others are glad of a breathing space, defining the difference between the life they have come from and the therapy hour. A therapist I supervise used to begin sessions himself, fearing to 'retraumatise' his patient by initial silence. He disliked my initial silence when we first met. Equally, a patient may feel traumatised by a therapist starting the session, experiencing this as an intrusion. A similar gap occurs when there is silence in a session. A gap may be felt as an intrusion, an absence, or both – an intrusive absence.

Student therapists are (we hope) anxious about their ability to understand the patient and make interpretations; here, much of the supervisor's task is encouraging the student to listen and wait, gradually becoming comfortable with the gap. American psychoanalyst Hilde Bruch's paper (1974) 'On talking and listening' addresses this issue. I give this to student therapists especially in the National Health Service: they are usually not in therapy, so have no personal experience of therapeutic listening.

The gap is in the in-between parts of sessions, the non-verbal communications which underline or belie what is said. These include use of the therapist's room, couch, lavatory, objects such as tissues and, in private practice, bills, cheques and cash. In health care settings they include use of the secretary, building and waiting room. These are immensely important as they communicate what cannot be said or symbolised directly (Chapter 6). They are frequent areas of 'acting out': paying early or late, not signing the cheque, giving the wrong amount of cash, losing the bill. Arriving hours early, refusing to use the waiting room, talking to the secretary: each patient shows us something about themselves which cannot yet be articulated.

One of my supervisors, London psychoanalyst Gerald Wooster, commented that the beginning of sessions relates to attachment, the end relates to separation: the way the patient or therapist begins and ends sessions tells us how they handle attachment and separation. For example, arriving or leaving early or late or saying the important thing before the session 'starts' and after it has 'finished'. This behaviour may leave the patient open to feeling rejected: a complex is being unconsciously enacted. Patients who end sessions themselves may dislike the therapist's control over separation. It may be they are denying being in therapy, trying to make themselves a colleague rather than a patient.

Tissues are something concrete a therapist provides. Patients use tissues in many interesting ways. They may refuse to use them, use their own, or make things out of them which may be presented to the therapist as a gift or taken away. They may take handfuls or even the box away. They may tear them into little bits which they leave all over the consulting room – a mess for the therapist to clear up before the next patient arrives. Bills are also given by the therapist. Therapists handle bills differently, mailing or giving them, with or without an envelope, perhaps adding information such as holiday dates or fee increases. Patients may keep them as transitional objects or lose them, indicating a difficulty holding on to anything from the therapist. They may seek to control the therapist by paying late. They may pay exactly on time as a way of never owing anything. They may overpay or underpay. They may pay in cash, which can cause problems if the wrong amount is given. Or, if paying by cheque, they may forget to sign it.

In an institutional setting, non-therapy staff may be used as transferential objects. The secretary may be confided in, leaving the therapist as the transferential 'bad' object. The secretary may be spoken to before or after sessions, diminishing the therapist's importance and denying the beginning and end of the session. The building may be felt as a container, the patient arriving very early or leaving very late. Or, it may be criticised and denigrated, a displacement of contemptuous or angry feelings about the therapist. Other patients may be approached in the waiting room for gossip about therapy. As with more obviously symbolic imagery, the meaning of 'gap' events emerges during the course of therapy. Supervisors encourage therapists to watch for these liminal events and hold them in mind until it is possible to speak about them. As Redfearn (1978) says, patients may learn a symbolic attitude from the therapist.

Pets such as cats or dogs may contribute to therapy and/or supervision. My cat acts as a barometer of patients' mental states: if she appears when the patient is present I know they are in a bad way. Patients relate to her in their unique way: pleased to see her, feeling rejected when she leaves the room, jealous of her imagined relationship with me. A patient with a negative transference related positively to my cat, which made it possible for him to continue seeing me. At his last session, the cat waited in the room until he came, said her goodbyes, then left.

Gifts are not strictly speaking 'gap' events. Nevertheless, as a concrete intrusion, they are often a source of anxiety for the therapist, who may look to the supervisor for guidance. A discussion of gifts before therapy begins provides an opportunity for considering how to respond to this eventuality. Patients give gifts before or after therapy breaks, at particular moments during the work, and most commonly at the end, out of gratitude. Therapists may in their confusion and embarrassment resort to formulaic utterances when presented with a gift.

David, a mental health professional working in the NHS, refused a gift at the end of therapy, telling his patient the institution did not allow him to accept gifts. Recounting this, he felt sad, realising he had rejected his patient's gratitude. I felt sad too; David, who was warm and caring, resorted to defensive coldness when confronted with the separation and the gift.

Gifts given during therapy may have many meanings. Like 'gap' events they may not be symbolised at the time but may be understood many months later.

One of my patients regularly gave me gifts, which I accepted, as well as seeking, together with him, to discover their meaning. They ranged from flowers and plants

to wine, cheese, boyhood treasures, and a brush resembling a broomstick. He did not give me a gift at the end, which I considered a healthy outcome of our work: a development of the symbolic attitude.

The symbolic container

The alchemical idea of the Hermetic vessel (*vas Hermetis*) symbolises the containers of supervision and therapy. The vessel

> must be completely round, in imitation of the spherical cosmos . . . It is a kind of matrix or uterus from which the *filius philosophorum*, the miraculous stone, is to be born . . . Hence it is required that the vessel be not only round but egg-shaped . . . one soon learns that this is an inadequate conception since the vessel is a mystical idea, a true symbol like all the central ideas of alchemy.
>
> (CW12 para. 338)

Figure 7.1 shows a vessel within a vessel within a furnace – a depiction of therapy and supervision. The heat required for transformation comes from the emotional energy of the work, in the therapist–patient and therapist–supervisor couples.

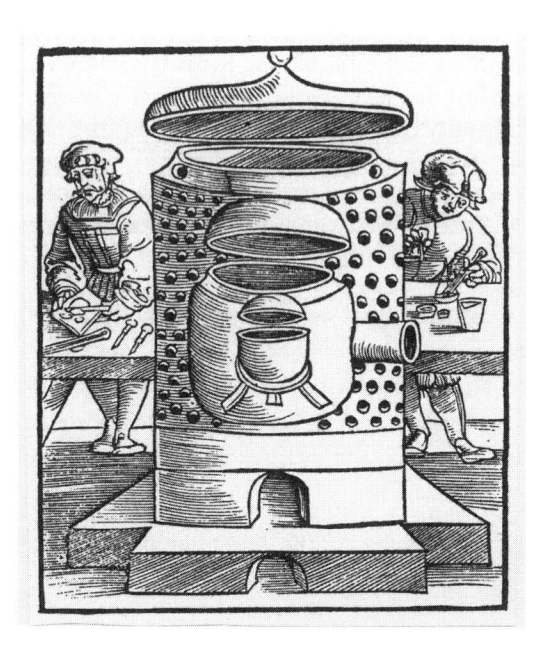

Figure 7.1

Redfearn (1978: 233) describes the alchemical vessel as an 'analogue of the body-ego' since the ego must be strong enough to contain the energy of the clash of opposites so a life-enhancing symbol may be born. Similarly with supervision: therapist and supervisor trust that the supervisory situation can symbolically represent the therapy. The therapist trusts the supervisor to sometimes act as an auxiliary ego. The supervisor trusts the therapist's integrity. The supervisory container, like the therapeutic container, requires firm boundaries and ethical principles so both participants feel safe (Chapters 2 and 3). American psychoanalyst Robert Langs (1997: 123–125) describes the importance of 'ground rules' for supervision which are as clear as therapeutic boundaries. In practice, some supervisory couples know each other before supervision begins, some supervisors offer tea or coffee. Keeping the supervisory frame consistent and predictable is essential for a safe container to form. When the container is safe the therapist can rely on the supervisor's reflective capacity, allowing images and symbols to arise.

Therapist and patient at the beginning of the work may be in unconscious union, with the supervisor experienced as a foreign body breaking into the couple (Searles 1986). The therapist has, as yet, little idea of what is going on. The therapeutic container is being slowly formed. Therapist's and patient's unconsciouses are getting acquainted (see Jung's 'Gate' diagram, Figure 11.1, on p. 167). The supervisor may have clues from his unconscious or from the therapist's way of presenting the patient. Images or symbols may be taken to supervision yet their meaning cannot be discovered. The supervisor may have to restrain beginning therapists from premature interpretations which may lead to closure and loss of space for playful exploration. Attention to boundaries helps the therapist experience the supervisor as providing a safe holding space: a womb-like 'maternal' container. This evolves into a 'paternal' space: thinking, challenging, questioning. At best, the supervisor 'nourishes' the therapist, trusts in the therapeutic process, pays attention to and is concerned for the therapeutic couple and the evolving therapy. The therapist's transference to the supervisor helps or hinders this process.

As the supervisor holds the therapeutic couple in mind, so the therapist is able to hold the patient in mind. Patients who are 'hell in mind' (Mathers et al. 2006) require frequent supervision, being difficult to hold and producing ambivalence in the therapist and countertransferential acting out. However, this acting out may provide valuable information. It is neither condemned nor condoned, but held in the vessel until the meaning emerges.

Beginnings in supervision are important. How a therapist approaches a supervisor is likely to shape the symbolic container. If a specific patient is to be supervised, the beginning may shed light on the therapy, giving information, by parallel process, about the patient's unconscious dynamics. As mentioned in other chapters, the symbolic container is differently constellated when a therapist is training and has never before been supervised, than when a therapist is experienced with previous supervisors. With a trainee, the supervisor will be aware of projections such as magician, wise teacher, or loved/hated parent, and a wish to be told how to conduct the therapy. As a trainee will be in therapy, there are inevitably split transferences between training therapist and supervisor, perhaps with pressures on the supervisor to behave as a therapist. Additionally, the supervisor may be chosen for the therapist, or the therapist may be given a choice which is not actual, as in geographical limitations, or those imposed by the training organisation. With an experienced therapist the supervisor knows she will be compared to previous supervisors, and may be told about styles of supervision that don't suit. There may be, as with second therapies, supervisory hurts to be healed. Martin Stone (Chapter 5) writes about the 'fit' between patient and therapist, and between therapist and supervisor, using typology. Some writers state it is good practice to change supervisor every five years to avoid therapist and supervisor feeling too comfortable, and perhaps colluding, when unconscious processes merge.

Symbols, dreams and transformation

Symbol formation and use is a complex issue. A symbol may exist in the collective, such as the Great Goddess. For example, a patient may dream of a wolf suckling her young. In therapy she explores her relationship to the personal and archetypal mother. Or she may dismiss the dream imagery as simply a day residue. Her therapist may attempt to open a dialogue about wolves, pups and mothers. The patient may work with the symbol or be unable to make sense of it. The therapist hopes her supervisor can help her understand why the patient has a dream rich in symbols but cannot work with it. From their knowledge of the patient's history and current life situation, the supervising couple will consider possibilities such as inadequate early maternal care, sadomasochistic object relations, defences against the therapy, or mistrust of the therapist. In the example above the patient could not work creatively with the symbol in the session because she envied her therapist and would not allow anything good to occur within sessions. Later she let the therapist know she thought deeply about the dreams on her own.

Sometimes the therapist may be temporarily unable to work symbolically.

Alex, an experienced therapist, brings to supervision evocative dreams from a patient with strong intellectual defences. The dreams are rich in symbols of death, destruction, secrets and cover-ups but the patient is too defended to work with them. Alex comes to supervision unable to think, feeling blocked. Alex uses her intuitive function, the patient uses primarily thinking. As we work, exploring Alex's feeling intimidated by the patient's intellect, Alex becomes less blocked and more hopeful of working with the images. The symbolic container allowed Alex to regain her reflective and thinking capacity.

When therapists make use of the supervisor's capacity to reflect, images and symbols emerge, leading to transformational processes within the therapist which the patient unconsciously picks up.

Sonia has a strong sensation function and relies on bodily and emotional experience. She tells me how she feels in relation to me or the session, and I share my feelings if appropriate. We can usually trace her countertransferences back to the patient. Once she complimented me on my skirt, adding, 'but of course it isn't silk'. I said it *was* silk, which took us straight to the patient being presented, who is often contemptuous but unable to bring the negative transference to consciousness. On another occasion Sonia was drifting away in the session, feeling dissociated from her body. We looked at the split in her patient who was afraid of going mad ('split mind') because his mother suffered from schizophrenia.

Symbols may be progressive or regressive, or both simultaneously. For example, the erotic transference may be regressive, symbolising the infantile wish to be close to mother, or merged with her in blissful union. At the same time it may be progressive, indicating the need to feel validated as a desirable sexual being and experience adult relating, via a resolution of the oedipal complexes. Progressive symbols, such as alchemical images of the *coniunctio oppositorum* (the marriage of opposites), or water, immersion, and washing, may be brought. They are distinguished from regressive symbols – the *uroboros* (the snake eating its own tail), death or incest fantasies. So-called progressive symbols may be used regressively by the patient and the same for so-called regressive symbols. The supervisor will be aware of the to-ing and fro-ing of progression and regression throughout the work, even within one therapy session. Any unknown may be symbolised, such as parapraxes by supervisor or therapist (see example on p. 110).

For Jung, dreams were highly significant psychic phenomena: 'one of the basic principles of analytical psychology is that dream-images are to be understood symbolically; that is to say, one must not take them literally, but must surmise a hidden meaning in them' (CW5 para. 4). The meaning of dream symbols is not fixed, otherwise they would be signs, but depends on the dreamer's individual situation: 'It is an especial inconvenience that one cannot recount a dream without having to add the history of half a lifetime in order to represent the individual foundations of the dream' (CW5 para. 7).

Dreams help patients begin exploring symbols: the dream 'does not conceal, it teaches' (CW8 para. 471). Initially patients may relate to dream images concretely.

> we come upon something of the utmost importance for the ability of dream-analysis: the dream describes the inner situation dreamer, but the conscious mind denies its truth and reality, or admits it only grudgingly.
>
> (CW16 para. 304)

Therapists are often anxious about working with the concrete, considering they ought to be working with symbols.

Henry told me his patient dreamed her car was about to break down. He worked with her on what this might mean symbolically. She was adamant it meant she should sell the car. A few days later the car did break down. She triumphantly told Henry this was what the dream meant and nothing else. He was downcast he hadn't helped her reflect on the dream symbolically. However, this event did show her the power of unconscious processes. She began taking more notice of dreams, parapraxes and apparently chance events. Gradually, she became aware her intuitive function was stronger than she'd thought.

By describing their dreams to an attentive listener, patients become more confident about listening to their dreams themselves. Unconscious processes are encouraged and a fruitful relationship to the symbolic life results, both in patient and therapist. The same is true with active imagination.

Therapists are often shy of bringing dreams about their patients. The dream may reveal too much about themselves. Nonetheless, dreams may be a useful commentary on the work. Jung describes dreaming about a patient: 'I began to feel I was no longer getting at the correct interpretation of her dreams, and I thought I . . . noticed an increasing shallowness in our dialogue' (Jung 1989: 133). He decides to talk to his patient about this. The night before he is to see her he dreams:

> I was walking down a highway through a valley in late-afternoon sunlight. To my right was a steep hill. At its top stood a castle . . . on the highest tower there was a woman sitting . . . In order to see her properly I had to bend my head far back. I awoke with a crick in the back of my neck. Even in the dream I . . . recognised the woman as my patient.

His interpretation: if he had to look so far up to see the patient, in reality he had been looking down on her. 'Dreams are, after all, compensations for the conscious attitude'. He further comments on compensation as being sometimes obscure:

On the basis of compensation theory, one would be inclined to assume, for instance, that anyone with a too pessimistic attitude to life must have very cheerful and optimistic dreams. This expectation is true only in the case of someone whose nature allows him to be stimulated and encouraged . . . But if he has a rather different nature, his dreams will purposively assume a much blacker character than his conscious attitude.

(CW8 para. 489)

Here Jung reminds us the dream is purposive, part of psyche's self-regulating functions.

I learnt in supervision about Tom, who believed he was self-sufficient, needing no-one: his conscious attitude to therapy. Gradually, he started trusting his therapist, who was well aware of Tom's dependency needs. The therapist worked hard to reach Tom; on two occasions when he did, he dreamed Tom was his therapist. We understood these dreams as showing us how Tom dealt with moves towards trusting the therapist: immediately reversing the therapeutic situation. Jung's use of his dream describes a process of self-supervision. Reflecting on it led him to discover and refine his conscious attitude.

Experienced therapists use self-supervision as well as collegial and peer supervision. Self-supervision depends on openness to imagery and symbols. These may arise in the course of the day when the therapist is thinking about the patient as she washes up or drives her car, for example. They may be consciously sought out, such as using the I Ching, Tarot, Astrology or other mythopoeic systems.

London psychoanalyst Patrick Casement (2002) finds patients can be accurate supervisors:

> When we are getting something wrong, either in our understanding of the patient or in how we are handling the therapy or analysis, we are frequently given helpful prompts towards recognising this if we are willing to notice these. It is therefore fortunate that we are not entirely alone in our endeavour to understand our patients. The patient is also present in the consulting room, though some analysts seem to work as if the only source of insight will be found within themselves.
>
> (Casement 2002: 21–22)

Quoting Langs (1978) writing about unconscious supervision by the patient, Casement (2002) enlarges this to discuss patients offering 'unconscious criticism'. Being alert to this allows therapists to discover mistakes. He also stresses the importance of being open to conscious critical remarks from patients without defensively interpreting these as negative transference:

we can miss something important if we too readily regard a patient's attempts at correcting us in terms of some assumed pathology of the patient: for instance, trying to castrate the analyst, or to render the analyst impotent. But it can happen that, with a particular patient, some change in how we are working may genuinely be appropriate: even essential.

(Casement 2002: 6–7)

Neumann (1989: 7) pointed to the importance of beginnings. He reminds us: 'Symbols gather round the thing to be explained, understood, interpreted'. Creation myths are active in all beginnings, be they the physical or psychological birth of the individual or the couple (consider how couples enjoy narrating their first meeting). The same is true for therapeutic and supervisory couples. Such symbols may appear in the consciousness of the supervisor and/or therapist in the form of dreams or fantasies. These may involve any of the senses. An anxious novice therapist may interpret images the patient brings according to a formula, as in the ocean symbolising the unconscious, or a cave symbolising the personal or archetypal mother. Since a living symbol represents something as yet unknown, the supervisor will remind the therapist they are speaking about signs rather than symbols. If an unconscious union between patient and therapist lasts overly long there may be resistance to the supervisory process, with consequent difficulty bringing the symbolic. If the resistance is not overcome the therapist may never bring this patient. This may lead to the breakdown of the therapy.

All the participants' complexes may be activated at the beginning. The supervisor may seek supervision. To understand the therapist–patient couple, the supervisor wants to know how therapist and patient got together. Who was the intermediary? A website, a public list, a professional in the field, a previous patient, a friend, a relative? A referral from a trusted person such as a friend or relative is more likely to support the future therapy than a website or public list. Patients feel more held by a personal recommendation. The supervisor will be alert to boundary issues in the case of relatives, friends or the therapist's former or concurrent patients making referrals. An assessor adds an extra dimension, such as when the patient is an adopted child, who is passed from assessor to therapist.

For example, if the complex around being given away by the biological mother cannot be symbolised, the therapy may not survive, as the therapist 'becomes' the adoptive mother. The supervisor's task here is to facilitate a symbolic, an 'as if' transference rather than a concrete transference where the patient experiences the assessor as the actual historical rejecting mother and therapist as the actual rejected adoptive mother. If a symbolic transference can be facilitated the assessor can be thought about as an 'as if' rejecting mother and the therapist as an 'as if' loved and hated adoptive mother. Or the assessor may be a man referring the patient to a woman therapist. The supervisor will be alert to parental dynamics in the patient's narrative and a residual transference to the assessor as, possibly, an absent, rejecting or indifferent father with the therapist as a tired mother struggling alone to cope.

When I worked as consultant psychotherapist in the NHS, I was fortunate in assessing patients for individual therapy, then supervising the therapist. I noticed how differently patients related to male therapists having seen me, a female assessor. Occasionally there were references to me in the therapy, indicating a residual transference. The psychoanalyst Nina Coltart, who assessed for many years for the London Clinic of Psychoanalysis, considered assessors should be somewhat rejecting in order to minimise residual troublesome positive transferences to the assessor which could interfere with therapy (Coltart, personal communication 1993).

When does the symbolic fail?

A neat parapraxis occurred when the publisher sent me the contract for this chapter. The title given was 'the symbolic *constrainer*'. Supervision felt as constraining restricts or obliterates reflective space. The imaginal world is collapsed and unavailable. The supervisory couple is sterile and uncreative. Many factors lead to this. Apparent symbolising may be an intellectual defence by therapist, patient or supervisor. Jargon can be used to avoid exploring deeper individual meanings as opposed to collective ones. Or, the supervisory couple collusively assume they know what each other is talking about. A therapist who has difficulty using symbols may speak in a theoretical language which appears to make sense and can intimidate a supervisor with a less developed thinking function. The supervisor needs to make sure the therapist understands what they are talking about rather than speaking theory in an undigested way.

The therapist may be anxious and/or narcissistic, experiencing any challenge from the supervisor as wounding, personal criticism; or they may have borderline traits experiencing supervision as persecutory, reacting with outward compliance but inward rebellion. Descriptions of sessions may be distorted, verbatim accounts avoided, lies told. Trainees may defensively try to use their supervisor as therapist and vice versa. If they succeed, therapeutic and supervisory boundaries have been violated and the symbolic container of both spaces damaged or broken. Therapists who have not had therapy may do good work if they are empathic and naturally gifted. If they are not, the symbolic container may be effective enough to hold them even though they struggle with exploring the patient's symbols through dreams and fantasies.

When supervisor and therapist have therapeutic styles or theoretical backgrounds which are too divergent, supervision may break down. As Hauke (2000: 198) describes, making a generalisation, a psychoanalytic therapist is more likely to elucidate and explain unconscious processes while a Jungian therapist is more likely to watch and wait for unconscious processes to unfold. When the supervisory couple are too much at odds, the patient notices. For example, a patient once told me I seemed much more relaxed. This occurred soon after I changed from a Kleinian to a Freudian supervisor.

Mark was ambivalent about working in private practice. He felt persecuted in a previous supervision which had lasted some years. On first seeing me he was anxious and guarded, gradually relaxing and becoming more confident. His ambivalence was mirrored in our work: he came infrequently and often planned to leave. His patients left one by one; at the same time he found work in a mental health setting. At our last supervision Mark mourned the loss, aware he had not fully used the potential of supervision.

Therapy may fail when a therapist is caught in a concrete experience with the patient which is not worked through in supervision.

Helen describes supervising Jane and her patient, a young woman with anorexia nervosa. The supervision took place by telephone, during which Helen noticed Jane's voice fading. In telling me, Helen began to feel confused and disorientated, which she had not felt with Jane. I asked who's who, as I was now confused. Instead of saying Jane was the patient, Helen replied, 'Jane is the supervisor', putting herself into this murky melee: all three of them symbiotically merged. In this undifferentiated state no thinking was possible, yet Helen's parapraxis allowed a gap for thinking and eventual understanding.

London Jungian analyst Joy Schaverien (2006: 61–63) describes a situation where two supervisors remained with the concrete problem of a female therapist's erotic countertransference in relation to her male patient. The first ignored the therapist voicing this timidly; the second became alarmed and told the therapist to terminate the therapy, which she did without giving the patient a reason. In this case, the symbolic was not retrieved, the therapy failed and the patient may have been harmed.

Jung, in 'Two kinds of thinking' (CW5 paras 11–25), describes and distinguishes between directed, logical or reality thinking and dreaming or fantasy thinking. Supervisors employ both kinds of thinking when hearing about sessions and considering theoretical hypotheses (diagnostic formulations, personality structure, complexes, defences), therapeutic process (transference/countertransference, concrete/symbolic, boundaries) and the supervision process (psychological availability of therapist, their use of supervision, parallel process). Therapists may have problems with one of these two kinds of thinking: highly intuitive or feeling therapists may have difficulty with directed thinking; highly sensate or thinking therapists may struggle with fantasy thinking. Supervisors concentrate on helping therapists develop their inferior functions. By doing so in a non-judgemental way, the therapist feels valued and held, experiencing their ideas about the patient as named and worked with: here, supervision is working as symbolic container. Or the therapist may feel threatened by looking at theory and construing it as 'dogma', a theoretical straitjacket. There may be unnamed anxiety and negative transference to the supervisor. Here, supervision is not functioning as symbolic container.

A therapist whose primary function is thinking may feel deskilled by the supervisor's encouragement to free associate to the patient's material and suggestions to tolerate not-knowing, waiting and allowing silence so the unexpected may emerge. Or such a therapist may feel liberated from the pressure of having to know and understand the patient quickly and to make early interpretations. As Jung says (CW5 para. 25), dream thinking is regressive, tending to the past, and infantile memory. We are in a regressive position when employing dream thinking. A defence against this regression occurs when we use only directed thinking. Directed thinking is progressive, adapted to reality.

Mary sees me for supervision of her supervision. She feels frustrated with Tony, a trainee. He has recently moved to another supervisor, but left her a telephone message requesting urgent advice about his patient. Returning the call, she discovers the problem is not urgent. She had worked hard to contain Tony, helping him adhere to boundaries, and feels she has failed (directed thinking). As we talk about the work, Mary feels pain in her abdomen identical to menstrual discomfort. She suddenly realises her supervisee felt abandoned when the supervision ended (dream thinking). Her frustration changes to understanding and regret at their work together finishing, which she had not felt before. The pain goes.

Next time we meet, she tells me she met Tony at their training institute. They spoke about ending and how it affected them. Mary suggested the telephone call was Tony's way of making sure she survived the ending. Later he sent a card thanking her for her help. This example shows dream or fantasy thinking can have bodily manifestations. Mary had not worked through the ending, and Tony unconsciously knew something had to be done urgently to remedy this. In the supervision Mary's body showed us the problem, providing a symbol of the absent mother (menstruation here meaning a lack of pregnancy, therefore a loss). An experienced therapist, she quickly understood the symbol. Her feelings of failure were misdirected before the symbol appeared, but became known afterwards. She recognised the importance of Tony's transference to her. There arose a flexible interplay between directed thinking and dream thinking as a symbol emerged, first experienced literally in the body.

Conclusion

I discussed several ways in which symbols manifest. The imaginal world is continuously present: we are constantly dreaming, whether asleep or awake. Symbols both appear and are created in individual psyches and between psyches. Yet symbols cannot be used creatively without conscious work. There may be synchronicity, the patient echoing what the supervisor said. Or the fruits of supervisory work may be long delayed. I assert the work requires a safe container and emotional investment by all parties, as pictured in the alchemical *vas*, the well-sealed vessel, and furnace. The supervisor puts herself into the vessel with the therapist and patient, regulating the heat so transformation may take place, sometimes turning up the heat, sometimes cooling it down. This is an ideal to aspire to and, as with therapy, does not always materialise. We struggle to resist regressing to concrete and collective forms, we work towards individuating and living the symbolic life.

References

Bion, W. R. (1974) *Bion's Brazilian Lectures, 1: São Paulo, 1973*. Rio de Janeiro: Imago Editora.
Bruch, H. (1974) *Learning Psychotherapy: Rationale and Ground Rules*. Cambridge, MA: Harvard University Press.
Casement, P. (2002) *Learning from our Mistakes*. Hove: Brunner-Routledge.
Colman, W. (2007) 'Symbolic conceptions: the idea of the third.' *Journal of Analytical Psychology* 52: 565–583.
Hauke, C. (2000) *Jung and the Postmodern*. London: Routledge.
Jung, C. G. (1953–1973) *Collected Works*, ed. Sir H. Read, M. Fordham, G. Adler and W. McGuire, 20 Vols. London: Routledge & Kegan Paul.
—— (1989) *Memories, Dreams, Reflections*. New York: Vintage.
Langs, R. J. (1978) *The Listening Process*. New York: Jason Aronson.
—— (1997) 'The framework of supervision in psychoanalytic psychotherapy.' In B. Martindale (ed.) *Supervision and its Vicissitudes:*. London: Karnac.
Mathers, D., Palmer Barnes, F. and Noack, A. (2006) '"Held in mind" or "Hell in mind": group therapy in Poland.' *Journal of Analytical Psychology* 51: 191–207.
Neumann, E. (1989) *The Origins and History of Consciousness*. London: Karnac.
Redfearn, J. (1978) 'The energy of warring and combining opposites: problems for the psychotic patient and the therapist in achieving the symbolic situation.' *Journal of Analytical Psychology* 23: 231–241.
Schaverien, J. (2006) *Gender, Countertransference and the Erotic Transference*. Hove: Routledge.
Searles, H. (1986) *Collected Papers on Schizophrenia and Related Subjects*. London: Maresfield Library.

Chapter 8

Representation, evocation and witness

Reflections on clinical scenes and styles of presentation in supervision

Richard Wainwright

> Jung thought that psychology writing should aspire to the greatest authenticity by including unconscious psychic creativity *within* writing, not limit it to outside, to what psychology is *about*.
>
> Rowland (2005: 2, original italics)

Introduction

This chapter will present a series of supervisory scenes and some brief reflections that emerged from experiences of being in them, inviting the reader to make use of them as imaginal spaces for further elaboration. In this sense it is conceived as a stimulus to imagination rather than as a didactic tool. In considering a few of the ways in which the supervisory relationship can assist the process of evoking 'the sense of something human' in supervision, I shall be speaking from experiences of work with four supervisees, who in quite different ways are struggling with the challenges of representing their work. The last of these will be concerned with a supervisee's use of supervision to explore the interpenetration of some personal and professional experiences that bear upon his capacity for self-representation in his professional world.

I shall pay particular attention as to how supervisees can be encouraged to release themselves from a sense of obligation to offer slavish recitals of what happened, born of anxiety to get things right, which is often betrayed through premature flights into knowing and understanding. The work privileges a willingness to disinter conversations in supervision from the official language of clinical discourse in the interests of cultivating a capacity to evoke experiences of persons and scenes in the spirit of dreaming with another. This could also be described as a way of thinking about presentations as imaginative fictions. In this sense supervision is a creative collaboration in the service of fictions that emerge from a *feeling for what happened*. It is an opportunity for play in the creative sense of allowing something, or anything to be seen, to have a voice, a presence in contrast to the self conscious work of showing, or demonstrating knowledge.

Prelude

Supervision as an analytic process involves the participants in conversations, or at least certain kinds of conversations which allow for the seen and unforeseen to play into each other. The ambition of showing or demonstrating tends to close things down. When dialogue becomes monologue the feeling of being in a state of play is suspended, perhaps provoking a suspicion of an imaginal policeman having turned up.

Conversation, deriving from the Latin word *conversare*, involves us in a process of turning things over, or turning them round. Analytic conversations, although occurring in an atmosphere of intimacy and confidentiality, will (it is hoped) discover traces of common ground with so-called ordinary conversations that allow for disclosures of the self in a multivocal play of mutualities generated by involvement in the pleasures and difficulties of turning over and turning round.

When two people, an I and a you, are involved in a conversation, they are involved, or potentially involved in a process of representation, evocation and witness. For instance one of them begins with a brief description of the journey to the room, restaurant, or bar where they are meeting. It will be a re-presentation of what has happened, taking account of time, place and event. If I am the speaker I will no doubt be aware of the quality of your interest, which is likely to enhance or diminish my capacity not only to make available something of interest but also to find something of interest in what I hear myself saying. In other words our co-presence at the time of my speaking, your listening response and my hearing what I say in the here and now of this place are indispensable constituents to a feeling for something happening, evoked by a feeling for something that has happened – an event, which has a past and a present. We could say there is a collaboration, which turns representation towards evocation of something witnessed by something other than itself.

In the most ordinary conversation the three processes are built into each other. It may begin with an intention to tell another something quite unremarkable, but in the telling something unexpected might arrive whether in the form of a response or an unintended thought we call a free association. In an obvious way conversation is the foundational ground of psychotherapy, which we understand as a process of inviting and responding to the unexpected. It is an essentially evocative process. Like art, film, drama, poetry, music, story and dance, it evokes feelings, emotions, memory and a sense of multiple directions. Evocation connects us to presence, the presence in imagination of an embodied now and the presence in the body of an imagined then, generating in the process a feeling for future selves and states of mind. We use the world and its objects to bring parts of ourselves to life. Evocation means calling forth. Evocative speech (as Heidegger had it) 'discloses our being in the world'.

There's a lot to do

She spends a few minutes informing me how we shall use the session. We are to consider three clients. She's been busy and there's a lot to do, she remarks, as she lifts three immaculate files from her case, placing two of them beside her chair and opening the one from which she will read to me in a single and accomplished movement. She checks that I am in place and ready to listen. I guide a mild cocktail of irritation and amusement with her style of management to a safe place in the third chair on the other side of the room, hoping for good weather. She has begun.

The work is twelve weeks old, once a week, but I am hearing about it for the first time. We begin at the beginning. I hear about the referral process at the counselling centre, the first phone call, the making of the first appointment, the first meeting. She allows herself a moment to tell me what impression the client made when she walked into the room. She is middle aged and dowdy, appearing through the gap allowed by the sense of a semi-colon. I am interested in 'dowdy' and quickly squeeze her into the chair with the cocktail before she is dismissed in the service of narrative progress. In a few minutes I am informed about her childhood, the parents who didn't protect her from her brother's abuse, 'her father was a womaniser', her leaving school, her career as a secretary and latterly personal assistant to various successful men. I am left in no doubt she is a 'puella' with a 'weak ego' who needs to find 'a sense of agency' if she is to have a chance of becoming more 'individuated'.

Before we get any further I suggest we pause and look at the various persons who might like to come in. She tolerates my intervention with the proviso she will be able tell me about the rest of the work since the first session. I suggest we need to go a little more slowly so we can attend again 'a bit more freely' to what was going on between therapist and client and what it felt like when the parents, the brother and various others arrived. Feeling slightly disconcerted by her pen, which is clearly ready for action, I add that it might help her to keep this consideration in mind as the work unfolds. She records what I've said, letting me know in the process how 'useful' it is. I am hoping to have a conversation and find I am an authority. It's difficult to have a conversation with an authority, but you can defer to it, take dictation from it, undermine it, compete with it and defend yourself against it. If you are the authority, watch out for the monologues lining up to be recorded for future retrievals in some other time and other place. She's right, there is a lot to do. There is a lot for both of us to do. For instance the supervisor will need to keep open the offer of conversation and the supervisee will need time to distinguish between an invitation and a demand.

Commentary

The person who is anxious to get the material in and is glued to their notes might indicate a defensive refusal to engage with the other (supervisor). It might also reflect the supervisee's assumption about what they are expected to do, particularly if they are a trainee, or perhaps a therapist with a new supervisor whose ways they don't know. They may also have learned this way of presenting the material, as if they weren't there, from their training institution. The feeling of transference anxiety is obvious, but as supervisor and supervisee get better acquainted, we hope that things will loosen up.

Writing notes is obviously useful for grounding experience and aiding reflection, but they don't have to become the basis of a recital. Having written them it would be more valuable to second sight what they contain by loosening the author's grip in order to allow other voices to come in. In supervision the process of imagining with another allows for the play and interplay of thoughtful associations. It can allow the supervisee, like the actor who is situated between the author and the text in another kind of play, to reappropriate the text in the interests of revealing not only what the author might intend, but more importantly – what the author may be suppressing.

Notes used as aids for the defence might be constructed to address the supervisor in a language the supervisee assumes to be correct. It might also reflect something of work with a patient, or client who is anxious about the prospect of trusting their own mind. Perhaps the therapist might have difficulty in dealing with a demand from a patient or client to explain, know or understand. One of the biggest impediments to creative exploration and experience is an anxiety about getting things right, as if there was a right way to do things. If that's the conviction then the supervisee is under huge pressure to demonstrate they know what it is. The supervisor will need to assist the anxious supervisee to distinguish between showing and allowing something to be seen. Clearly the supervisor's supportive attitude and capacity for encouraging the supervisee into a state of play will be essential. Trust takes time to establish.

Representation and evocation

> Perhaps the function of psychoanalysis in the future will not be to inform but to evoke.
>
> (Phillips 1994: 164)

There are some interesting implications for the practice of supervision in the way analytic psychotherapies have redefined clinical practice by giving priority to therapeutic interactions between therapist and patient as the focus of the work. Instead of privileging the fiction of analytic objectivity and non affected neutrality psychoanalytic theory situated itself in the relational field analyst/patient in which both are participants in a mutually engaging process. This shift of emphasis has a long history and was anticipated by Freud as early as 1916: 'what turns the scale [for the patient] is not his intellectual insight, which is neither strong enough or free enough for such an achievement – but simply and solely his relationship to the doctor' (Freud 1916–1917: 497).

Jung put it even more explicitly in emphasising mutuality as the organising principle of analytic endeavour: 'By no device can the treatment be anything but the product of mutual influence, in which the whole being of the doctor as well that of his patient plays its part' (CW16 para. 163). The psychic necessity of mutuality is at the core of Winnicott's notion of a 'holding environment'. In the context of the more recent contributions of attachment theory and neuroscience to analytic endeavour the process of mutuality is acknowledged as indispensable to the incremental accumulation of 'implicit relational knowledge' yielding in the process, as one commentator has it, 'focussed attention on implicit models and explicit autobiographical narratives' (Fosshage 2004: 54).

There is however a problem in professional therapeutics concerning how experience is represented. If I pick up a professional journal I am often inclined to read a few paragraphs and lay it aside. The clinical reporting is efficient, the theorising seems to fit and the writers show me they know what they are talking about. They are not defensive in the sense of concealing difficult material, it is there, but I have little or no feeling for it and am left with a sense there's something I haven't understood, as if understanding is the issue. My experience is one of being denied access to experience so I remain un-in-formed.

I think professional representation has little to do with what happens in a therapeutic encounter, but not because writers are trying to mislead. They are not able to communicate the experience perhaps because they are representing it with a view to what it means. Representation subjects the body to the semantic and semiotic. It orders it into a certain form. In evocation the body becomes itself as a subject, in representation it's an object. Evoking involves us while representation keeps its subject at a distance. No matter how detailed, representation raises fundamental questions about power. Who and what is being represented? Is anybody there?

In contrasting representation and evocation I am referring to how speaking *about* and speaking *from* experience derive from two different discourses, the semiotic and phenomenological. In the mode of speaking *about*, language and experience are polarised for it is assumed experience can only be represented. This polarisation is a function of a representationalist theory of language that largely predominates in analytic discourse. Of course the word *representation* resonates with a different sense if it is thought of as *re-presenting* or making present again. In the latter sense re-presentation is informed by an evocative mode that discloses the presence and aliveness of experience. In this sense 'language gives access to a world of experience in so far as experience comes to, or is brought to language' (Csordas 1994: 11).

It is something of a paradox that the analytic project of whatever provenance should situate itself in opposition to the Cartesian epistemology of unminded bodies and unbodied minds, while continuing to prioritise a discursive style of keeping the experiencing body at a distance from the perceiving mind. For Jung there were implications in writing psychology – *a logos of the psyche*, involving the writer in a responsibility towards 'words that respond to the *whole* of the mind and not just its well mapped territories' (Rowland 2005: 2). He was not for the abstract prose that is the preferred idiom of what modern cultural practice sanctions as scientific.

The supervisory alliance as an essentially allowing process will encourage both the willingness and the creative effort of allowing something to be seen rather than something to be shown. It allows the speaker and listener freedom to inter-imagine, to collaborate in the work and play of finding and being found in language that registers the idiom of experience. In this 'potential space', as Winnicott coined it, both supervisor and supervisee might renew their relationship to language as a living field rather than an already fixed box of meanings. A creative relationship to language is not about searching for new words but of attending to the significance of the words we already use and to the life they authorise when speaker and listener are open to the shape, feel, rhythms and reverberations of words. Thomas Ogden reflecting 'on the art of psychoanalysis' captures this I–Thou dimension of 'sensing something human' in the relationship between writer and reader:

> What it means to bring a person, a feeling, an idea, to life in writing is to be found in the reader's experience of reading or hearing the words and sentences being said (written) by the writer. This is the challenge of all literature and of all analytic writing since both are fundamentally concerned with the task of using language to capture something of human experience. If we as readers cannot sense something human, however faint, in the experience of reading an analytic paper, poem, an essay or a novel, then we come away empty handed. The work of the analytic writer, like the writer of poetry or fiction, begins and ends with his effort to create *in* language the experience of human aliveness. If an analytic writer contents himself with talking 'about' aliveness or deadness, his efforts will certainly be in vain.
> (Ogden 1999: 5–6)

Losing it

A large and well-used canvas bag disgorges notes and files on to the coat she has shed beside her. With a resonant in-breath she picks up the file and helps it on to her lap with an extended sigh. She apologises for what I am about to receive. In the brief silence that follows she soothes her head distractedly with both hands, before confiding that she feels there is so much left 'undone'. The dishevelled canvas bag may not be elegant but it is undoubtedly eloquent.

I ask what interests her about her client. She confides she admires her selfishness in running her own business. Yes she feels there is some hope in her aggression, 'but there is such an emptiness and so little self awareness'.

A brief catalogue of symptoms follows which her voice embellishes with a tone of soured boredom and frustration as she recites the evidence of her client's 'lack of confidence', her 'lack of concentration', her addiction to distraction signified today by the guitar taken up only to be put down through lack of application. 'She doesn't play – she doesn't stay with anything.'

We are entering the affective atmosphere or 'felt sense' of the transference/countertransference here in the supervision space. The client thwarts the experienced therapist's notion of a good life in refusing to come round. In conversations we turn things over and turn things round. That's what conversations are. It occurs to me we don't question the value of self awareness in our profession, we take it for granted – as a value. I ask what it would be like to value the unselfconscious life. She looks at me and breaks into a radiant smile: 'I don't know. I can't imagine.' We both hear what she's said. She repeats, 'I can't imagine.'

'Yes I lose my imagination and that's what she does. It's not that she hasn't got any, but she loses it.' Becoming quite animated she speaks of her client's longing for a partner in her life and a partner in her work. She adds: 'That's her idea of a solution.' I announce the obvious: 'Perhaps that what's she's after with you.'

A brief silence allows space for her thoughts to reverberate: 'There's a bit missing inside her, so I can't speak to it, the bit I need to speak to.'

She is following the course of her unfolding thoughts and it feels enlivening to follow her, as thought follows impulse and word follows close upon thought. There is space for a hitherto unspoken thought to announce itself to the imagining ear of the supervisor: *The place needed is always somewhere else off stage in another scene so it feels impossible to engage with what's here.*

She speaks of her need for help in engaging with what's here rather than engaging with something that isn't: 'Then perhaps what's gone missing might come back' arrives somewhere in between us.

The conversation allows us to explore thoughts about fear of solitude and the need we have of being alone with another. It is reassuring to have Winnicott here as a witness, reminding us of how the supervisory space and the process of evocation, released within it, can recover the patient from the therapist's premature resort to despair and recover the therapist from the patient's appropriation of her as a refuge for despair.

Witness

The notion of witness is indispensable to the work of privileging the idiom of speaking from and of allowing something human to be seen. In both therapeutic and supervisory spaces, it invites the 'witness' to find themselves devoid of preconceptions that distract attention away from whoever is here, or there. It is akin to the state that Bion commends as being without 'memory or desire'. As witnesses we need to re-imagine our habits of perception and give undivided attention to what comes towards us without moving to impose sense or meaning. We suspend what Husserl calls the rule of the vertical, ordering in hierarchies, for the rule of the horizontal where things are allowed equal weight. To witness is be a natural phenomenologist. You surrender to complexity.

In reality of course we cannot have experiences, however acute and unexpected, which are bracketed from assumptions, or concepts. Experience comes already informed with meaning, because meaning is inseparable from experience. The work of the witness could be understood as dedication to speaking *from* experience, rather than speaking *about* it. In attempting to speak *from* experience we need to keep in mind both Jung's and Ogden's acknowledgements of a need for the discernment that mediates with in-between space if we are to move beyond the confines of our habitual perceptions (CW8 paras 131–193; Ogden 1994: 97–106). Being open to whatever is present is perhaps a gift of being *good enough* to be free enough and still enough to divine the delicate and epiphanic nature of imaginal bodies inhabiting our temporary recoveries of *inner sense*. That's probably the best we can do in order to surrender to complexity.

Words and knowing

> It is of course not the actual information acquired, but the conformity which the accumulation of knowledge is apt to impose, that is harmful.
> (Eliot 1920: 319)

It is often suggested that analysis is limited because of its dependence on language as if language in itself were the problem. What I am drawing attention to here is a use of language, or relationship to language in which the speaker or writer betrays a kind of deference to discursive styles that overdetermine meaning and understanding.

Analytic discourse becomes problematic in being susceptible to appropriating a sense of the scene we might be in with a language of knowing. Discursive thought, while being indispensable for us to function in the world, is often resistant to approaching language as the stuff of exploration, improvisation (encountering the unforeseen) in acts of speech that *mediate* with the unconscious rather than converting it into consciousness. It

Representation, evocation and witness 121

can easily be commissioned into the service of a species of hermeneutic imperialism.

Jungians have sometimes been prone to adopting a species of nominalism, disposing the speaker to explain by naming the complex, as if the naming of the parts will somehow tame the phenomenon. *What would it be like if trainees were not required to show evidence of their theoretical acumen by these means?* The effect is to divest the phenomenon of whatever it is that gives it life. I am thinking particularly of those solemn summonings of the puer, persona, the shadow, inferior functions and the stultifying literalism that so often misconceives and de-ranges the psychology of types (see Whan 2005: 181–192 for a critique of the misuses of typology).

Evocative speech gives voice to the idiom of the self, which is neither fixed nor singular. The implication of subject and object, of 'me and not me' constellates both and neither. That is what it is to encounter another. We do not remain the same, neither does the object, or other. The process of appraisal is reciprocal. We need the other to call forth, to come into being by *inter being* with others. In states of interest, *inter-esse* inter-being, we lose consciousness of our habitual selves in revealing what is other. We may not be able to recreate our encounters as they happened, but we can place ourselves in the present in our speech, so whatever it is we have encountered has a chance of being more immediate, more in the midst, more present.

Transference and countertransference

In speaking of transference and countertransference scenes we try to keep in mind the play between

- the patient as seen through the therapist's eyes
- the patient as seen through the patient's eyes
- the therapist as seen through the patient's eyes
- the therapist as seen through the therapist's eyes.

If we now move these into the supervisory space we have an even more complicated composition, which other chapters in this book explore. The only point that needs making here is to draw attention to the play of representations and evocations as they move across each other, drift in to each other, clash and resonate with each other, or reverberate as we encounter their repercussions in realising the depth and complexity of reference in our exchanges.

I am reminded of what happens in a bell tower when the tongue of the bell makes the bell resonate. There may be three, four or more bells in the same tower. When the first is set in motion it begins to swing back and forth until the tongue inside strikes the wall of the bell and the first sound is created. As the swing expands the moving bell touches another which in swinging brings forth a new voice and different rhythm. Gradually all the bells are engaged. In the play of their tones and rhythms the receiving ear is allowed to sense the shape and size of the different bells. The undistracted listener is not just available to the music, but in a sense becomes the music in being awakened to the emerging mutuality of resonance and structure. Other bells from other places might be summoned to follow in a polyphonic procession each calling forth and answering the other.

Chewing bus tickets

In the analytic space you can be transformed in a few minutes or even less by an emotion, or knotted cord of emotions that often have no overt connection with what is being said, seen, or heard. The motion in emotion translated as imagination of the body. The experience is often destabilising and part of the process of being in a situation, or relational field that is moving you into new alignments, often prompting questions like 'Who's here?' – or 'Where am I?', which are prior to the notion of 'Who am I?' Discomfort has a way of urging us towards premature understanding. If we can keep in with the emotional texture without needing to understand it, there is space for the unforeseen to enter.

The following vignette derives from moments in two supervision sessions in which the supervisee's experience of being baffled and bored made it possible for supervisor and supervisee to reimagine the client. The process of evocation does not require poetic eloquence, but more likely a capacity to allow difficulty to emerge in broken phrases, irritation, pauses, sighs and involuntary gestures to constitute the process of exploration and collaboration. It will pick up on the tension between the therapist's need to understand which disposes her to draw from her repertoire of analytic understandings in the hope of ordering and clarifying the material and her sense of helplessness when she feels unable to do so.

She pulls a familiar envelope of notes into position on her lap, running her fingers abstractedly along its edges. Her way with making and breaking eye contact, with looking towards and looking away, with rocking slightly back and forth as she smoothes the surface of the envelope betrays the presence of a dilemma. An artificial smile presented and withdrawn registers the irritation of indecision augmented by dis-ease.

I find myself thinking of T. S. Eliot and *Prufrock*, although being visited by an image would be nearer to my experience of thinking as she rustles her notes, apprehensive at the prospect of daring to make a decision and risk disturbing, if not the universe, a fog of impressions that seem immune from transformation into experience.

She confides that she doesn't know who to bring and would like 'to know what that's about', adding that she needs 'to know how it feels'. A brief pause allows for a different kind of thought and a hint of emergent composure: 'I think I have to wait to see how it pans out', I record a thought on the empty page facing my notes: *Supervision is about giving time for experience, allowing space for understanding to arrive in its own way.* With the thought recorded I return to Prufrock, but say: 'Perhaps you feel coerced by your clients to understand them, which might have the effect of distracting you from any possibility of understanding.'

She replies she doesn't know what to think and resumes her smoothings for a while: 'Yes I suppose I do feel coerced . . .', the upward intonation of her voice declares the sentence unfinished. Turning the envelope over on her lap she makes a desultory reference to two clients, though her avowed intention had been to present only one of them. 'I do a lot of thinking and they do a lot of I don't know.' After a few moments I draw her attention to the different registers of her concern with knowing and not knowing: not knowing who to bring, wanting to know what that is about, needing to know how it feels, the clients not knowing – and her not knowing what to think. 'Can you imagine what it might be like to live in a world where you had to know what to think before you thought?' She responds with a sudden smile saying: 'Yes, it's all a bit bewildering like being in a fog. I suspect I want you to give me directions.' I ask what that feels like. She smiles and on the point of laughter says: 'I want to say I can't be bothered.' We catch the sense of a double reference to both the lassitude of Prufrock's world and the possibility of ironic distancing from it.

A familiar literary reference with its atmospheres of yellow fog and estrangement emerging from the interpenetration of conscious/unconscious between supervisee and supervisor offers an opportunity to reconsider her phrases as reflections of her experience of her clients. She recognises which of the two clients she had wanted to speak about and realises she has been speaking not *about*, but *from* her experience. The difficulty in distinguishing one person from another, the feeling of 'can't be bothered' contrasting with the desire 'to know how it feels' allow us to think together about what it might feel like for one's experiences to be devoid of meaning as they would if one had little sense of identity from within. The supervisee's predicament of not knowing who to present could be recognised and thought about as a communication of the client's predicament of feeling not known, or knowable and, it follows, of her corresponding need to be recognised and thought about.

Two months later. She announces she didn't want to come today, adding from somewhere in between timidity and audacity she feels embarrassed about bringing 'the same old stuff'. Opening her file she closes her eyes and turns away before returning with a pale smile: 'Oh well.' I'm aware of my recent dream of an old bent woman in a state of spectacular dishevelment putting down a bulging plastic bag while she rustles in a dustbin and remember the recurring image of *la vieille* in Kieslowski's Three Colours trilogy, reaching from her chronic stoop to feed the bottle bank. The unreconstructed Jungian in the supervisor has a vision of Hecate, shit stirrer divinity, goddess of the waste, the rubbish, the despised and rejected of the world – the thirteenth and forgotten fairy whose way with depression promises a long wait on the margins.

For a moment the supervisee's attention is arrested by midsummer light playing on the roses outside the window. 'Aren't they lovely. I caught their scent while I was standing at the door.' Open windows allow muffled voices from the street to insinuate themselves. The room is murmurous with memoria. It seems the supervisor and supervisee basking in the warmth have gone on holiday. She allows herself a moment more to savour the experience and relinquishes her pleasure by rubbing her hands together vigorously as if to keep them warm: 'Oh well, I better get on with it.'

She doesn't know whether her irritation, born of boredom, is a 'symptom of being tired' or whether it's an indicator of how 'flattening' it is to be faced with the same moves and preoccupations, the same refusals of life-giving opportunities. 'I don't sense any desire to change anything. I don't know how to get any emotional leverage on the situation. I just don't know where to start.' I reply: 'Perhaps you feel you should know where to start.' She feels she is expected to know how to 'unlatch things'.

Accepting an invitation to describe the last session, she lets me see how her attempts to be the good therapist offering analytic commentaries and interpretations have the effect of leaving her feeling trapped in endless repetition. Like her client she is vulnerable to feeling stuck in the same understandings and knowings. Today she is describing her client's conviction that she has to perform to gain acceptance. 'It's always been like this, nothing will ever happen unless I make it happen.'

The word 'always' hangs in the air signifying a sense of the chronic. The therapist is struggling to make a difference, perhaps unable to bear her client's assumption that there's no one there. I comment: 'It feels like chewing bus tickets.' She pauses and allows herself to laugh lightly and repeats the phrase: 'Chewing bus tickets, that's interesting.' She moves immediately into speaking about her client's relationship with a man who she longs for but can't have. 'He's never available when she wants to see him.' She dismisses the relationship as 'being offered crumbs'. The therapist, replying, 'wondered' whether this predicament was familiar in her client's experience as a child.

I experience this plausible connection as being something of a distraction from experience which we could use to reflect together on the relational atmosphere of the transference/countertransference scene. Chewing bus tickets is an obvious metaphor for substitute food devoid of nourishment, a way of distracting oneself from a hunger for real food and the terror of being aware of one's appetite. Abandoned refugee children, unseen, unknown and forgotten, eating paper to appease the rage of hunger, emerge by association with this image. It is a grim signifier of boredom, emptiness and desolation. Emerging as it has in the supervisory space, it brings the supervisor, supervisee and client into relation with each other. It is a speaking from experience that has the potential to provoke thoughtful attention. The supervisee begins to pick up on her client's hunger for the holding of relationship, allowing herself to re-experience her own terror of a hunger that might never be met. In the space disclosing itself for associations with personal experience she recognises that the disclosure about the longed for lover speaks right into the transference scene. Her client wants her unavailable lover/other 'to attend to her needs' – whether or not she knows what they are.

The bus tickets image allows the supervisor and supervisee to collaborate further. Does the supervisee have a sense of what she means to her client? She's unsure, but she thinks she likes her. I say it feels as if her client has little or no experience of being pleasurable either to herself or another. We enter into another reverie linking the moment with the sunlight, the open window and the roses with an image of a mother and infant taking pleasure in each other. She says she can't imagine her client ever having had such an experience and that makes her feel a bit helpless and overconcerned with trying to help. 'Is there a chance that your attempts to link her complaints with her experience of being a child feel to her like attempts to persuade her to accept your way of seeing, rather you accepting her?' She feels this makes sense of what she has often felt as rage and aggression that are 'never allowed out', adding 'I know what that feels like'.

Unsolicited help, however well intended, is likely to be experienced as an impingement. The supervisee's recognition of this dilemma helps her to re-imagine the nature of her client's requests for a more flexible arrangement with session times, as she often has overwhelming working commitments. She wonders now if meeting these requests might be more helpful than her customary way of interpreting them as instances of taking refuge in work as an unquestionable authority and depriving herself of herself in therapeutic space. 'Cutting the client some slack' can also be understood as a form of interpretation, rather than mere collusion.

Imagining the patient in supervision: some essential requirements

Louis Zinkin has represented the fictive nature of the supervisory process as 'shared fantasy' (Zinkin 1995: 247). The proposition that supervision works best if supervisor and supervisee (who is a trainee in his picture) 'both remain aware that what they are jointly imagining is not true' is perhaps more completely articulated by Ogden's reflections on the collaborative and transformative process of fact becoming more real in becoming fiction in the supervisory space. 'It is an essential part of the task of the supervisor and analyst to dream (to do conscious and unconscious psychological work with) the interplay of the supervisory and the analytic relationships' (Ogden 2005: 1266).

The process of 'dreaming up the patient' in supervision will entail a variety of interrelated requirements: for instance, disclosure of clinical material, descriptions of work, reflections on personal process, tracking of free associations to material presented, attention to the shape, texture, rhythm and cadence of what is said – and often unsaid, thus cultivating a sense of having eyes in our ears. We need all of this for supervision to give us a handle on realising what we say through the process of second hearing, or second sighting of what can only be located in dialogue with another or others. When the supervisory alliance is enlivened by feeding and feedback, the patient is more likely to come to life and draw forth a host of bodies who might otherwise not turn up, but whose presence keeps us open to new meanings and new possibilities.

Just as the analyst's 'act of freedom' encourages change, the supervisor has a responsibility to encourage responsible thought by her or his freedom of mind (Symington 1986: 253–270). One of the most valuable functions of the supervisory alliance is to be able to refresh theory in the particulars of clinical and analytic encounter. The idea of dreaming together to dream things on in the supervisory/analytic space allows access for con-versions of revered others into the idiom of the self by turning pre-scribed versions over and turning them round in the light and dark of experience. In other words, freedom of thought requires dedication to particulars if the familiar, defined by the habitual, is to be approached in the spirit of exploration rather than confirmation. Supervision is not a confirmation class.

Supervision and self-representation

Turning things over, turning them round and turning with another in the process allows for the interplay of representation, evocation and witness. They need each other. I will conclude by offering a final vignette to re-present an experience of the supervisory relationship being used by a creative therapist to assist with giving support to a project of self-representation in the interests of personal and professional self definition. It picks up on some key moments in work with an experienced and very talented dramatherapist working in a forensic setting.

George asked if he could supervise with me having heard a paper I gave concerning the relevance of Jungian thought to the practice of drama therapy. His first presentation was exclusively focused on the image of a fragmented institution in which communication between departments was either blocked or subverted by people who were either unable or unwilling to understand each other's work. It concluded with a reference to a consultant psychiatrist referring patients, who couldn't or wouldn't respond to psychiatric 'treatment', commenting: 'I don't know how you do what you do, but carry on doing it.' In adopting the reported speaker's tone of sunny-side-up patronage, George allowed me to hear what I might otherwise have missed. By disclosing his experience of this address he allowed his apprehension of not being taken seriously in the supervisory space to be felt and thought about. The comment, as I heard it, suggested the psychiatrist was telling George he thought his work had more to do with magic and revelation than with communicable, or transferable thought.

In subsequent supervisions George presented examples of his clinical work. His descriptions were acute and empathic, showing me how successful he was at finding ways of relating to some very dissociated patients. He showed me how he worked, but I was unsure as to what he understood about what he did. I suggested that we might explore this further and he responded by giving further examples in which the voices, gestures, ways of moving and rhythms of speech of various patients were re-created by George with an acute feeling for the disclosing detail. His capacity to show and model at that time was an obvious strength in his work and I confided that it perhaps enlists the intuitive artist rather than the clinician. In other words it seemed there was a gap between revelatory intuition and containing thought which was likely to inform his use of supervision.

As we explored this, further material began to emerge concerning his difficulties with authority in the setting. The emergence of transference feeling colouring his communications was palpable. A colleague, who couldn't understand how he worked, was represented by George as telling him she didn't feel safe with him and was inclined to distrust him. He was annoyed and there was hint of despair in his 'I can't be bothered to try with people like that.' I connected his avowed difficulties with colleagues and authority figures and his frustration with lack of communication with his choice to come to an analytic supervisor who both understands the language of drama and has access to experience of discursive, clinical reporting. We were able to think about the supervisory space together as a kind of research and rehearsal space for something aspirational. I was reminded of my own experience of using the supervisor as a form of 'transformational object' (Bollas 1987).

The word 'translation' became very important in the work of following George. It struck me that he was being recruited to work as a daring performer in a dangerous world and said: 'If you're cast as a magician you need to know what you're doing, because you don't know what will happen if your tricks desert you.' He used this to speak freely of his doubts about the value of what he did and his sense of inferiority in a professional situation where he felt the arts therapies were exoticised, which meant work like his would 'always' be regarded as inferior, or at best, supplementary.

In free association he recalled how his father came to England from abroad, got a job and brought the rest of the family to join him. Father remained almost impervious to English, relying on his children, particularly George, to translate for him. George had made it possible for himself to openly link the personal with the professional. He recognised that the blocks in communication, which he often referred to, could be understood as the magician's fear of losing his magic on the one hand and the desire to have conversations with people (outside the family) on the other. He was very open about his fear of mis-recognition if he translated his acute capacity for responsive action into discourse. I understood him to be saying that that which he fears will happen, has been happening for a long time. Clearly this was not something to be explored in the transference as in analysis, but it could be used as an opportunity for him to enrich and strengthen his capacity for reflection upon professional life and identity. He could recognise the disclosure about his father as being offered in the service of an aspiration to become more integrated into society when understood against the background of the power, status and mis-communication tropes that recurred in his presentations of the work setting.

Coda

> The models and theories of subatomic physics express again and again, in different ways, the same insight – that the being of matter cannot be separated from its activity.
>
> (Capra 1979: 62)

In this chapter I have tried to keep in mind some of the ways in which the analytic process of whatever provenance involves patients–clients, therapists–analysts, supervisors–supervisees in an ongoing relationship between language and experience. Analytic representations involve us in a paradox. For instance the analyst's body is the site of vivid images, sensations and impressions, but the conventions of discursive speech often trap the analyst in the grammar of objectivity. Whether in speech or in writing, the representation of bodies as nouns objectifies active processes. When bodies are allowed to be reimagined as verbs, the speaker or writer might remain more open to what is active in imagination and therefore more able to mediate with the ambition *to know* that often intrudes when he/she submits to the distractions of the 'box seat' position from which bodies are more likely to be objectively perceived. When the analytic space of whatever kind is open to the *nature* of imagination speakers and writers might conceive of bodies as nouns and verbs at the same time. It is the basis of poetics. To echo Jung, poetics 'arise in the depths of the body'. If the body is objectified we need to ask what and how does the object think or feel. How this question is posed and registered keeps negotiations open with the possibility that when something gets through something unforeseen might come back. When the body of whatever kind is objectified 'like a patient etherised upon a table', the circuit breaks, the dance of entrances and exits, of implicit and explicit, of *himeros* and *anteros* (gesture and response), of noun and verb, of I and Thou is suspended. No dance – no transformation.

References

Bollas, C. (1987) *The Shadow of the Object*. London: Faber.
Capra, F. (1979) 'Dynamic balance in the subatomic world.' *Parabola* 4(2): 60–65.
Csordas, T. J. (1994) 'Introduction: the body as representation and being in the world.' In T. J. Csordas (ed.) *Experience and Embodiment*. Cambridge: Cambridge University Press.
Eliot, T. S. (1920) 'William Blake.' In T. S. Eliot, *Selected Essays*. London: Faber.
Fosshage, J. L. (2004) 'The implicit and explicit dance in psychoanalytic change.' *Journal of Analytical Psychology* 49(1): 49–65.
Freud, S. (1916–1917) 'Lecture 27 – Transference.' In S. Freud, *Introductory Lectures on Psychoanalysis*, vol. 1, London: Pelican.
Jung, C. G. (1953–1973) *Collected Works*, ed. Sir H. Read, M. Fordham, G. Adler and W. McGuire, 20 vols. London: Routledge & Kegan Paul.
Ogden, T. H. (1994) 'Projective identification and the subjugating third.' In T. H. Ogden, *Subjects of Analysis*. London: Karnac.
—— (1999) 'On the art of psychoanalysis.' In T. H. Ogden, *Reverie and Interpretation*. London: Karnac.
—— (2005) 'On psychoanalytic supervision.' *International Journal of Psychoanalysis* 86: 1265–1280.
Phillips, A. (1994) *On Flirtation*. London: Faber.
Rowland, S. (2005) *Jung as a writer*. London: Routledge.
Symington, N. (1986) 'The analyst's act of freedom.' In G. Kohon (ed.) *The British School of Psychoanalysis: The Independent Tradition*. London: Free Association Books.
Whan, M. (2005) 'Supervision as self questioning.' In C. Driver and E. Martin (eds) *Supervision and the Analytic Attitude*. London: Whurr.
Zinkin, L. (1995) 'Supervision: the impossible profession.' In P. Kugler (ed.) *Jungian Perspectives in Clinical Supervision*. Einsiedeln, Switzerland: Daimon.

Part III
The collective

Chapter 9

Working with organisations

James Bamber

Introduction

There are many facets to supervising in organisations and, for clarity, this chapter is divided into four sections. The first section considers the defining issues in supervision when it takes place in organisations. It presents a global view of the underlying factors which any supervisor contemplating working in an organisation should be considering and expecting to meet. The second section examines what the organisation expects both from the supervisee and from the supervisor. It demonstrates that for the organisation, supervision can become a problematic activity. The third section looks at organisational ponderables, such as the impact on the supervisory activity of the way the organisation functions and how, if at all, the supervisor can address the problems which arise from this. The fourth section is specific to supervision taking place in group settings. In such settings the supervisor has to navigate the psychodynamic challenge arising from both individual and group unconscious processes.

The defining issues

An activity takes place in organisations which is called sometimes 'supervision' and sometimes 'consultation'. Although these terms tend to be used loosely and synonymously there is a need to clearly distinguish between them. I take 'supervision' in the organisational context to include a line management responsibility whereas 'consultation' refers to facilitating reflection on practice in which there is no line management accountability. In agencies where there is confusion between the terms crucial questions concerning tensions between managerial accountability and professional autonomy can become obscured. In this chapter the word 'supervision' will be used in order to maintain compatibility with the other chapters but will strictly imply 'consultation'.

Supervision used in the sense denoted above enables the activity to be described following the London Jungian analyst Zinkin (1995) as a 'shared fantasy', by which he implied the supervisee is trying to imagine what went on between himself and his client while, at the same time, the supervisor is trying to imagine it too. Where I work at the Highgate Counselling Centre in North London, the 'shared fantasy' is spelt out as a situation where one individual (the supervisor) takes an informed interest in the professional work of another (the supervisee), which involves reflecting with the other on that person's work and on their psychological states while undertaking the work. The supervisor is the 'third eye' in the development of a relationship between two other people (or between one person and a group of people) of which the supervisor is presented with only one person's perspective of that relationship and from which perspective the supervisor has to reconstruct the dynamic of the relationship. Part of the process of reconstruction necessarily involves the dynamic taking place in the relationship between the supervisor and the supervisee, the parallel process (Chapter 11). Supervision is one of a quartet of interlocking activities. The other activities are

- the supervisee's work with the client or client group
- the supervisee's own personal development, especially where it has involved being a client
- the supervisor's history of personal development and experience of being a supervisee.

Each of these components influences the other three so that 'supervising' activity is concerned not only with the supervisee's professional work but also with the influence their personal development and that of the supervisor has on the process. In an organisational context, supervisory activity is influenced by psychodynamic forces which drive and distort the effective functioning of organisations as collectives. The sacred space of supervision can be swept along and battered by the organisational weather system. The effect of this on the supervisor is to raise the question of how to enrich the professional work of the organisation without the supervisor role becoming overwhelmed and made impotent by unconscious forces in the organisational matrix. As Hughes and Pengelly (2002: 6) point out, the functioning of the supervision activity can become 'inextricably linked to the way the organisation manages the tension between needs, resources and rights'.

The turmoil of change which has taken place in the large public institutions of health, social services and education in the UK since the early 1990s, including the introduction of radical restructuring, new job titles, new tasks, and new ethos has left staff finding themselves 'lost in familiar places' (Shapiro and Carr 1991) as one new fashion in public policy follows another. Similar fashions in the fields of psychology, psychotherapy and counselling have produced continual change in professional training organisations. Since these organisations in turn produce many supervisors employed by the public institutions, the sense of being 'lost in familiar places' permeates both aspects of the supervision dyad. The link between supervision and organisation has been conceptualised by Hughes and Pengelly (2002) in terms of two triangular interactions:

- between the participants – supervisor, supervisee and service-user
- between the three functions of supervision – service delivery, facilitating the supervisee's professional development and focusing on the supervisee's work.

Mattinson (1981) pointed out that in these triangular relationships the functions most likely to be avoided are those causing most anxiety to the supervisor and/or supervisee at any given time. Hughes and Pengelly (2002: 43) noticed that 'supervisors or supervisees can become anxiously attached to their most worrying corner, unable to risk leaving it for another equally important, but less specifically anxiety-provoking corner'.

Organisations can be conceptualised as collections of groups where one group embraces another, like Russian dolls. Among the nodules at the core of such a collection are the supervisory functions of the organisation. They can manifest themselves either as dyads or as groups, the latter tending to be more usual format. The supervisory space can be usefully conceived as a *temenos* (sacred space) in its psychological application (Samuels et al. 1986). In the supervisory context, it is a psychological container shaped during the activity of supervision and distinguished by mutual respect for unconscious processes, confidentiality, a commitment to symbolic enactment (an acknowledgement of the presence and power of unconscious motivation while withstanding its pull by neither regressing nor allowing oneself to be overcome by it) and trust in one another's ethical judgement. It can be experienced also as either a womb or a prison, as the dictionary authors describe it. The latter qualities can reinforce either avoidance of what is causing most anxiety in the supervisory triangle or anxious attachment to the most worrying corner (Chapter 7).

A further defining issue when considering supervision in organisations is identifying the organisation's primary task. Some organisations are primarily service providers, others are devoted entirely to training; a percentage are hybrid, combining both service provision and a training function. The rationale for this classification is that a distinction needs to be drawn between the status of supervisee either as practitioner or as trainee. For the trainee, supervision carries additional complexities to those pertaining to the practitioner. These can be listed as follows:

- The relationship between the trainee and the training body. For the supervisor this can sometimes be the poisoned chalice of supervision. What the supervisee needs of the supervisor and what the organisation

expects from the supervisor could be at odds unless the trainee, the supervisor and the organisation have scope for dialogue.
- Facilitating the trainee's understanding of the work and skill perspectives of the organisation through the actual experience gained by them of the emotional and unconscious processes in the work as well as its practical activity. Through supervision that theory becomes linked with practice. The supervisor becomes like the 'mother-in-reverie' in Bion's scheme of psychodynamics, converting the supervisee's raw beta elements into alpha elements which are then returned to the supervisee to increase the latter's understanding (Bion 1984).

Bion (1984) provides a succinct statement of the relationship between beta and alpha elements when he states that beta elements are a way of talking about matters which are not thought at all; alpha elements are a way of talking about elements which, hypothetically, are supposed to be part of thought (Bion 1994).

The trainee can experience the emotional and unconscious processes and the practical activities like a bombardment of undigested, raw sensorial impressions which cannot be stored as memory but only as accumulations of facts (beta elements). This bombardment of facts hinders them in thinking clearly about the clinical situation. The job of the supervisor is to help transform these beta elements into thoughts which can be stored as memory or used for thinking (alpha elements). Thus the alpha function of the supervisor provides the trainee with an apparatus which can afford the trainee's personality the kind of experience from which comes a feeling of confidence. There is discernment through understanding the following:

- The organisational or professional model being encouraged by the supervisor and the model as it is experienced by the trainee, in terms of skill and psychodynamic attitude. For the trainee, this creates a dilemma as to whether they should practise in what they perceive to be the style of their supervisor or in a style individual to them, emerging and developing through their involvement with the work. Because their own style can be at a fledgling state, the trainee can experience anxiety and uncertainty in clinical situations and so needs the reassurance of supervision. At this point the trainee's anxiety can become heightened if their emerging style is at variance with their supervisor. The London analytical psychologist, James Astor (1995), describes this situation well when he likens the training process to the trainee arriving in a fragmented state, being taught ideas which underlie the practitioner's organised fragmentation, and being expected, as a trainee, to integrate what the trainers have failed to integrate themselves.
- How to establish a place of containment for the trainee's work and furthering their aptitude. This highlights the essence of supervision;

a container for the duo of trainee and their client or clients; a vessel within a vessel (see Figure 7.1 on p. 102), functioning like the chrysalis of an insect which protects psychological development as it is taking place.

Organisational expectation

What is expected of the supervisee

How much contact with a patient does an organisation expect from a supervisee? If the supervisee is a staff member then this could be the basis of the supervisee's contract with the organisation. If the supervisee is a trainee then contact with patients will depend on the nature of the training; it is likely that some contact is involved. It falls to the supervisor to ascertain the extent of the supervisee's involvement with patients and to support that involvement. Nevertheless this obligation is not without its tensions: the supervisee may become the advocate of the patient when the organisation places limitations upon what it will offer the patient; the supervisee may question the type and method of service delivery; the supervisee may be tempted to offer an out-of-hours supplementary service to the patient on a private fee basis; the supervisee may have reservations concerning the patient's entitlement to the service; or the supervisee may become progressively disillusioned with the service.

In such situations the supervisor is confronted with the ethical questions of moral obligation (Chapter 3). The supervisor may privately share the supervisee's attitude and stance on some of these issues and this may come across in the way the supervisor facilitates reflection on the supervisee's practice. The triangle of *supervisor–supervisee–patient* is, however, encased within the triangle *supervisor–supervisee–organisation*. A parallel triangle is *supervisor–professional code–organisation*. The supervisor thus has a moral obligation to the supervisee, the patient, the organisation and to his or her professional code.

There is no easy resolution to this ethical situation; if the organisation pays the supervisor, is the supervisor then its agent? To resolve the situation on the basis of paymaster may compromise the supervisor's relationship with the supervisee. To fudge the supervisee's struggle with the organisation may bring the supervisor in conflict with their professional code. In my view, the primary obligation of the supervisor is to their professional code. The supervisor is appointed on the basis of having a particular professional expertise. That expertise is likely to be encompassed within a set of professional rules of conduct. It is whether or not the supervisor has complied with the professional code that might be the basis of any complaint against them.

The supervisee will be expected to conform to organisational culture: meetings, referral procedures, managerial oversight, clerical and administrative procedures, record keeping, and the form of presentation in supervision. Facilitating reflection on these areas may be helpful for the supervisee but requires the supervisor to be familiar with the organisation's culture. Some organisations recognise this and appoint only supervisors who themselves have been service providers at some point in their career. However, many organisations ignore this and leave the supervisor to become familiar with the culture through simple trial and error learning. The supervisor's learning curve helps determine the value of supervision for the supervisee and ultimately for the organisation and the patient.

Developing professional competence is expected by an organisation of its professional staff. This is usually recognised through giving staff grades or titles and allowing time for continuous professional development (CPD). In small organisations grades or titles may not reflect developing professional competence or exist at all. The CPD component may be entirely the responsibility of the staff member including not only the financial outlay but also providing time from private life. Whether the organisation is part of a large public institution like the NHS or is a small independent organisation like a counselling centre, the supervisor will have a role in its development through facilitative reflection. The nature of this will vary depending on whether the supervisor belongs to the same professional group as the supervisee, or to another. As professional groups become more specialised it is increasingly likely the supervisor can belong to an associate group (for example, a psychodynamic psychotherapist supervising art therapists, or a psychologist supervising nurse therapists). A supervisor's own CPD activities can help stimulate professional competence in their supervisee as well as through the role adopted and the attitudes presented. Positive interest and active curiosity encourage professional competence as effectively as professional knowledge.

What is expected of the supervisor

To say that through supervision theory becomes linked with practice implies that it has a role in teaching a method. This leads to expectations that the professional area of the supervisor is compatible with the method practised by the supervisee. When budgets are tight in organisations, existing supervisors can sometimes be asked to supervise in areas with which they share little affinity, the assumption is that the task of supervision is generic and depends little upon a particular professional background. This is often associated with supervisors having little say in the selection of supervisees, which remains a prerogative of management.

Both issues, assuming a generic concept of supervision and the preselection of supervisees, raise the question of the supervisor's scope to liaise within the organisation. Organisations do not necessarily think through either issue, relying more upon availability and convenience; supervisors are often only too grateful to have paid work. The extent of and forum for debate can be ill defined. The supervisor can become professionally compromised without clear recognition of possible consequences both for supervisee and patient. In such situations good line management becomes essential.

An associated area is clinical responsibility. What clinical responsibility does the supervisor carry? This is not always clarified by organisations irrespective of whether the supervisee is a trainee or staff member. In continuing clinical work supervisees will be expected to seek advice on particular aspects of their work. Is this given or does the supervisor encourage consideration of a spectrum of possibilities and their consequences? In either case what is the supervisor's responsibility if a particular action results in a complaint being made by a patient?

The supervisor should ensure that the question of clinical responsibility is clarified in the initial contract. However, some consciously omit to clarify this, lest it imply they have poor clinical judgement or they do not have a clear understanding of their role.

Organisational ponderables

The activity of supervision within an organisation can, in itself, generate organisational issues. Patients may be provided with services which are, in a prevailing organisational climate, contributing to tensions between needs, resources and rights. An example can be the organisation's attitude towards different forms of psychotherapy. External influences may direct an organisation towards a type of psychotherapy which appears more efficient in terms of resources. It may not always meet the particular needs of some patients nor may it accord with their right to a degree of choice. At the same time, the organisation continues to provide a range of psychotherapies despite some receiving little external endorsement. In such circumstances, the supervisor may be placed in the role of defending advocate of the out-of-favour therapy. They become a focal point in an organisational tension without an impartial judge to determine the case for their professional specialism.

To maintain the health of the supervisory *temenos*, there needs to be an adequate source of referrals. The number of referrals and their appropriateness are factors usually not under control of the supervisory duo but determined by an internal referral system which can reflect various tensions within the organisation and between the organisation and its environment. Whenever there is a decrease in referrals or an increase in the level of inappropriateness there is a corresponding increase in the anxiety experienced within the *temenos*, generating self-doubt and frustration – an example of the poisoned chalice referred to earlier. The supervisor has to ensure the health of the *temenos* but may have little influence over the input from the organisation. In such a situation the supervisor's personal resources become critical for the survival of the *temenos*.

Earlier, I said that supervision is a nodule lying at the core of the organisation. A corollary of this nodal position is supervision can become multiple for any given supervisee. Within any particular organisational or professional grouping, staff or trainees may be part of more than one supervision arrangement overlapping to various degrees. As can be expected, overlapping arrangements become fertile grounds for confusion, contradiction and splitting to flourish. As in the situation regarding referrals, the supervisor is caught between organisation and supervisee. The supervisor has to contain confusion, a desire to contradict and tendencies to split in order to enable the supervisee to make sense of confusion, understand apparent contradictions and recognise splitting as a defence against anxiety. Some organisations understand the practical and psychological difficulties arising from multiple supervision and make efforts to organise regular meetings of supervisors where confusion can be identified and contradictory responses minimised. Others, alas, do not.

Also, supervision within organisations has to contend with relocation, staff changes and restructuring. The *temenos* must be portable, flexible and able to survive organisational surgery. Once again, these problems are usually at an operational level one or more steps removed from the *temenos*.

Such problems generate anxiety, anger and helplessness in the recipients and the organisational matrix. They can also threaten to overwhelm and make impotent professional roles. While a supervisee has the supervisor for support and the *temenos* for containment, how is the supervisor to be supported? The Institute for Group Analysis (London) has, for a number of years, offered work support groups specifically created to help professionals, such as supervisors, work through their own feelings related to the problems they experience at work and help them by providing containment. Group supervision of supervision is good practice.

Supervising in groups

More often than not supervision in organisations takes place in a group. A group begins when there are more than two persons in a room. Thus three or more people become a model for a new dimension which introduces multipersonal phenomena with its own network of communication and disturbance (Foulkes 1964).

The group has implications for the supervisor as it stretches the *temenos*. At one level (Level I) there is a supervisor and a group of supervisees, at another level (Level II) there is a group which includes both supervisor and supervisees. The supervisory *temenos* in its group format thus oscillates between these two levels, and it is this oscillation of which the supervisor must be aware. I referred earlier to the pulling power of unconscious motivation within the *temenos* which has the potential to overcome those encapsulated within it. The supervisor is much more able to help the group withstand its pull at Level I than at Level II where the supervisor can become as helpless in the face of unconscious motivation as their supervisees.

Bion (1961) described the dynamics within a group as 'an interplay between individual needs, group mentality and culture'. By 'group mentality' he is referring to the unanimous expression of the will of the group to which group members contribute anonymously and thereby establish a system of evasion and denial. The concept of 'group culture' refers to those aspects of the behaviour of the group which are born of the conflict between 'group mentality' and the desires of the individual.

When the *temenos* is at Level I the supervisor is exercising some direction over the interplay between supervisees' needs, group mentality and culture. At Level II it is postulated the couple within the *temenos* are mutually taken over by the conflict between 'group mentality' and the desires of all those present, that is, they have succumbed to the forces of 'group culture'.

The advantages of group supervision

A supervision group at Level I can allow the advantages of group supervision to flourish, namely mirroring of relationships; encouraging proxy learning; enabling the corrective input of peers; and offering a wide range of ideas and experiences. Mirroring in the group can operate at various levels; vertical and horizontal, between colleagues, and with clients. Foulkes (1964) describes the 'mirror reaction' in groups as a situation where the group member

> sees himself, or part of himself, in particular a repressed part of himself in the other members. He can observe from the outside another member reacting in the way he himself reacts, can for instance see how conflicts and problems are translated into neurotic behaviour.
> (Foulkes 1964: 81)

In a supervision group, the supervisee presenting clinical material can observe the transference and countertransference aspects of this material as it is played out in other members of the group. For the supervisor it is akin to observing a spontaneous piece of psychodrama. The 'shared fantasy' of supervision comes alive and exists in the room. This is what Foulkes (1964) calls 'translation' – the group equivalent of making the unconscious conscious.

The 'mirror reaction', however, has an aspect which Zinkin (1998), a group analyst as well as an analytical psychologist, calls 'malignant mirroring' and is a product of deception. The deception is generated by the inherent qualities of the mirror. Zinkin (1998) describes this deception as arising from the premise that 'the mirror can never show us as others see us because it reflects back either ourselves looking in a mirror or caught unawares, never ourselves relating to another person', and 'the mirror cannot take part in a true dialogue' because the mirror does not allow for more than responses (Zinkin 1998: 231). It can be observed between two individuals while the rest of the group becomes a paralysed onlooker. Zinkin (1998: 232) refers to 'the uncanny atmosphere which is generated . . . seeing two participants locked in a mutually destructive battle'. The supervisor may 'like a referee at a boxing match, have to part the combatants before too much damage is done' (Zinkin 1998: 232). At this point the *temenos* can easily move from Level I to Level II, as described earlier, with the result that the supervisor is equally paralysed; the combatants are not parted by the supervisor and damage is done to the group, to the process and to the individuals themselves.

The drawbacks of group supervision

The drawbacks of supervising in groups all have the potential to swing the *temenos* into the Level II position.

Collective non-confrontation

Collective non-confrontation is an example of Bion's 'group mentality'. No group member can be identified as initiating 'non-confrontation' and its existence in the group establishes an atmosphere of evasion and denial. No statement contributed by a group member will be challenged and may not even arouse comment. The group adopts the qualities of the three wise monkeys so anything contentious is greeted with refusal to hear, to see and to speak.

Crowding each other out

Crowding each other out ensures there is no space for anything which can generate anxiety and confrontation. Bion (1961: 47) describes this: 'the atmosphere of the group is heavy with fruitless effort . . . there is the determination of the individuals to make the session what they would consider to be a success'. In supervision this becomes an avoidance of the clinical material. In its place there is enthusiastic discussion of organisation issues, personal activities, diffuse grievances, and generalised comments about clients and the state of mental health provision. The discussion never flags but it never leads anywhere. It is all too easy for the supervisor to be swept along in this tide and to feel impotent about returning the group to the work task.

Acting out rivalries from other contexts either within or without the organisation

Acting out rivalries can come to dominate the supervision group in much the same way that the rivalry between Jung and Freud (McGuire 1974) dominated the Association of Psychoanalysis. Progoff (1973) refers to styles of thinking as one source of the rivalry; the Apollonian Freud and Dionysian Jung. Styles of thinking and attitudes can provoke resentments in the group because underlying issues in relation to persona and shadow are not being addressed.

Jung recognised the persona as a compromise between a collective identification and the necessity for a person to individually express himself in the social arena (Campbell 1978). Personas in the supervision group are compromises between job titles and how members wish to represent themselves. There is a danger, however, that the persona and the individual become as one; always the art therapist, the nurse, the occupational therapist. At this point the persona feigns individuality. If it is accepted completely rather than worn loosely, the individual becomes out of step with their inner psychic reality. The consequence is the shadow, their persona's opposite, becomes active. Hence the advice offered by Jung that the mantles of name, title, office and so on should be worn lightly (Campbell 1978). As the shadow emerges the power of unconscious motivation can create regression in the persona. The consequence is a person's essence will haunt him from the shadow. This will add positive reinforcement to the group becoming overcome by unconscious motivation producing a Level II situation.

The desire *to bond with* the supervisor turns the supervision group into the Dependent Group which Bion (1961) has so carefully explored. It is only by engaging with the leader that a group member can gain any benefit from attendance:

> The dependent group, with its characteristic elevation of one person, makes difficulties for the ambitious, and indeed for anyone who wishes to get a hearing, because it means that in the eyes of the group, and of themselves, such people are in a position of rivalry with the leader.
> (Bion 1961: 79)

Such a group engenders a powerful emotional drive which will obstruct and divert the supervisory activity. The goal of the group for its members changes from meeting to benefit from supervision to meeting 'in order to be sustained by a leader on whom it depends for nourishment, material and spiritual, and protection' (Bion 1961: 147). Any new idea is suppressed 'because it is felt that the emergence of the new idea threatens the status quo' (Bion 1961: 155).

Conclusion

The chapter aimed at presenting a picture of what is entailed when a professional takes on the job of being a supervisor within an organisation and, especially, a large public sector institution. Apart from relevant professional training and experience, the job involves political skills, maternal attributes, entrepreneurial abilities, psychological insight and a psyche capable of weathering the persecutory anxiety of others. The supervisory psyche must not

- underestimate the shame dynamic
- be too controlling
- be careless with time boundaries
- be inflexible
- be drawn into personal antagonisms
- be inappropriately psychotherapeutic.

Especially in organisations, the supervisor should bear in mind the advice given to Mary Ann Mattoon (1995) by her Zurich analyst: 'It isn't what you do that counts; it's what you are'.

References

Astor, J. (1995) 'Supervision, training and the institution as an internal pressure.' In P. Kugler (ed.) *Jungian Perspectives on Clinical Supervision*. Einsiedeln, Switzerland: Daimon.
Bion, W. R. (1961) *Experiences in Groups*. London: Tavistock.
—— (1984) *Learning from Experience*. London: Karnac.
—— (1994) *Cognitions*, ed. F. Bion. London: Karnac.
Campbell, T. (ed.) (1978) *The Portable Jung*. New York: Penguin.
Foulkes, S. H. (1964) *Therapeutic Group Analysis*. London: Allen & Unwin.
Hughes, L. and Pengelly, P. (2002) *Staff Supervision in a Turbulent Environment*. London: Jessica Kingsley.
McGuire, W. (ed.) (1974) *The Freud/Jung Letters*. Princeton, NJ: Princeton University Press.
Mattinson, T. (1981) 'The deadly equal triangle.' In *Change and Renewal in Psychodynamic Social Work: British and American Developments in Practice and Education for Services to Families and Children*. London: Group for the Advancement of Psychotherapy in Social Work.
Mattoon, M. A. (1995) 'Historical notes.' In P. Kugler (ed.) *Jungian Perspectives on Clinical Supervision*. Einsiedeln, Switzerland: Daimon.

Progoff, I. (1973) *Jung's Psychology and its Social Meaning*. New York: Anchor.
Samuels, A., Shorter, B. and Plaut, F. (1986) *A Critical Dictionary of Jungian Analysis*. London: Routledge & Kegan Paul.
Shapiro, E. and Carr, A. (1991) *Lost in Familiar Places: Creating New Connections between the Individual and Society*. London: Yale University Press.
Zinkin, L. (1995) 'Supervision: the impossible profession.' In P. Kugler (ed.) *Jungian Perspectives on Clinical Supervision*. Einsiedeln, Switzerland: Daimon.
—— (1998) 'Malignant mirroring.' In H. Zinkin, R. Gordon and J. Haynes (eds) *Dialogue in the Analytic Setting*. London: Jessica Kingsley.

Chapter 10

Seeing the point of culture

Begum Maitra

> This, broadly speaking, is what both parenting and culture are for: luring people into seeing the point.
>
> Adam Phillips (2005: 135)

Introduction

After over two decades living and working in Britain, I am startled by the difficulties I continue to experience 'understanding' surprisingly everyday encounters with British friends and colleagues. Having now amassed a large number of 'facts' about British values, choices and ideals, and having spent a great deal of time (mostly enjoyably) reading, discussing and exploring cultural meanings, I must concede that cultural difference may not be open to understanding. However, since the many problematic consequences of cultural separatism are fairly obvious, this chapter looks at the conditions necessary if difference is to be made to yield something other than discomfort in a supervisory setting.

A few months into my first post at a British psychiatric hospital, I struggled to understand the motivation of a white British woman in her sixties who had taken a significant overdose of painkillers. Clearly distraught (and possibly angry) she explained that her 'boyfriend' (in his seventies) had invited her to spend the summer with him in the south of France, but remained obdurately set against an engagement (to marry). A 'girlfriend' some years her senior (to my ears these were incongruous, even insulting, uses of 'girl' and 'boy' for persons their age) had recently announced her engagement. What made her despair sharper (and by now, mine too) was the prospect of appearing in beach wear, the young and perfect bodies at a fashionable resort confirming to her the loss of her own youth and desirability.

Thoroughly bemused and struggling to conjure up some empathy I tried, with an overwhelming sense of the absurdity of such a notion, to see my grandmother in India in the same predicament. Widowed and almost totally dependent on her adult children, she was the central figure in a large extended family and, beyond what may have been owed her by virtue of this hierarchical position, was loved for her unshakeable enthusiasm for the family and its welfare. A beauty in her youth, she retained a delight in personal beauty and romantic love, but in accordance with cultural ideas about the desires and preoccupations of age, no longer considered these personally relevant. To do otherwise, or to contemplate suicide because these desires had not been met, would have seemed to be unthinkably egotistical. Ideas about the lifespan and the reality of a not-too-distant death would have made suicide seem absurd.

Now that I am nearer my patient's age, I am more sympathetic towards the dilemmas of ageing and loneliness. Despite this, and the fact that the choices I now live by are wider than those I was socialised into, owing as much to the multiple cultures I now inhabit, I find many ways in which the body and gender contribute to my sense of self (and self-esteem) appear less easily available to conscious negotiation. Cultural belief systems are closely related to the social realities and choices available in a society.

Notwithstanding the rapid advances in Indian technology and the wider range of life-choices these hint at (though out of reach to all but the most affluent, urban, and pro-western set) the shorter life-expectancy in India (than in the west) contribute to different attitudes towards desire, and what is considered sensible and morally appropriate with increasing age. What remains important, however, is the force of the negative emotion aroused by unbridgeable cultural value systems. What is at stake is nothing less than the entirety of how we experience ourselves and the world. The question is whether such differences may be made sufficiently bearable, through exploration of contexts and meanings, so as to allow therapeutic engagement. Hidden within this are other questions – of professional 'taste' (or preference for one patient group or another), of varying degrees of personal confidence at addressing particular problems, and the degree to which one's political beliefs about citizenship, relations between cultural groups and tolerance of differences are relevant to one's practice as a psychotherapist or supervisor. Even if we were to agree that cultural supervision had a vital role in psychotherapy, it cannot address these questions for a supervisee; nor can it begin until these matters have been considered sufficiently by any supervisor.

Components of a culturally astute supervision

I hasten to reassure those irked by the self-congratulatory tone of much of the language in this field (cultural sensitivity, cultural competence, intercultural competence) I am not proposing to add 'cultural astuteness' to the list, but merely to emphasise a process of critical analysis has to be a premise of supervision. A willingness to be extravagantly self-critical could be the best antidote to the stifling political correctness which clings to questions of difference. I suggest a set of strategies which, when used in combination, may trigger sufficient curiosity to create a reflective space when faced with unpalatable or incomprehensible cultural difference. In trying to understand how cultural worlds, set in fluctuating political, economic and social contexts, interact with individual worlds I have found ethnography, and the analytic frameworks of the social sciences, to be particularly useful. As a result, many of the writers referred to are anthropologists and sociologists, or psychologists and psychiatrists who cross boundaries between social sciences, psychology, psychotherapy and psychiatry.

The place of personal experience in professional practice

As any supervisor knows, the line between addressing the personal development and professional skills and responsibilities of a supervisee can be difficult to spot. These boundaries are likely to be more anxiety-laden in the supervision of trainees who are also in personal analysis as a training requirement. (The dreaded 'take this back to your analyst' comment from a supervisor can trigger absurdly persecutory fantasies about implied incompetence in all three, trainee, supervisor and personal analyst.) Despite this, it is difficult to imagine how supervision can progress without consideration of the relationships between personal experience and professional development.

The heady rhetoric of evidence-based practice invites one to equate therapy and how it works to the chemical effects of giving a pill. Driven by the demand that the therapist–patient relationship be cleansed of the unpredictable effects (mainly those concerning power and desire) of its unprecedented intimacy, there has been a preoccupation in recent times with the technical elements of therapy and attempts to standardise, indeed even manualise, treatments. While debates rage about the nature, quality and methodology of outcome research, several studies show *who* the therapist is accounts for a greater degree of variation in outcome than *what* is being practised (Rønnestad and Skovholt 2002). Jennings et al. (2003) found the most important factors in therapeutic expertise were the personal characteristics of the therapist, experience, cultural competence, and comfort with ambiguity. In research at the Tavistock Clinic in London, Jensen (2007) found the personal experience of the therapist to be a significant influence on what happened in therapeutic sessions. This was true for both naive and experienced therapists, even if they believed it to be contrary to properly professional behaviour.

Among the kinds of personal experience which promote a greater openness to cultural diversity, childhood exposure to multicultural societies can provide a head start, at the least making the fact of difference ordinary, even if not pleasurable. On the other hand, while childhood within a homogenous cultural group and marked by an emphasis on conformity (such as, closely knit groups united by occupation, religious faith or social class) may make difference seem desirable, even 'exotic', this may be no less problematic. When disappointment and disillusion strike, the positive fantasy can be abruptly replaced with fear and revulsion.

After an idyllic start to therapy my English patient, who had spoken with admiration of the spirituality she had discovered among Indians, had a frightening dream. She dreamt she was being inducted into a collective ritual by a priestess, and would have no way of refusing to participate in something she feared could involve unspeakable cruelties.

A similar anxiety about the unpredictable and alien may be discovered among western tourists in Islamic and eastern countries, namely, particularly grave offence may be given in these cultures, famous for their hospitality, by a refusal to accept what is offered. Specifically, the fear is hospitality is merely a disguise for hostility. Anxiety about the unpredictable is functional, a useful safety valve. Childhood exposure to experiences of cultural variety allows exploration unhindered by adult considerations of polite behaviour, and the development of observational and other skills which increase confidence. Given encouragement, children easily learn to be multilingual; discovering other children who look, smell and sound different, who live in different contexts can conduct the business of life in different, but equally effective ways.

Throop (2003) reviews the contributions of psychological anthropology to an understanding of the intra-, inter- and extra-psychic processes underpinning culture and its internalisation, which he calls the 'crafting of a cultural mind'. Unlike psychoanalysts, who tend to treat the past as a fixed objective foundation structuring the present (as in transference), psychological anthropologists attempted to steer between cultural determinism and psychoanalytic universalism, emphasising the unpredictable directions of influence between the past and present. Throop considers the work of Obeyesekere, Briggs and Chodorow among others. Obeyesekere (1990) emphasised the fixity and fluidity of cultural representations, noting public symbols are often tied to unconscious motivation. Private symbols may be patterned by cultural images 'to an extent *where cultural templates may actually help to shape the individual's experience of "reality"'* (Throop 2003: 114, emphasis mine).

Based on direct observations of a 3-year-old Inuit child, Briggs (1998) described the personal and impersonal mechanisms which constitute the socialisation of children into culture. Chodorow (1999) emphasised the central role of the non-verbal, non-linguistic aspects of earliest caregiver–infant experience in how personal meaning is structured, noting cognition is inevitably infused with emotion and unconscious fantasy. It is scarcely surprising then individuals are so entrenched in cultural ways of experiencing others and the world. Nor that conscious, rational processes which underpin contextual understandings, while allowing greater choice of meanings and action, have such limited power to change the emotional impact of first impressions. This must necessarily raise questions about how transference and countertransference are perceived and interpreted both to oneself and to one's patient.

Non-verbal communication: language, embodiment, (ir)rationality

A white (European) colleague and I visited a Bangladeshi mother to plead with her to reconsider her decision to stand by her husband. His physical chastisement of their son (indisputably abuse in British law and in the eyes of child protection agencies) had precipitated the removal of all four children from the couple's care. Obviously distraught and maintaining a civil manner with some difficulty, she sat tight-lipped as we explained for the umpteenth time the rationale behind professional decisions. The brittleness of her grief was painful to watch, and we swung between the helpless pity of women watching the suffering of a mother, and an attempt to remain professional. Situations such as these highlight painful contradictions between my own cultural beliefs and professional obligations.

Suddenly, as she sat before us on the settee, this diminutive woman in sari and black headscarf threw out an arm and flung her head back in a declamatory stance immediately recognisable to me, and burst into some kind of oration. My colleague looked at me in alarm, believing the need for our empathic abilities had now been superseded by a need for my skills as a psychiatrist. Slowly, given the context of a council flat in East London on a cold afternoon, I recognised snatches of what she spoke, identifying the words of Kabi Nazrul Islam, a famous Bengali poet. The poem belonged to a revolutionary genre of regional literature which united Bengalis, Hindu and Muslim, against British rule in pre-independence India.

While I was able to reassure my colleague that this woman had not, in her grief, collapsed into psychosis, I was aware that episodes like hers were easily misunderstood and prone to being misdiagnosed as evidence of mental illness (Maitra 1995). I doubt that our patient was aware of the poignant ironies she invoked as we faced each other, two Bengali women (Muslim mother and Hindu psychiatrist) united by culture, and separated by the legacies of colonial influence and regional conflict. In her declamation of poetry – emotion couched in an essentially embodied and culturally unmistakeable form – we saw a keenly expressed sense of agency, rather than its fragmentation.

This vignette draws attention to the value of indirect communication, and embodied experience, especially when intense feeling is inexpressible in language, or when the explicit nature of language is believed to endanger a balance of complex social relationships and networks. Christensen et al. (2001) describe communication among agricultural families in northern England, where links between community and the material world are expressed by silence as much as by verbal means. They note explicit talk about certain matters is proscribed, especially if it threatens the unarticulated, unacknowledged interdependencies which, ideally, constitute the community. However, respondents did engage in talk with outsiders such as the researchers. I wondered whether the apparent irrationality of the Bangladeshi mother's resort to poetry was a way of circumventing similar cultural prohibitions. Poetry allowed allusion to potentially divisive influences 'within' the Bengali community (represented by the differences between her and myself), while picking a careful path between open rebellion and the submissive acceptance of defeat and humiliation; the loss of her self as mother, the threat to her self as loyal wife.

If both professionals had been non-Bengali speakers would the services of a Bangladeshi advocate or interpreter have averted misinterpretation? As I discuss elsewhere (Maitra 2004), the fact of shared cultures does not in itself guarantee better identification of complex cultural and psychological processes. Further, in a multicultural context of contested, and politically imbued, meanings the degree of imaginative hypothesis-testing (and implicit risk-taking) necessary is harder to accomplish through interpreters.

To those who chafe at the psychotherapeutic preoccupation with remaining non-directive, the exuberant exhortations of family therapists to curiosity and questioning may appear liberating. However, it is worth bearing in mind that family therapists trained in the west, with deeply ingrained western codes of privacy and polite behaviour, may not find it easy to divest themselves of their cultural restrictions. Even with a robust willingness to interrogate cultural premises, would any series of questions, however skilful, have enabled this Bangladeshi woman to stand outside her cultural map of gendered, embodied experience to comment on the influences of regional, linguistic and educational difference, collective history and inequitable allocations of power? The greater likelihood is, of course, misinterpreted first impressions and the entrenched emotional responses these give rise to on both sides would grow exponentially.

The frustration generated by ideas or emotions which elude words, let alone allow translation into the words of another tongue, have become clearer through personal experience of immigration. I noted for years, with equal measures of perplexity and amusement, that release from the highly restricted styles of communication with which I felt compelled to comply, mainly in professional relationships with English colleagues, triggered a sort of 'acting out'. These emotionally charged irruptions – of muscular postures, facial expressions, verbal styles, accents, and hybrid forms of Indian English – expressed in the safety of solitude or the company of non-English friends, may be attributable to the unavoidable task minority ethnic persons must endure; either trying to understand or to explain.

What has become clearer, as increasing ease and authority replaced my uncertainty as a new immigrant, is the unalterably embodied character of emotional experience, and the extent to which bodily repertoires learned long ago are inseparable from the feeling itself. In fact, suppression of bodily expression in emulation of the emotional restraint considered appropriate by British colleagues seemed to cut at the very base of a Self that feels, and giving rise to the urge to 'act' these out with a compensatory heightening of both verbal and non-verbal expression. Indeed, the humorous element of 'hamming it up' both reveals and masks the underlying anxiety of being discovered as different. This may well have been true for both the Bangladeshi mother described above, and myself; based as much on our perceptions of the British other, and our attempts to read their acceptance and rejection of our bodies, and of how we expressed ourselves through them.

Codes of linguistic behaviour mark membership and position in social groups. This is well documented, for example in descriptions of intracultural variation due to social class. Ethnicity, especially in the generation born in Britain, merely adds another layer to class stratification. Despite having been socialised into both ethnic and mainstream cultures, minority ethnic young people may be as occupied with strategies for negotiating difference as their parents. New, hybrid linguistic genres (Kirmayer 2006) allow the speaker to position themselves in a new relationship to the dominant form, thus questioning the legitimacy of the frames imposed by the majority.

Among immigrant communities which experience a loss of language and identity following colonisation these new language forms arising among their youth serve, through appropriation and reconfiguration of the languages of the coloniser, to support new identities. This may be one way of interpreting Mrs T's 'breakdowns' in the following vignette.

Embodied selves, memory, nostalgia

While in my office I overheard an excited babble of voices in the clinic corridor. Identifying one voice easily and unmistakeably as Indian (urban, educated and 'northern') I emerged to investigate, but seeing no one who fitted my expectation, I returned to work. Some hours later, in my general adult psychiatry out-patient clinic, I was introduced to a new patient diagnosed with recurring episodes of manic disorder for which she was on very large doses of medication. Mrs T was a middle-aged woman, white, attractive and well-dressed. It was only when she spoke I realised it had been her voice I had identified so unquestioningly, then failed to find a matching physical appearance among the cluster of people in the corridor.

I discovered Mrs T was of 'mixed race' – with an English mother and Indian father – and grew up in a major Indian city, arriving in Britain in her early twenties. Light skinned, sandy haired and easily able to 'pass' as European, she had no reason to question the British 'identity' she, as many others among the Anglo-Indian communities in India, had assumed. The migration to Britain was then a return home, to 'the mother country'. She settled, married an Englishman and had three daughters. Mrs T had no reason to revisit the question of her cultural origins until several years later, when her youngest, favourite child grew into her teens, becoming increasingly Indian in appearance. I never heard what was made of this by the family. Mrs T, however, displayed a sudden and dramatic change from her usual pleasantly ebullient personality. Much to the family's consternation, and the surprise of the quiet English suburb they lived in, the police had to be called in one summer afternoon when Mrs T climbed onto the low garage roof to sing the Bollywood musical classics of the 1950s at the top of her lungs. Hauled away by a slew of police officers and hospitalised, she calmed considerably, but only to 'relapse' into a 'rapidly cycling manic disorder'.

I took on Mrs T's care after her fourth relapse. We discovered that we had grown up in the same Indian city. This, and the fact that I was Indian, had a powerful impact on her. She immediately launched into a passionately emotional account of her childhood. Once a week for some months Mrs T spoke, almost without taking breath, about the mango trees at the corner of one set of roads, the tram tracks on another, the corner *beedi* (Indian cigarillo) shop (she was sure I would know it), the heaviness in the air before a monsoon storm, *ayahs*, *maalis* (domestic staff in a middle-class Indian household), school-teachers. I understood she had never spoken of these memories before, and had never returned to India. She had apparently not thought to tell her family in Britain about her Indian childhood, and it seemed they had little curiosity about her past. It seemed enough that she had been an English girl who had 'stayed on' in India after the country's independence from colonial rule, as many British families had for a while.

The unexpected part of Mrs T's progress under my care was unlocking these memories, which seemed to make it possible to reduce her doses of medication to the very lowest. (I thought it unwise to withdraw medication completely in the relatively short period we had together as it would arouse the anxieties of a biomedical system, and have unpredictable implications for Mrs T.)

Mrs T has many reasons to remain in my memory. That a sort of urgent 'nostalgia' was her self-cure in these sessions reminded me of using the same device for years, when paralysed by home-sickness and embarrassed about disclosing so childish an affliction, I spent weekends conjuring up comforting hallucinations of the past like Mrs T. Unlike her, I had regular access to India and contacts with the people I had left behind. The loss of Self accompanying the other losses of migration may be one which, because largely registered in embodied experience, is overlooked and not easily available to verbal recall or reminiscence.

In attempting to link the wider matrix of culture to individual lives I will draw on the work of anthropologists with a significant interest in psychoanalysis. Antze and Lambek (1996), in their edited volume on memory and trauma, note the role of memory in broader discourses on identity and the dialectical relationship between experience and narrative. 'People emerge from and as the products of their stories about themselves as much as their stories emerge from their lives. Through acts of memory they strive to render their lives in meaningful terms' (Antze and Lambek 1996: xviii). Rasmussen (2002) draws attention to the ways diverse viewpoints on the past, whether through narrativisation or production and engagement with material artefacts, mutually engage. She emphasises the part played by hegemonic discourses, past and contemporary, on how memory is constructed in the re-telling. This makes it essential for the therapist and supervisor to bear in mind the impact of historical relationships, 'real' and perceived, between the cultures of the patient, therapist and supervisor on the patient's account of past experience. For the psychotherapist, Rasmussen (2002: 125) is right on the button when she writes: 'the past is perceived to be unfinished business, becoming the present and the future'.

Narvaez (2006) discusses collective memory and its transmission through everyday techniques of embodiment; noting it may be inaccessible to consciousness and explicit statement. Cultural enactments are 'part of our embodied rhetoric, which we deploy – on the brink of habit, rite and choice – to put our social exchanges on a conventional footing' (Narvaez 2006: 64). On gender, Narvaez writes:

> And being a man or a woman involves many aspects of embodiment: techniques of the (engendered) bodies, gendered affects, management of desires, culturally contingent gestures, sartorial standards, standards of bodily beauty, phonetic dispositions, etc. Each of these – partaking from the bodily, the mental, and the cultural – is often charged with collective significations, and hence conveys 'retail' consistency to social groups – including psychological consistency; for many people will feel assured when they can see and hear that men and women are men and women proper.
>
> (Narvaez 2006: 64)

The vignette about Mrs T suggests the degree to which errors are possible when interpreting signs to arrive at a single 'truth' about others' lives, especially when cultural distance (whether intra- or intercultural) makes it hard to guess at past experience (Maitra 2006). The interrogation of such largely pre-conscious cultural habits relies on the therapist having sufficient cues. These may be derived only through active exploration of available cultural information (from the literature, and other sources, discussed below). The question that Mrs T's previous psychiatrists did not appear to have asked her, or a cultural consultant, was 'Why Bollywood?' It is true I did not do so either, in the same way I did not ask the Bangladeshi mother about the poem or its author. I read the cues she gave, about place, social background, verbal styles and thought these sufficient to form a working hypothesis.

For example, the fact that she spoke with a clearly identifiable Indian accent only during her manic phases suggested its significance. It referred to the conflict posed to her core identity when well, namely, of the possibility of being both English and Indian. Mrs T's choices, unconsciously selected from a range of deeply embedded memories from a distant past, expressed complex positions of unspeakable loss and repressed conflict about race, 'passing' and social hierarchies (British and non-British, Bollywood Indian and Anglo-Indian). She did so with a psychological consistency recognisable to a knowledgeable observer, but only if simplistic dichotomous categories were suspended in favour of an interpretive framework allowing multiplicity of meaning (cultural displacement, psychological conflict, biomedical illness).

The academic context

The culturally bound nature of western psychoanalysis must come as no surprise, given its acknowledgement by its earliest thinkers. To the accusation that psychoanalysts were merely drawing on 'old wives' psychology', Cunningham and Tickner (1981) note that Freud, who never quite succeeded in reconciling his divergent interests in neurological and psychological issues, was unable to explain his interest in explorations more reminiscent of the Jewish mystical traditions than of science. Jung's response was to defend his return to ancient traditions as conscious and deliberate, attributing the western emphasis on ego-development to cultural traditions in philosophy, specifically to the emphases on rationalism, Cartesian dualism and the impact of the Protestant faith. This drive to widen the cultural base of western psychology has persisted, even if not as a dominant form, as is evident in Abramovitch and Kirmayer's (2003) enumeration of Jung's contributions to contemporary cultural psychiatry. In its psychological redescription of religious experience and its pluralistic emphasis (for example, the psychic autonomy of archetypal structures) analytical psychology presents an important balance to the dominant monotheistic, monological and individualistic cultures of the west.

It is curious that so much criticism has been levelled in recent years at the Eurocentrism implicit in western health policy and practice. The expectation that a set of health beliefs and practices can, or should, aim to be culture-free is clearly flawed. Of greater concern is how this reveals the lingering hegemony of a colonial mind-set in its yearning for the coloniser's highest values – the post-Enlightenment European ideals of equitable provision for a universal formulation of human need. The note of outrage in the accusation of Eurocentrism seems curious, until one sees it as a response to the discovery of how well we had been, and continue to be, intellectually colonised (Pieterse and Parekh 1997). Accusations based on historical wrongs contribute little to contemporary multiculturalism. This is evident in the responses these provoke – ranging from the belligerent 'None of our black patients are complaining', to the plaintive 'How could we possibly learn about all the cultural groups that have migrated here?'

It is worth bearing in mind that as long as health discourses on race and culture are dominated by demands for equity (in service provision) and rights, we may merely be implicitly and paradoxically transposing the hierarchical relationships of master–subject onto 'white provider–black patient'. In place of a demand for equity of cultural viewpoints we could consider the nature of professional obligations, specifically the obligation to practise only when one is reasonably certain of one's skills in that particular field.

Therapeutic trainings in and for multicultural societies must consider what exposure to and experience of other cultural lives and points of view consists of, and which frames of research and analysis would widen the frameworks of theory and practice. No one member of the supervisory triangle can claim 'cultural superiority', despite each, naturally, having an embedded sense of their own 'rightness'. In addition to lessons from personal experience and early exposure, the ways we are socialised by culture shape all our discussions. Openness needs to be reinforced by a robust adoption of a diverse literature base.

There is extensive ethnographic literature describing non-western cultures from without and within. Psychotherapists would do well to grow comfortable with it. The diversity of ways history, politics, geography and, most importantly, the social sciences contribute to newly evolving ways of thinking about experience and mental functions is reflected in the number of publications currently available. Interdisciplinary dialogue and exchange has been extremely slow to influence psychotherapy. This may in part be the reason why our discipline appears sadly moribund to potential trainees. Broadening the literature base from disciplines focused solely on 'internal' psychological preoccupations or reinforcing 'theory' attributed to worthy ancestors, to consider the unavoidably porous boundaries between inner and outer, would not, as some fear, weaken professional confidence. It could help increase it by opening discussion with supervisees and patients about the premises of treatment, what they choose as their goals, and why. I will next briefly touch on cultural concepts of the self to show how, far from being an outer layer over a core universal self (the metaphor of onion rings, or the cultural icing on the universal cake) notions of the person are impossible to dissect out of the cultural worlds in which these are embedded.

The self in western and non-western therapeutic discourses

A great deal has been written about the differences of therapeutic focus which arise from how a group demarcates the 'person', defines the nature of the mind, essential self (or soul), the location of personal attributes, and so on. The western self, Kirmayer (2007: 240) writes, is 'agentic, rationalistic, monological, and univocal', with American individualism having undergone changes to appear in two new forms – expressive and utilitarian individualism. Expressive individualism defines 'real' persons as those who give full expression to their emotional life, idiosyncratic aesthetic and moral values. The utilitarian view of full personhood is revealed in the pragmatic pursuit of one's own well-being and of one's immediate family (not of higher order groups such as the community) through an instrumental control of power and the material world. Participants in these beliefs see them as natural and inevitable ways of speaking of the self, not as cultural constructions peculiar to their history, and context.

Western psychotherapy is distinct from other forms of psychological healing in requiring the patient to show an ability and willingness to talk explicitly about private events, emotions or interpersonal relationships – to objectify the processes of their own mind. As the London psychoanalyst Nina Coltart's (1988) seven features of 'psychological mindedness' show, criteria used to identify patients who will be able to engage in and benefit from therapy reflect shared cultural meanings and goals which unite western patient, therapist and supervisor.

Other cultures define the self according to vastly different constructions of the world, and man's place in it. In many 'non-western' parts of the world (Africa, the Middle East, South Asia and further East) the self is essentially relational. This is sometimes simplified into depictions of 'traditional' cultures as polar opposites to western cultures – collective, hierarchical, dominated by religious or spiritual concerns, and essentially antithetical to the uniqueness, and the rights to choice central to individualism even when these are dominated by consumerist pressures towards uniformity. Kirmayer (2007: 239–246) presents cultural configurations of the self – egocentric, sociocentric, and cosmocentric, separated by dominant values which shape each group's constructions of the self, locus of agency and healing systems. Shamans, healers, and others who deal with emotional distress work within different boundaries between the body, mind and spirit, between individual roles and interdependent collectives, between the living and the Spirit World, constructing different therapeutic goals (Pakaslahti 1998). Such ways of construing the self are not mutually exclusive as, depending on their situations, people move between a range of self-concepts. And patients from cultures defining well-being in terms cutting across western categories may experience the goals of western therapy as deeply alienating, even when the attention and empathic intentions of the therapist are gratefully received.

The following example shows the possibility of misinterpretation even when the apparent distance between cultural worlds is not great.

A colleague from Latin America, a vast region of hybrid cultures incorporating the European, spoke of a recurring misinterpretation in his personal analysis. At the end of each session, he reported, his final act was to turn and glance at his (British) analyst as he opened the door. In the analyst's view this suggested a persecutory anxiety, the glance searching for the anticipated attack from the analyst or attempting to counter it. My colleague's strong feeling was of being unable to leave without the backward glance, this serving as a ritual of 'closure' in place of the culturally Latin parting kiss.

We wondered whether the sharpness with which boundaries to the individual Self are protected in British culture predisposed to a persecutory bias in dominant interpretations of the transference. Such preoccupations may predispose the British analyst to anticipate, and guard against, perceived threats to personal or professional boundaries, and to attribute to the analysand's actions a set of meanings drawn from the cluster of envy, counterattack and rejection. In similar situations an analyst whose cultural construction of self is less laden with boundary concerns might call up other realms of meaning. To an Indian analyst, for example, the importance of the collective and role-relationships in how self is defined, as well as cultural models of relationships as between *guru* and disciple. This privileges other meanings. For example, an acceptance of the hierarchical nature of the relationship between guru and therapist and between disciple and patient places a primary focus on reciprocal obligation. Perceived threats would be more likely to involve the relationship rather than the person of the guru, and would appear as disrespect. The expectation of dependency as a central element of such a hierarchical relationship would give to the parting sequence enacted by my Latin American colleague the meaning, for example, of a claim for the analyst's continuing interest at the point of separation. Clearly, the same argument would apply between guru and supervisor and between disciple and supervisee.

Multicultural groups and supervision

After many years presenting workshops on culture and mental health to multidisciplinary teams, I proposed an experiment at group supervision of intercultural work. Set up in 2004 the Cultural Psychology Workshop is a monthly meeting open to anyone in the Inner London Child and Adolescent Mental Health Service where I work, who has a case, or curiosity about culture they wished to explore. The focus was determined by the work of Richard Shweder, an anthropologist who made important contributions to the dialogue between psychology and cultural anthropology. He describes cultural psychology as an interdisciplinary science 'premised on human existential uncertainty (the search for meaning) and on an "intentional" conception of "constituted" worlds' (Shweder 1991: 74). The principle of intentional or constituted worlds, he elaborates, 'asserts that subjects and objects, practitioners and practices, human beings and sociocultural environments, interpenetrate each other's identity and cannot be analysed into independent and dependent variables'. Our workshop's core activities include focusing on cultural contexts in clinical material; examination of policy and organisational matters which impact on intercultural practice or equitable service provision; and critical reading of related papers.

The workshop is attended by mental health professionals and trainees from psychology, child psychotherapy, family therapy, psychiatric nursing and child psychiatry. Months were spent discussing 'safety' – mainly, concerns from white colleagues about venturing thoughts which might reveal unconscious racism, and concerns among non-white colleagues that they would be thought poorly trained (in 'white' mental health thinking), or might reveal thoughts or feelings overly-critical of white culture, systems and individuals. In a bid to direct the focus away from exotic minority ethnic cultures, the agenda for the first year was focused on exploration of white British culture and all its variety. Perhaps unsurprisingly, this did relatively little to ease potential tensions, intense disagreements arising about social class and regional variations in cultural practice.

A major concern centred on the difficulties that seniors, as supervisors, felt exploring culture in their clinical work, and discussing it with supervisees from minority ethnic cultures. Equally, trainees did not feel able to disagree with their supervisors about claims of universal relevance made by their academic disciplines and training. The group proved useful in establishing greater confidence than felt heretofore, in developing new frameworks for analysing observations, and taking considered clinical risks in intercultural contexts.

'Matching' patient, therapist, supervisor and world-view

It is important to note that cultural variety is not located in our patients alone, but also in our professional groups. Immigrant psychologists, psychotherapists and psychiatrists may have qualified in disciplines dominated by western intellectual and folk traditions, with a wide range of different understandings. Translated with varying degrees of accuracy and incorporated into non-western systems of belief, these hybridised forms re-enter contemporary western therapeutic discourses in unpredictable ways (Maitra 2007). Supervision needs to address cultural diversity between supervisee and patient, as well as between supervisor and supervisee. The greatest complexity is presented when patient and supervisee have similar cultural backgrounds. The task of supervision is to track process with relatively little information about how cultural content relates to form, to different components of an alien world-view.

How would a European colleague (not my supervisor) in the vignette of the Bangladeshi mother know whether or not my reading of her behaviour was adequate? What were the risks of an over-identification with the mother, and her obvious literary sensibility and gendered dilemmas? As supervisor of a bicultural worker, recruited from the Turkish and Kurdish community in East London, I am aware of the difficulties of promoting their independence and skill at understanding how culture affects their patients, while simultaneously preventing premature closure to the processes of hypothesis-making and testing. It is crucial to keep alive in them a taste for multiple rather than single explanations, and for thoughtful tentativeness rather than premature certainty. Considering the fluidity of global influences on local contexts immigrant cultures in particular are marked by multiplicity and hybridity. The most useful frame in cultural supervision is to maintain a focus on the context-specificity of individual positions, interactions and meanings: to promote open meaning-systems rather than ones prematurely closing (Mathers 2001: 9, 231).

Consultation and community networks

The final element in this cluster of strategies is the necessity for dialogue between therapeutic institutions and culturally diverse communities. This may be achieved by close liaison with bicultural professionals who have experience in the difficult art of interpreting culture in terms comprehensible to western institutions. Unfortunately, setting up 'cultural experts' who speak for 'the community' poses other problems – representation, vested interests, and the putative expert's ambitions. These must be balanced by wider efforts at engagement with cultural groups, and the diversity of community organisations within them. As minority communities may have little, if any, interest in being comprehensible to western institutions it becomes necessary to reverse the direction of explanation-making; for the therapeutic disciplines and provider organisations to make their ethos comprehensible to their users. This applies many times over in therapy. Open relationships may help therapy keep pace with a rapidly changing social context, and restore a measure of humility to its claims.

Conclusion

The significance of cultural encounters between therapist–patient and therapist–training organisation–supervisor is strikingly, even poignantly, made in a biography of the Pakistani analyst, Masud Khan. Linda Hopkins (2006) reports from correspondence between Khan and 'a former friend' who charged him with believing 'more and more in feudalism and less and less in psychoanalysis'; Khan responded, 'I do not believe more and more in feudalism. I never lapsed from a total belief in it.' He added, while he had for some two decades 'exercised a "willing suspension of disbelief"' toward psychoanalysis, he now disowned it totally' (Hopkins 2006: 358). As Hopkins notes, it is difficult to know how to take this obviously cynical comment from someone who wrote passionately about psychoanalysis for so long. However, it raises interesting questions about the apparent failure of the psychoanalytic world around Khan to take this conflict between two cultural systems into account. What makes her biography of this extraordinary man so curious is that Hopkins continues to read him as though Khan's cultural origins and his keeping his eastern and western selves hermetically separate and non-interacting were largely irrelevant.

'Setting aside the cultural considerations, it is fair to say', Hopkins writes with a breath-taking recklessness (no less impressive than Khan's alleged arrogance) towards the end of her book, 'that much of Khan's life can be addressed by Western thinking. Almost anyone in the West would agree that he was "mad"' (Hopkins 2006: 388).

While psychotherapy does not (in the way psychiatry might) express a yearning for objectively verifiable truths, its theory-making is no less coloured by a similar desire for universals. Fortunately, questions about universals have been superseded by a curiosity in local worlds, and the influences of distant events and global processes on them. This trend suggests a wider frame on what is considered relevant to psychotherapeutic trainings. I encourage psychotherapists to venture into the rich ethnographic literature, and into new fields of interdisciplinary research. Inevitably, this information will blur and redraw the boundaries between western cultural categories constructed in response to the concerns of an earlier period, of limited use today. Globalisation and the multicultural character of the societies within which psychotherapy is practised – whether New Delhi, Oaxaca or London – has made the risks of stepping outside our own cultural premises necessities, no longer merely matters of individual taste. Supervision, aided by flexibility and a self-critical awareness of limitations, whether in personal ability or in theoretical beliefs, can make a significant contribution to a culturally responsive style of psychotherapy.

> In the mixing and matching of two largely unknowable histories (of genetic endowment and personal experience) the only sane foregone

conclusion about any relationship is that it is an experiment; and that exactly what it is an experiment in will never be clear to the participants.
(Phillips 2005: 231)

References

Abramovitch, H. and Kirmayer, L. J. (2003) 'The relevance of Jungian psychology for cultural psychiatry.' *Transcultural Psychiatry* 40: 155–163.

Antze, P. and Lambek, M. (1996) 'Introduction: forecasting memory.' In P. Antze and M. Lambek (eds) *Tense Past: Cultural Essays in Trauma and Memory*. London: Routledge.

Briggs, J. (1998) *Inuit Morality Play*. New Haven, CT: Yale University Press.

Chodorow, N. (1999) *The Power of Feelings*. New Haven, CT: Yale University Press.

Christensen, P., Hockey, J. and James, A. (2001) 'Talk, silence and the material world: patterns of indirect communication among agricultural families in northern England.' In J. Hendry and C. W. Watson (eds) *An Anthropology of Indirect Communication*, ASA Monographs 37. London: Routledge.

Coltart, N. E. C. (1988) 'The assessment of psychological-mindedness in the diagnostic interview.' *British Journal of Psychiatry* 153: 819–820.

Cunningham, A. and Tickner, D. (1981) 'Psychoanalysis and indigenous psychology.' In P. Heelas and A. Lock (eds) *Indigenous Psychologies: The Anthropology of Self*. Berkeley, CA: University of California Press.

Hopkins, L. (2006) *False Self: The Life of Masud Khan*. New York: Other Press.

Jennings, L., Goh, M., Skovholt, T. M., Hanson, M. and Banerjee-Stevens, D. (2003) 'Multiple factors in the development of the expert counsellor and therapist.' *Journal of Career Development* 30(1): 59–72.

Jensen, P. (2007) 'On learning from experience: personal and private experiences as the context for psychotherapeutic practice.' *Clinical Child Psychology and Psychiatry* 12(3): 375–384.

Kirmayer, L. J. (2006) 'Culture and psychotherapy in a creolizing world.' *Transcultural Psychiatry* 43: 163–168.

—— (2007) 'Psychotherapy and the cultural concept of the person.' *Transcultural Psychiatry* 44(2): 232–257.

Maitra, B. (1995) 'Giving due consideration to families racial and cultural backgrounds.' In P. Reder and C. Lucey (eds) *Assessment of Parenting: Psychiatric and Psychological Considerations*. London: Routledge.

—— (2004) 'Would cultural matching ensure culturally competent assessments?' In P. Reder, S. Duncan and C. Lucey (eds) *Studies in the Assessment of Parenting*. London: Routledge.

—— (2006) 'Culture and the mental health of children: the "cutting edge" of expertise.' In S. Timimi and B. Maitra (eds) *Critical Voices in Child and Adolescent Mental Health*. London: Free Association Books.

—— (2007) 'Post-colonial psychiatry: the promise of multiculturalism.' In C. I. Cohen and S. Timimi (eds) *Liberatory Psychiatry: Towards a New Psychiatry*. Cambridge: Cambridge University Press.

Mathers, D. (2001) *An Introduction to Meaning and Purpose in Analytical Psychology*. London: Brunner-Routledge.

Narvaez, R. F. (2006) 'Embodiment, collective memory and time.' *Body and Society* 12(3): 51–73.

Obeyesekere, G. (1990) *The Work of Culture*. Chicago, IL: University of Chicago Press.

Pakaslahti, A. (1998). 'Family-centered treatment of mental health problems at the Balaji Temple in Rajasthan.' In A. Parpola and S. Tenhunen (eds) *Changing Patterns of Family and Kinship in South Asia*, vol. 84 of *Studia Orientalia*. Helsinki: Finnish Oriental Society.

Phillips, A. (2005) *Going Sane*. London: Hamish Hamilton.

Pieterse, J. N. and Parekh, B. (eds) (1997) *The Decolonization of the Imagination Culture, Knowledge and Power*. Delhi: Oxford University Press.

Rasmussen, S. (2002) 'The uses of memory'. *Culture and Psychology* 8(1): 113–129.

Rønnestad, M. H. and Skovholt, T. M. (2002) 'Learning arenas for professional development: retrospective accounts for senior psychotherapists.' *Professional Psychology: Research and Practice* 32: 181–187.

Shweder, R. A. (1991) *Thinking through Cultures: Expeditions in Cultural Psychology*. Cambridge, MA: Harvard University Press.

Throop, C. J. (2003) 'On crafting a cultural mind: a comparative assessment of some recent theories of "internalization" in psychological anthropology.' *Transcultural Psychiatry* 40(1): 109–139.

Chapter 11

'Spooky action at a distance'[1]
Parallel processes in Jungian analysis and supervision

Gottfried Heuer

> No man is an *Iland*, intire of it selfe; every man is a peece of the *Continent*, a part of the *maine*.
> John Donne (1624/1945: 538)[2]

Introduction

This chapter is about the specific transference phenomena between analysis and supervision that are called parallel process. Since the 1950s we have become used to working with this and other modes of transference. Up to now, only descriptive terms were available for these phenomena which we could experience, observe and use in analytic work and discourse, but for which we lacked any real explanation. Only now, with recent discoveries in quantum physics and neurobiology, have scientific explanations become possible; so, perhaps for the first time, this chapter provides insights for a scientific explanation for some of our most basic clinical tools. After briefly introducing how I understand the clinical place of parallel process phenomena and the development of this concept, I shall present a Jungian perspective on analysis, supervision and their links, before discussing current research in quantum physics and in neurobiology in so far as they are relevant.

In the 1900s, with initial uncertainties as to their analytic and therapeutic value, transference and countertransference manifestations were discovered, as analysis gradually began to be understood more and more in relational terms. Initiated by Otto Gross, as I show elsewhere (G. Heuer 2004), this development culminated in the mid-1940s in Jung's 'Gate' diagram (CW16 para. 422) of a mutual dialectic between equals. For Freudians, cut off from Jungian theory, it took another fifty years to develop what they correspondingly call interpersonal or relational psychoanalysis, or intersubjectivity (G. Heuer 1996). Appropriately, during this time, based on experience and observation, ever finer differentiations were discovered and new descriptive terms needed and found for an ever greater variety of relational experiences. When supervision evolved, further technical terms were coined not only for the discourse on what happens in the supervisory relationship, but subsequently also for the relationship between analysis and supervision.

The chapter falls into four sections. First, I shall trace the history of the use of these transference dynamics in analytic theory and therapeutic practice: from Freud's early recommendations, via Gross's and Jung's work on mutuality to initial descriptions of parallel processes by Searles and others in the 1950s, then to Doehrman's seminal dissertation on the subject in the early 1970s. Second, beginning with animal behaviour, I shall use aspects of research in quantum physics, and third, neurobiology to provide parallel process phenomena for the first time (as far as I know) with a contemporary scientific basis by introducing some of the findings in these fields. I conclude with clinical vignettes of the use of parallel process in present day Jungian psychodynamic supervision and historical research.

Parallel processes in Jungian analysis and supervision

> A thousand fibers connect us with our fellow men.
> Attributed to Herman Melville (in Campbell 1995)

I understand parallel process to be the unconscious influence of the transference/countertransference between analyst and patient on the supervisory relationship and vice versa. The emotional dynamics between supervisor and supervisee parallel those of the analytic situation under discussion. Aspects of the analytic psychodynamics are being transferred into those of the supervisory relationship by the analyst or supervisee. Parallel process can thus be understood as one of the ways in which a certain kind of transference is described. Considering these parallels between the two processes allows me to use current knowledge about transference for an understanding of parallel process.

In paralleling the psychodynamics of the analytic relationship within those of the supervisory relationship, *either* supervisor or supervisee can take on the role of *either* analyst or patient. This means that if I, for example, have a patient who is angry with his father and, in the transference, angry with me, in presenting my work to my supervisor, we may suddenly find ourselves having an angry argument. In this either of us may feel as the not-understood-son who sees the other as a father-to-be-angry-with. In that situation, I thus may become my client and turn my supervisor into myself-as-analyst, or the other way round. If our work goes well enough, we become conscious of what we have unconsciously enacted and can use our immediate emotional experiences in the here and now to more fully understand and solve problems which previously arose in the analytic setting.

Before I focus on the current usage of this concept, let me briefly look back at the history of the ideas which led to this perspective which emphasises relational interactions in analysis, and, later, in supervision. One hundred years ago, the psychoanalyst Otto Gross laid the foundations for a relational psychology with his emphasis on self and other, a central focus of his work from 1907 (Gross 1907) onwards, with what he called 'the will to relating' (Gross 1919). In contact with both Freud and Jung, and influencing both, Gross opened the way from a one- to a two-person psychology focused on the relational aspects of analysis rather than on the pathology of the patient. Jung and Freud then fully developed the concepts of transference and countertransference, gradually recognising them as important tools rather than hindrances to the analytic work.

Initially, corresponding psychodynamics in the supervisory relationship were also understood as a hindrance, indicating feelings of competitiveness or immaturity and inexperience on either side (Sachs and Shapiro 1976). In 1955, Harold Searles first described what he called 'reflective processes' between analyst and patient on the one hand and analyst and supervisor on the other (Searles 1986). Eckstein and Wallerstein (1958) first used the term 'parallel process' for the unconscious transfer of feelings from the analytic to the supervisory situation. In the same year, John Gustin criticised: 'supervision that does not make use of the unconscious interaction between the therapist and his supervisor is dealing only with the superficial aspects of learning' (Gustin 1958: 69). The theories of these pioneers were expanded on, researched and described in Margery Jean Gross Doehrmann's 1971 dissertation, 'Parallel processes in supervision and psychotherapy' (Doehrmann 1976).

My own understanding of the psychodynamics of parallel processing is based on Jung's concepts of relational processes as described in his seminal 1945 text 'On the psychology of the transference' (CW16). Though not using the term countertransference, Jung understands both analyst and analysand as entering their relationship with transferences towards each other. This perspective starts from a basis of equality and mutuality that Jung found not only in his study of alchemy but also in his work with Otto Gross who introduced him much earlier to these ideas, based on the anarchist concepts of Proudhon and Kropotkin (cf. G. Heuer 2004). In the mid-1940s Jung created the diagram in Figure 11.1 (CW16 para. 422), sometimes called the 'Gate' diagram.

To Jung's Latin terms from an alchemical treatise I have added descriptive terms from analytic practice. Already here in this diagram we can, strictly speaking, observe a number of parallel processes as every interaction (shown by a double-headed arrow) resonates with each of the others. The external, interpersonal relationship thus corresponds to, resonates with and hence parallels the intrapersonal relationship between conscious and unconscious of each partner.

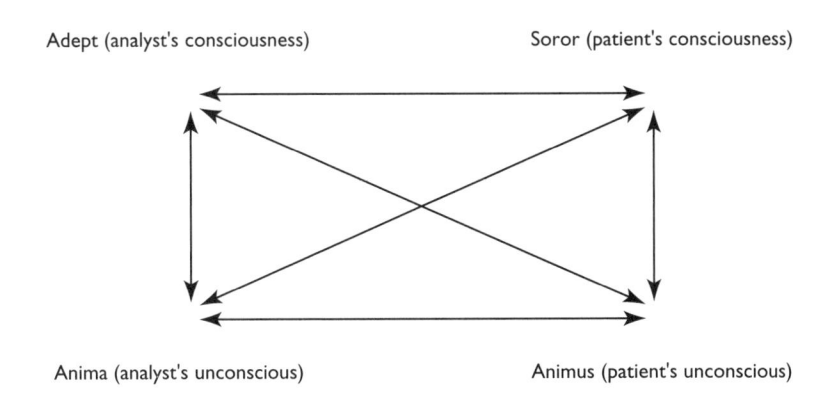

Adept (analyst's consciousness)   Soror (patient's consciousness)

Anima (analyst's unconscious)   Animus (patient's unconscious)

Figure 11.1

These interactional psychodynamics are believed by some analysts to begin long before analyst and patient initially contact each other. If we do not believe in meaningless coincidence, then the way analyst and analysand choose each other can be said to be based on a kind of unconscious resonance between the two in terms of what each requires on their paths towards healing and greater wholeness. We can speak, with reason, of the analytic relationship as starting at the time when the prospective patient first considers going into analysis. This is confirmed by how psychodynamic couple therapists understand the mutual choice of partners (Hendrix 1993: 3–82).

This dyadic diagram includes only analyst and analysand. Yet the therapeutic couple does not exist in isolation. In order to truly consider the complexity of the situation, the same multidimensional and mutual links exist, resonate with and parallel each other not only between each of the participants but also between them and every significant other in their respective lives. In psychic reality, it seems, everybody can be seen and understood as being interlinked and resonating with everybody else. In the 1930s Jung said, 'When you analyse a person, you have not only that individual on your hands, but it is as if you were analysing a whole group.' He continues, almost echoing Einstein, 'It has magic effects in the distance, even in people who are not immediately related to the patient' (Jung 1930–1934: 475).

We can use Jung's diagram of mutual interrelating as a model for the supervisory relationship. The dyadic relationship of the therapeutic couple then changes to a triadic one, involving analyst, patient and supervisor, forming a pyramid (Figure 11.2).

In expanding the diagram by including a third person, it is possible to understand the complex conscious and unconscious transference interactions and parallel processes between all three participants in their relational

168 Gottfried Heuer

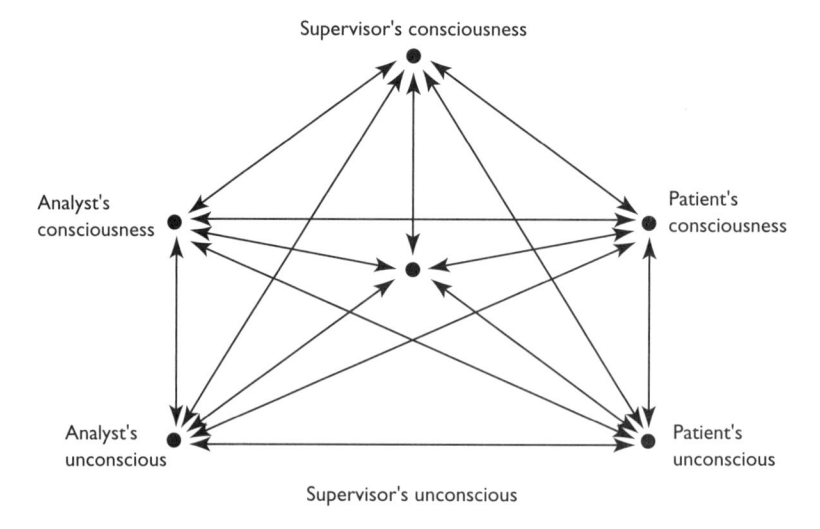

Figure 11.2

triangles. We might put a question mark beside the conscious relating between patient and supervisor, yet more and more, being in continuous supervision for the duration of one's professional life is a requirement of which patients may well be aware. Or the analyst may choose to disclose this aspect of their work in the beginning when they discuss confidentiality, to which supervision is an exception.

Just as in analysis the analyst needs to be open to understand every verbal or non-verbal communication in its transference aspects, the supervisor needs to be open to understand every communication in terms of it being a parallel process communication. For example, when a patient's dream contains a two-person interaction, I need to be able in my mind to creatively play around with the various possibilities present: our external relationship might be symbolically represented with either of us in either role, paralleling relations between the patient's consciousness and unconscious, as well as between various aspects of their or my inner self. The *same* applies to the supervisory relationship, only here the primary relationship has become even more complex as it is triadic.

This becomes particularly clear when the supervisee brings a dream about a patient. Primarily, we might say, this concerns the personal life of the supervisee. Yet it certainly also relates to their role as analyst in relation to their patient. In addition, from a parallel process perspective, such a dream also concerns the supervisory relationship and portrays specific aspects of it.

If the analyst is a candidate in training, then this turns into a four-person relationship of mutual interrelating and parallel processing (Figure 11.3).

Parallel processes 169

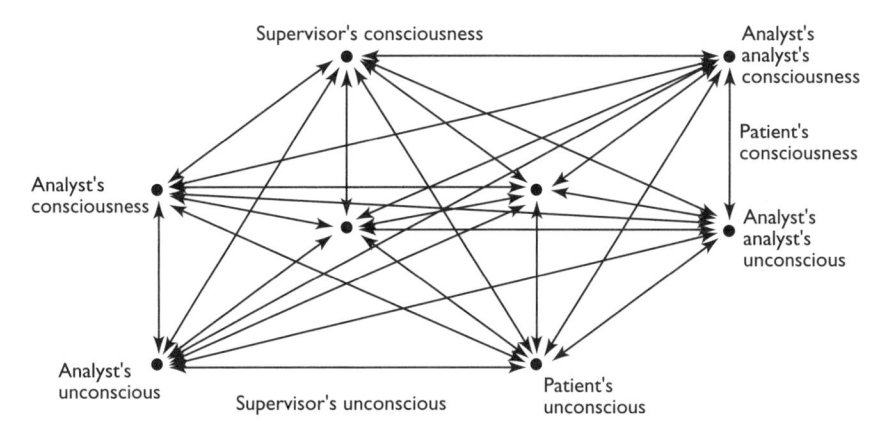

Figure 11.3

Again, in this diagram, the double-headed arrows of mutual interrelating show the complexity of transference links the supervisor could be aware of and creatively play with in order to arrive at the most appropriate, meaningful and mutative interpretation.

There is yet another way to read Jung's diagram: if we realise this kind of transferential influence of the supervisory process by the analytic one does not happen in one direction only, we can also take the two sides of the diagram as each representing the totality of the analytic and the supervisory process respectively, or each specific situation of either at any moment, relating – resonating – with each other in dialectic mutuality (Figure 11.4).

The upper horizontal double-headed arrow then stands for what is consciously transferred from the analytic to the supervisory situation and vice versa, whereas the lower horizontal double-headed arrow depicts the corresponding two-way communication on an unconscious level. Used in this way, the diagram portrays and draws attention to yet another 'spooky action at a distance': the frequent and sometimes uncanny experience by an analyst in an analytic session following a supervision, that the patient almost seems to have been present in the preceding supervision session. Thus a patient may start the session with a statement or even a specific term which seems to relate directly to the supervisory discourse, almost as if the patient had been able to follow that discussion; or the patient may bring a dream which appears to symbolise a conclusion just arrived at in supervision.

It is reasonable to assume that on an unconscious level parallel processing is happening all the time in supervision. In Jung's diagram, the lower horizontal double-headed arrow denotes a permanent two-way communication between the analyst's and the patient's unconscious. The vertical and diagonal double-headed arrows denote the analytic process of raising material from the unconscious into consciousness. This is what analysis is

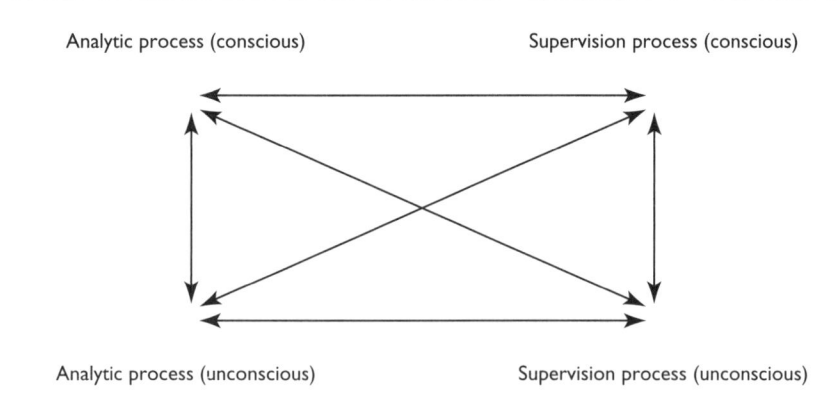

```
Analytic process (conscious)          Supervision process (conscious)

         ┌─────────────────────────────────┐
         │◄───────────────────────────────►│
         │▲▲                             ▲▲│
         │ │ ╲                         ╱ │ │
         │ │   ╲                     ╱   │ │
         │ │     ╲                 ╱     │ │
         │ │       ╲             ╱       │ │
         │ │         ╲         ╱         │ │
         │ │           ╲     ╱           │ │
         │ │             ╲ ╱             │ │
         │ │             ╱ ╲             │ │
         │ │           ╱     ╲           │ │
         │ │         ╱         ╲         │ │
         │ │       ╱             ╲       │ │
         │ │     ╱                 ╲     │ │
         │ │   ╱                     ╲   │ │
         │ ▼ ╱                         ╲ ▼ │
         │▼                               ▼│
         │◄───────────────────────────────►│
         └─────────────────────────────────┘

Analytic process (unconscious)        Supervision process (unconscious)
```

Figure 11.4

about. Could we say that, correspondingly, in supervision it is a primary task to reflect upon the unconscious parallel processes which equally happen permanently between the analytic and the supervisory situations?

As mentioned, the terms used in the past hundred years to think and communicate about what happens in psychodynamic practice have been descriptive: resonance, transference, projection, introjection, and so on are attempts to name *what* is being observed. Yet, 'Little has been done to elucidate the mechanism at work' (Weiner et al. 2003: 236). What these descriptive terms do not tell us is *how* these phenomena work. By implication, they are based on classical Newtonian physics as they clearly denote distances in time and space that are being bridged: thus in 'transference' something is referred to as being transferred over time and space from one situation to another. In 'projection', something is being thrown forward across a distance and taken in – an 'introjection' – by someone else. When I have an idea, a felt experience, an emotion, and these affect someone else to the extent this other person 'catches' them, we use the psychodynamic terms mentioned above, or we can speak of 'resonance' (Stone 2006), 'thought transmission', 'extrasensory perception', 'psychic infection', or other descriptive names – although what actually happens remains 'spooky'. Gediman and Wolkenfeld (1980: 234–235) write, 'The phenomenon of which we speak partakes, in a word, of the "uncanny".' So far, we did not know what it actually is which moves at a speed greater than light through an unknown medium over seemingly limitless distances of time and space.

Spooky action at a distance

Before I consider some of the recent discoveries in quantum physics and neurobiology which may provide a physical and neurobiological explanation for some of our most basic clinical tools, giving these 'spooky actions at a distance' a scientific basis, I want to open up our range of vision to consider other areas of life where similar phenomena have been observed. This allows a contextualisation of the specific analytic concerns with 'the facts of life' in general as understood by contemporary scientific research and shows how these principles function in a wider context.

Let us start, then, with the birds and the bees, and work our way from there upwards the evolutionary ladder to human beings. Bees function as a single intelligence. In this, each individual bee is part of the decision making process, the whole swarm being in a state of constant mutual interaction. Referring to a colony of ants, David Attenborough speaks of 'one great super-organism' (Attenborough 2005b). It is interesting to recall in this context that, conversely, Rudolf Virchow, the founder of cellular pathology, in the 1850s likened the multicellular human body to a society, a 'unified commonwealth', 'multicitizened' (in Sontag 1989: 6–7). David Attenborough reports that, as larvae, the winged cicadas

> in the eastern United States spend 17 years [underground], and then, within a few days, a whole population emerges. There may be millions of them in a single acre of land . . . How do these cicadas all emerge simultaneously after 17 long years? Well, we know that they . . . are able to detect the passing of a year. But how do they count up to 17? We have *no* idea.
>
> (Attenborough 2005a)

Traditional science cannot provide an explanation. In an article entitled 'Swarm theory' in *National Geographic Magazine*, Peter Miller shows 'a tree ablaze with fireflies in Indonesia', that rhythmically 'blinks on and off'. The author calls this synchronised behaviour 'mysterious' and comments that each insect 'adjusts its flashes to match the others' (Miller 2007: 144), which is not really a satisfying explanation as to how the immediate synchronisation of the thousands of insects is actually achieved.

As with fish, you may well have observed whole swarms of birds moving in unison as they move and change direction as if one organism. The North American caribou is a migratory mammal which moves in herds of tens of thousands. Calves are born literally on the move. In order to minimise the danger of them being eaten by predators surrounding the herds, the caribou females, thousands of them, do what is called 'synchronised calving': within the space of a few hours, they all give birth at the same time (Turner 2004).

So far, phenomena like these have only been observed and described, but not adequately explained. Until recently, the connecting principles of interaction and resonance have been the white areas on the maps of scientific knowledge. In exploring these, let us first look at the inanimate aspects of these spooky actions from the perspective of contemporary quantum physics, before we add a neurobiological one which deals directly with animate beings, both animal and human. Physicist Gary Felder explains:

> Starting at the beginning of the previous century, our physical theories began to include aspects which ran counter to that common sense, and yet the theories consistently made accurate predictions of experiments which could not be explained with Newtonian physics. [One of the new results discovered is] called nonlocality. Its converse, locality, is the principle that an event which happens at one place can't instantaneously affect an event someplace else . . . I could put a particle in a measuring device at one location and, simply by doing that, instantly influence another particle arbitrarily far away . . . In short, locality is dead . . . Spooky action at a distance is part of nature.
>
> (Felder 1999)

Traditional quantum theory held that these new principles 'operate in an inanimate subatomic world' (B. Heuer 2008). Yet in the 1970s the 'German physicist Fritz Albert Popp was the first to discover quantum data in living cells' (ibid.). As Birgit Heuer (2008) writes, this means 'quantum laws cannot be neatly consigned to an inanimate world of small particles, but that they extend and underpin the living world and human consciousness also'.

A brief excursion into the history of these ideas: some 400 years ago, for Giordano Bruno, the Italian philosopher and Dominican monk, these concepts would not necessarily have been entirely new. He claimed that the whole universe was of infinite space and time, in which everything was interconnected. The universe was a cosmic body organised by a cosmic soul.

> For Bruno there was a continuous exchange [of] forces, mutual fertilisation . . . Bruno stood firmly in the subtle body tradition of the west . . . Members of the body are the limbs, the organs. The universe is a membership of beings . . . Attraction for Bruno is a kind of resonance between persons, between beings, between processes and events in the universe.
>
> (Boadella 1999: 121–123)

Bruno did not distinguish 'between persons, between beings, between processes and events in the universe'. For ideas like these, he was burned at the stake as an heretic. The body psychotherapist David Boadella (1999: 124) describes him in some sense as a forerunner of object relations theory, although, in Bruno's thinking, the relating, or 'attraction' as he called it, occurred between *subjects*. In a way, Bruno can thus be seen as having anticipated Jung's perspective of dialectical relating in mutuality. When it comes to analytic work, we speak of a field, an interactional field, or of a subtle body that is being created between two or more people – the modern scientific equivalent to Christ's, 'where two or three are gathered together in my name, there I am in the midst of them' (Matthew 18:20).

Deepak Chopra (1993) writes:

> Although each person seems separate and independent, all of us are connected to patterns of intelligence that govern the whole cosmos. Our bodies are part of a universal body, our minds aspects of a universal mind.
>
> (Chopra 1993: 6)

Jung was the first to introduce these concepts to the analytic discourse when he discovered the alchemical vision of the *unus mundus* (one world) as a ground for the *mysterium coniunctionis*, the mystery, one might freely translate it, of interconnectedness. He was also the first to link these alchemical concepts to the quantum theory of his time. In current quantum field research, the mystical experience and the explanations intuited for millennia in the past, are provided with a contemporary theoretical scientific basis. In a chapter entitled 'The sea of light', science writer Lynne McTaggart writes:

> To the religious or the mystic, it is science proving the miraculous. What quantum calculations show is that we and our universe live and breathe in what amounts to a sea of motion – a quantum sea of light . . . interconnected by waves which are spread out through time and space and can carry on to infinity, tying one part of the universe to every other part. The idea of The Field might just offer a scientific explanation for many metaphysical notions . . . It even echoes the Old Testament's account of God's first dictum: 'Let there be light' [Genesis I:3] out of which matter was created.
>
> (McTaggart 2001: 25, 29)

Having discussed scientific explanations for our physical interrelatedness, let us now turn to the biological correlates.

Neurobiology

> The body undoubtedly exerts 'action at a distance'.
>
> Wilhelm Reich (1999: 16)

Already in 1912 Freud suggested that the analyst:

> turn his own unconscious like a receptive organ towards the transmitting unconscious of the patient. He should tune in to the patient as

the telephone receiver is tuned in to the transmitting microphone. Just as the receiver converts back into sound waves the electric oscillations in the telephone line triggered by the sound waves, so the unconscious of the analyst is capable to reconstruct the unconscious as communicated by the patient.

(Freud 1912: 115–116; translation modified)

Developing this metaphor further by grounding the experience in the body, Martin Stone writes, 'I have found the notion of the resonance of a tuning fork helpful and I would suggest that resonance occurs when the analyst's tuning fork vibrates with the patient's unconscious material through the unconscious' (Stone 2006: 109).

Recent discoveries in physics may be understood as part of the answer to the mystery of resonance. We may have an explanation of the physical facts of mutual intercommunication, but what are its perceiving organs? Some of the developments in quantum physics have been matched by corresponding discoveries in neurobiological research. In the mid-1990s, the neurobiologist Giacomo Rizzolati and his team were able to ascribe specific actions to individual brain cells and those in their immediate vicinity. Working with anaesthetised monkeys, they were able to attach highly sensitive measuring devices to specific cells triggering highly specific actions. They could thus isolate a *single* cell that became active only when the monkey reached for a nut – and not as it reached for anything else. Subsequently the scientists made a groundbreaking discovery: the same cell would also become active when the monkey just *watched* another monkey reaching for a nut. This discovery proved the existence of a neurobiological resonance.

'Nerve cells capable of realising a certain program . . . that also become active from just observing a certain action or co-experiencing it in other ways, are called mirror neurons' (Bauer 2006b: 23). Noises typical for certain actions have the same effect. These mechanisms equally apply to humans. 'For human beings it is enough to hear a certain action being described for the mirror neurons to resonate' (Bauer 2006b: 24), or when asked to imagine it. The neurobiologist Joachim Bauer specifies:

This process of the mirror neurons happens simultaneously, involuntarily and without thinking. An internal neuronal copy is being produced, as if the observer was performing the very same action. He can decide whether he actually wants to perform this action, or not. He has, however, no control over his mirror neurons resonating with the perceived action and raising its program [required for its performance] into his imagination . . . By unconsciously experiencing what is observed as an inner simultaneous program, he understands, spontaneously and without thinking, what the other does.

(Bauer 2006b: 26–27)

Bauer concludes, 'Much that is ascribed to mysterious telepathic capacities can thus be explained' (2006b: 32). In an important paper, he focuses on 'resonance as modus of perception and source of information' (Bauer 2006a: 7). Contact between analyst and patient is here described as an emotional process of resonance rooted in the neurobiological processes mentioned earlier:

> With his metaphor of a receiver Sigmund Freud has actually recognised a process that has neurobiological correlates . . . The brain contains networks of nerve cells that have a characteristic double function. These are nerve cell-networks that get activated *both* when we ourselves feel, act or just think about acting, *as well as* when we witness corresponding events in *another* person present to whom we give our attention . . . Body language signals from another person are perceived by the five senses and then decoded in specialised regions [of the brain] – for example the emotional centres – to be subsequently passed on to the corresponding [nerve-]centres where they trigger resonant activity . . . Mirroring processes happen spontaneously and intuitively, i.e. pre-reflective. They are not dependent on whether the signals sent by the other are perceived consciously or not. This means that mirroring activity can also be induced by subliminally perceived signals . . . Thus as we engage with each other, we change . . . The empathic process described by Freud, which is necessary to perceive transference thus . . . is not only a process of *psychological* resonance, but also one with a neurobiological, i.e. *bodily* component.
> (Bauer 2006a: 8–9, 11–12, 15)

From this neurobiological perspective, parallel processing can be understood as follows: starting with the analytic situation, the patient's emotional state is being transferred to the analyst by the latter's mirror neurons resonating with those of the former – and vice versa, in the mutual psychodynamic process. When the analyst then brings this specific situation to supervision, the recalling of it consciously and intellectually also recalls the information picked up by the analyst's mirror neurons; these become reactivated. This, in turn, activates the corresponding mirror neurons of the supervisor so they resonate to the specific emotional vibrations – as Martin Stone (2006) described – like a tuning fork resonates to a sound it receives.

With the neurological mechanisms Bauer describes we are now finally able to scientifically ground these processes of mutual emotional relating in the biology of the body, just as Freud hoped in the early 1930s. In 1934 he said, 'So long as the organic functions remain inaccessible, analysis leaves much to be desired' (quoted in Wortis 1963: 111). Yet he had been confident that science would eventually confirm his findings. 'It is the biochemist's task to find out what this is, and we can expect that this organic part will be uncovered in the future' (Wortis 1963: 111).

In my understanding, the recent discoveries in quantum physics and neurobiology need to be seen as complementing each other. To me, neither alone can adequately explain the 'spooky action at a distance' – phenomena of intercommunication. Only if we consider a basic relatedness as given – as discovered by quantum physicists – in conjunction with the existence of mirror neurons as the perceiving organs in our bodies – as discovered by neurobiologists – can we get a scientifically satisfying explanation of the process as a whole.

At the same time, these discoveries, too, connect to yet another dimension: the spiritual. Corresponding to the recent findings in quantum physics, neurobiological research, situated also at the 'interface of the scientific-empirical and the symbolic' (B. Heuer 2007), enters the transitional space between science and religion, forming a bridge between the two. From this perspective, in relating with each other, as Andrew Samuels put it in 1989: 'the word and the image is being made flesh. Where that means that the Other (the patient's psyche) is becoming personal (in the analyst's body)' – and vice versa – 'I would conclude that . . . transference may be further understood by regarding it as a religious or mystical experience' (Samuels 1989: 165).

To briefly refer back to the animal behaviour mentioned earlier, before I come to the final section of my chapter, I would like to mention that, at the very end of his book on 'intuitive communication and the secret of mirror neurons', Bauer states, 'The intuitively attuned, instantly reactive behaviour of schools of fish and flocks of birds would be unthinkable without the mechanisms of the mirror neurons' (Bauer 2006b: 171–172).

Clinical examples

Here are some clinical examples of parallel processing: firstly, in analysis, secondly, in one-to-one supervision, thirdly, in group supervision, and fourthly in historical research outside the therapeutic context.

I shall start with an analytical situation in which a previous experience from the patient's life was unconsciously recreated. When Winnicott speaks of patients making him fail them according to their past history (Winnicott 1963: 258–259), I believe the transference dynamics involved too can be called a parallel process. Patrick Casement describes a patient, who

> had been traumatized as a child by her mother's repeated absences, in hospital with cancer, and (at the age of four) by her mother's death . . . One morning the therapist overslept. The patient came to . . . her . . . session, only to find herself shut out . . . Inevitably, [she] felt something

really serious must have happened. Perhaps there had been an accident. Perhaps her therapist was in hospital. Maybe she had died.

(Casement 1985: 89–90)

A whole traumatic situation from the past involving the client and a significant other was suddenly re-enacted in the present of the therapeutic relationship. Teleologically, it is assumed that this happens with the unconscious intention and hope of this time around finding a better solution to the problem originally posed.

This example of parallel process in one-to-one supervision comes from Jacob Arlow, who writes of supervising an analytic candidate who was treating a young, male homosexual patient.

> The patient was described as submissive . . . in relationship to perceived strong men . . . whose prowess he wished to grasp in the act of fellatio . . . In a dream the patient had . . . the patient saw himself lying on the couch, turning around to face his analyst and then offering him a cigarette. At this point in the supervisory session the therapist reached for a pack of cigarettes, took one himself . . . and asked, 'Do you want a cigarette?'
>
> (Arlow 1963: 580; Wolkenfeld 1990: 96)

Here, the unconscious content of the patient's dream is acted out in the session by the therapist with his supervisor. As noted, body awareness is an important and reliable tool in supervision. I am paying close attention to the emotional aspects of voice, facial expression, gestures and body posture of my supervisee, trusting that consciously as well as unconsciously the body of the supervisee can be understood as the carrier of the emotional expressions of the patient we are discussing. So I may say, in response to my supervisee directly quoting a key sentence their patient has said, 'Contentwise, the words were quite friendly, but the tone of voice and the facial expression with which "your patient" – i.e. you in this moment – spoke suggest an entirely different feeling.' My supervisee confirms that, at the time, he has observed the very same discrepancy in his patient, but had not yet been able to bring it into conscious awareness in the analytic work.

Another example follows.

My supervisee speaks of an injury her patient has suffered on his hand. In terms of a different right-hand/left-hand symbolism I ask, 'Which hand did he injure? The right one or the left one?' My supervisee does not remember. But I have seen her left arm and hand make a small movement as if frightened or startled. I share this observation with my supervisee and say, 'My guess is that it was the left hand.' In the next session, my supervisee confirms this (G. Heuer 2005).

From this way of using parallel process dynamics it is only a small step to apply them in role play in supervision where either analyst or supervisor can take the role of either analyst or patient. Here, we can both allow ourselves to be inspired by affects and words that result from empathising with either side of the analytic couple.

As supervisor, I might thus say to my supervisee, 'If I were you, now, in this analytic situation, what would you say to me if you were your patient?' or, 'So, I, as your patient, might express my distress about your taking a break by saying, "I don't want to be left alone in a dark place. – *And* I hate you! I hate you! I really, really *hate* you!" – What is your response to that?' Reacting to this will help my supervisee to get access to the patient's emotional state.

An example for parallel processing in group supervision comes from a 1985 article:

> On a supervision course for therapeutic community members, a . . . staff member presented a client with whom she had been having difficulties. After an initial enthusiasm and opening up, the client was either missing her sessions or hardly communicating. As soon as the worker began to resent her client, I found myself switching off. I just did not want to be bothered. However I kept going for about ten minutes asking seemingly appropriate questions until I could stand it no longer. I shared my feelings hesitantly – they just did not seem to fit and group members seemed very involved. In fact it turned out that the group was split roughly half and half. One half was very involved and the other half had totally switched off, too, but like me was trying to appear involved. The presenter was astonished to see how accurately her feelings for her client of both being very involved and identifying with her, and not wanting to know about her, were being mirrored.
>
> (Shohet and Wilmot 1985: 87)

In a group setting it is possible to make use of parallel process dynamics by one therapist briefly describing a situation from their practice, then choosing two other group members to be therapist and client in the described situation, and for them to continue dialoguing from within these roles. Uncannily, the actual therapist will find their own reactions and those of the client mirrored in the parallel process in ways that accurately go far beyond that communicated in the short briefing (see Chapter 9). These processes are used in psychodrama and, more recently, family constellation, a form of group therapy where one member chooses others to represent members of their family who then interact. Here too, hitherto unknown details of the emotional family constellation and history come to light in ways which make profound sense – for which the therapists do not have an explanation. 'From our experience, we only know *that* it works – *how* it works we don't know' (Anon., personal communication, 2005).

Elsewhere, using the American historian's Edmund Jacobitti's work, 'Composing useful pasts: history as contemporary politics' (Jacobitti 2000), I have described the close parallels between historical research and analysis (G. Heuer 2004: ch. 5 'The past is past – or: looking backwards to the future'). Robert Romanyshyn (2006) was the first to understand the relationship between a researcher and her or his subject in terms of a mutual transference process. In the next example, it is as if the emotional charge of an archetypal tension is, psychologically speaking, being passed on to a later generation. We can see the biographer and his subject as the analytic couple, with the critic in the role of the supervisor.

The situation I am thinking of involves the psychoanalyst Otto Gross. As an anarchist, he was engaged in a struggle of near archetypal dimensions with his father, a world authority in criminology and a pillar of the bourgeois establishment. When the Swiss psychiatrist and psychoanalyst Emanuel Hurwitz (1979) had published his comprehensive and balanced biographical study of Gross, the New York psychoanalyst Kurt Eissler started a correspondence with Hurwitz (Eissler and Hurwitz 1979–1980) because he felt Freud was unfairly criticised in the book. In the ensuing correspondence in a rather 'spooky' way the two polarised into positions which mirrored the father–son conflict Gross had lived – and sometimes also enacted with Freud and Jung. Reading these letters, it feels as if a powerful complex or archetype was reconstellated, reaching from the past of half a century ago.

Conclusion

Just like transference and countertransference aspects of analysis, parallel process is always present in supervision – and we need to turn our attention to it. As Martin Mayman (1976) puts it:

> I believe that parallel processing . . . is a universal phenomenon in treatment, and that the failure to observe its presence in supervision may signal only a natural resistance on the part of the supervisor and/or therapist against facing the full impact of those forces which *they* are asking the patient to face in himself [or herself].
>
> (Mayman 1976: 4–5)

For the first time in this chapter, as far as I can see, I have given the phenomena of parallel processes as they have been described in the literature since the 1950s, the startings of a scientific basis by referring to recent findings in quantum physics and neurobiology. I applied the Jungian understanding of the multidirectional psychodynamic processes in the transference relationship as a perspective from which to consider the complex interactions in supervision. In the process, I expanded the original Jungian diagram of mutual relating to take into account the even greater complexities of the supervisory relationship with its multidimensional links that arise when the dyadic relationship of the analysis changes into a triad or even one that may involve four persons whose conscious and unconscious interactional and parallel processes all need to be considered. I conclude with clinical vignettes from one-to-one and group supervision, linking the latter to current developments in group therapy, and with parallel process in historical research. I hope this has gone some way towards demystifying these uncanny and disturbing, 'spooky' actions at a distance. I would like to end as I started, by quoting Albert Einstein:

> A human being is part of the whole, called by us 'Universe'; a part limited in time and space. He experiences him self, his thoughts, and feelings as something separated from the rest – a kind of optical delusion of his consciousness. This delusion is a kind of prison for us ... Our task must be to free ourselves from this prison by widening our circle of compassion to embrace all living creatures, and the whole of nature in its beauty.
>
> (in Campbell 1995)

Notes

1 Albert Einstein, quoted in Felder (1999).
2 Emphases and spelling here and throughout, unless otherwise noted, are by the respective author.

References

Arlow, J. (1963) 'The supervisory situation.' *Journal of the American Psychoanalytic Association* 11: 576–594.
Attenborough, D. (2005a) *Life in the Undergrowth*, 2/6. Bristol: BBC 2 Television.
Attenborough, D. (2005b) *Life in the Undergrowth*, 5/6. Bristol BBC 2 Television.
Bauer, J. (2006a) 'Die Psychoanalyse aus der Sicht der Neurobiologie.' Freiburger Arbeitskreis Literatur und Psychoanalyse (unpublished manuscript).
—— (2006b) *Warum ich fühle, was du fühlst*. Munich: Heyne.
Boadella, D. (1999) 'The bonds of affect: the somatic psychology of Giordano Bruno.' *Energy and Character* 30: 121–125.
Campbell, E. (ed.) (1995) *A Dancing Star*. London: Thorsons.
Casement, P. (1985) *On Learning from the Patient*. London: Tavistock.
Chopra, D. (1993) *Ageless Body, Timeless Mind*. London: Rider.
Doehrmann, M. (1976) 'Parallel processes in supervision and psychotherapy.' *Bulletin of the Menninger Clinic* 40: 9–104.
Donne, J. (1945) *Complete Poetry*. London: Nonesuch Press.

Eissler, K. and Hurwitz, E. (1979–1980) *Correspondence*. May 1979 to April 1980. London: Otto Gross Archive.
Ekstein, R. and Wallerstein, R. (1958) *The Teaching and Learning of Psychotherapy*. New York: Basic Books.
Felder, G. (1999) *Spooky Action at a Distance: An Explanation of Bell's Theorem*. http://www.ncsu.edu/felder-public/kenny/papers/bell.html (accessed 2005).
Freud, S. (1912) 'Recommendations to physicians practising psycho-analysis.' *The Standard Edition of the Complete Psychological Works of Sigmund Freud*, vol. 12, pp. 109–120, trans. J. Strachey. London: Hogarth Press.
Gediman, H. and Wolkenfeld, F. (1980) 'The parallelism phenomenon in psychoanalysis and supervision.' *Psychoanalytic Quarterly* 34: 234–255.
Gross, O. (1907) *Das Freud'sche Ideogenitätsmoment und seine Bedeutung im manisch-depressiven Irresein Kraepelins*. Leipzig: Vogel.
—— (1919) 'Zur funktionellen Geistesbildung des Revolutionärs.' *Räte-Zeitung* 1, 52.
Gustin, J. (1958) 'Supervision in psychotherapy.' *Psychoanalysis and Psychoanalytic Review* 43: 63–72.
Hendrix, H. (1993) *Getting the Love You Want*. London: Simon & Schuster.
Heuer, B. (2007) 'The journey towards forgiveness: analytical, spiritual, and political aspects of healing.' XVIIIth IAAP Congress, Cape Town (unpublished manuscript).
—— (2008) 'Discourse of illness or discourse of health: towards a paradigm-shift in post-Jungian clinical theory.' In L. Huskinson (ed.) *Dreaming the Myth Onwards*. Hove: Routledge.
Heuer, G. (1996) Letter to the Editor. *International Journal of Psycho-Analysis* 77: 395–396.
—— (2004) 'The influence of the life and ideas of Otto Gross on the life and ideas of C. G. Jung.' PhD thesis. Colchester: University of Essex.
—— (2005) '"In my flesh I see God." Jungian body psychotherapy.' In N. Totton (ed.) *New Dimensions in Body Psychotherapy*. Maidenhead: Open University Press.
Hurwitz, E. (1979) *Otto Gross: Paradies-Sucher zwischen Freud und Jung*. Zurich: Suhrkamp.
Jacobitti, E. (2000) 'The role of the past in contemporary political life.' In E. Jacobitti (ed.) *Composing Useful Pasts*. New York: State University of New York Press.
Jung, C. G. (1930–1934) *Visions: Notes of the Seminar Given in 1930–1934*. Princeton, NJ: Princeton University Press.
—— (1953–1973) *Collected Works*, ed. Sir H. Read, M. Fordham, G. Adler and W. McGuire, 20 vols. London: Routledge & Kegan Paul.
McTaggart, L. (2001) *The Field*. London: HarperCollins.
Mayman, M. (1976) Foreword. *Bulletin of the Menninger Clinic* 40: 3–8.
Miller, P. (2007) 'Swarm theory.' *National Geographic Magazine* July: 126–147.
Reich, W. (1999) *American Odyssey*. New York: Farrar, Straus, Giroux.
Romanyshyn, R. (2006) 'The wounded researcher.' *Harvest* 52: 38–49.
Sachs, D. and Shapiro, S. (1976) 'On parallel processes in therapy and training.' *Psychoanalytic Quarterly* 45: 394–415.
Samuels, A. (1989) *The Plural Psyche*. New York: Routledge.

Searles, H. (1986) 'The informational value of the supervisor's emotional experiences.' In *Collected Papers*. London: Maresfield.

Shohet, R. and Wilmot, J. (1985) 'Paralleling in the supervision process.' *Self and Society* 13: 86–91.

Sontag, S. (1989) *AIDS and its Metaphors*. New York: Farrar, Straus, Giroux.

Stone, M. (2006) 'The analyst's body as tuning fork.' *Journal of Analytical Psychology* 51: 109–124.

Turner, J. (2004) *Wolves and Caribous*. Bristol: BBC 2 Television.

Weiner, J., Mizen, R. and Duckham, J. (eds) (2003) *Supervising and Being Supervised*. London: Palgrave Macmillan.

Winnicott, D. W. (1963) 'Dependence in infant-care.' In D. W. Winnicott, *The Maturational Processes and the Facilitating Environment*. London: Hogarth.

Wolkenfeld, F. (1990) 'The parallel process phenomenon revisited.' In R. Lane (ed.) *Psychoanalytic Approaches to Supervision*. New York: Brunner/Mazel.

Wortis, J. (1963) *Fragments of an Analysis with Freud*. New York: Charter.

Chapter 12

Afterword

Keven Hall

I write this chapter as an organiser of, and participant in, the Association of Jungian Analyst's course for potential supervisors, offering a dual perspective, to help consolidate what you, as reader, may gain from the book. The course was designed for supervisors from a range of settings, and for those wishing to be training supervisors within their organisations, this emphasis being a distinctive feature. As context, both Jung and post-Jungians are comfortable with the rational and the concrete, and also with a symbolic, non-linear approach to reality, trying to do justice to the multiplicity of variables, apparent and hidden, which make up the reality called 'universe', even 'multiverse'.

In the supervisory arena, triads, quaternities, parallel processes, symbolic equations and transference are taken seriously as descriptions of reality both in the consulting room and when supervisor and supervisee meet. There is a distinctive Jungian project when these perspectives are linked to the symbolic (giving depth to part and whole objects) using personal and collective unconscious as contexts for interpreting into paradigms of personal development, the worlds of myth and cultural story. Out of this a socio-political engagement with a moving and changing culture is incorporated, along with sensitivity to group process.

I had been working for four years in private practice when I joined the course. My thoughts about working as a supervisor were in an early form. Throughout the course I was struck by how much the science and art of analytical psychology is one of conjuration: apparently from nowhere, something unclear or seemingly absent, yet enormously important, becomes evident. There is the concrete, but also the other: as in a theatre, the magician, the hat, the rabbit and their context, all taken together expressing a quaternity. Like Samuels et al. (1986) and Hillman (1989: 71–91), I understand Jung's project less as the psyche proceeding 'scientifically' by hypothesis and model, more as imagistic, by myth and metaphor.

One day I read a poem 'Lone gentleman' by Pablo Neruda (1970: 49). It struck me as profound, but it was most complex, and I could hardly hold it in mind. Later, without reference to it again and unable to remember much of it, I experienced it as a non-verbal 'music', a sense though not like a sensation. But it was no less real for all that. And my experience of the words when I went back to them was accordingly enhanced. This is similar to my experience in consulting rooms as patient, as analyst and as supervisor. The craft of psychoanalytical supervision is about taking seriously strange yet meaningful phenomena, the 'spooky actions' of Gottfried Heuer's explication of Einstein (Chapter 11), alongside the relatively straightforward logic of reasoning around, for example, an Oedipal complex or an episode of infantilisation.

For me, supervision is a modern craft explicating existential essentials in the objective psyche from a Jungian setting and methodology, related to culture and politics. It is a commitment to wholeness, embodied in attending to fullest possible reality. I'll expand on this further with reference to the scope of supervision, the finding of coherence in the therapeutic matrix, and reconciliation as a primary goal for supervisory work.

But first in this context I like how Carola Mathers (Chapter 7) picks up on Christopher Hauke's description of not only the commonalities between Jungian psychology and the psychoanalytic psychotherapies, but also where they differ. Both seek change through an orientation to unconsciousness (note how the definite article when present gives a sense of the abstract being made concrete). Jungian psychology, however, sets a wider orbit for 'unknown'. This is Jung's contribution of the collective unconscious, which is itself not just an interesting theoretical concept, but also points to what differentiates his from other styles of depth psychology: a radical willingness to wait on the unconscious, to lay to one side the 'known' for the time being (not because the known is of less value, but because it is of different value); not to compromise, trusting the more qualitatively different gold of a living symbol can be found in the prima materia, as the leaven in the lump. This is an arduous craft, because the known is so alluring, so seductive. But the experience of a revelation through a symbol being born into life is worth waiting for. The import of this is that it is not what the rational ego thinks the Self should manifest that is significant but, as best this can be judged, 'what the Self wants'. This is a distinction which can be lost if the ego is blind to its true nature, that is, not in a proper relation to the Self.

Hauke (2000), in the same quote, seeking a parallel to Jungian psychology, cites Thomas Merton's view of Chuang Tzu, the ancient Chinese seer:

> he is not concerned with words and formulas about reality, but with the direct existential grasp of reality itself. Such a grasp . . . does not lend itself to . . . analysis. It can be presented in a parable, a fable, or a funny story.
>
> (Hauke 2000: 211)

In other words, through live symbols. This suggests Jungians and post-Jungians might not want to call themselves 'analysts' at all, as in everyday use the word points in the wrong direction: to taking apart rather than putting together.

The scope of supervision

Following assessment, during which (it is hoped) psychotic or neurotic states will be identified, the work begins. Then, by use of clear thinking and intuition, aided by supervision, complexes may become conscious. Using a certain free-floating quality of focus the minds of supervisor and supervisee attend to the patient's experiences and make critical sense of them for the patient's benefit, and hopefully for their own development. For example, a supervisee brings experiences and dreams of violence from a male patient. Thinking and playing imagistically brings the case to life, after which the supervisee can enable the patient to bring to consciousness connections between generalised feelings of being hated as a child, and his father. The son idealised his father in the face of the latter's resentment at his son being born. My supervisee and I were moved by his distress, resonating with our own experiences, enabling changes to take place in us.

Essentials of the craft of supervision include (at least) the following: even before the supervisee arrives, attention to the room and what the setting re-presents, presences within it, and willingness to discriminate truth from misconception. Re-presentation, attention and discrimination act as alchemical containers, permitting transmutations between inter- and intra-subjective states, transferences and countertransferences, inner and outer experiences, levels and nature of libido, authority and subservience, projections and identifications, logical and fantasy thinking, archetypes and inner guiding, and parallel processes.

At this point two risks exist: drowning in complexity on the one hand, and oversimplification on the other. But polarities can be held simply together in dynamic and positive relation to one another. Christopher Perry (2003), a Jungian analyst, uses the images of acoustic and luminous prisms, taken from Jung (CW8, para. 414):

> the material for supervision may . . . be brought as undifferentiated white noise or light which is then projected through the supervisory relationship, where 'noise' is broken down into its component sounds and 'light' into the colours of the rainbow.
>
> (Perry 2003: 191)

Using symbol and metaphor, structure and content are found and can be understood without losing depth. John Fowles, in his novel *The Magus* (1966), using the image of the labyrinth, has the lead character Nicholas

Urfe help make the walls of his own maze. This graphically illustrates how we both form ourselves and are formed. In the alchemical vessel of supervision we do not as much experience ourselves as in chaos as only semi-formed, still a kind of hell.

From the individual human experience which seems amorphous or cluttered, enough clarity emerges so the patient can be helped, be given something to hold onto, which can later lead to change; or learn to live more bearably (though not always) with their particular problem. Jung coined the word 'individuation' to name this movement toward becoming in-dividual (CW9i para. 490), which is less fragmented, more distinct, and pointed to the potential and actual impact in social, cultural, political and religious domains (Chapter 5).

Begum Maitra (Chapter 10) addresses the topic of culture in supervision. At the risk of compounding complexity with more complexity, she urges us to constantly question basic assumptions and seek a stance of informed neutrality arising from taking difference seriously. This is essential in any consulting room, and in any supervision, even though difference can lead to a desire to enviously attack. But desire on the part of the therapist for a particular outcome in the patient's life is nearly always experienced as invasive. This can be prevented by keeping a balance between affective thinking and reasonable feeling. Regardless of how we conceptualise the workings of typology, where these information gathering and processing operations are in relative balance, it is possible to let go of an investment in outcome so the patient or supervisee is freed to find their own truth.

Another chapter encouraging greater flexibility of thinking is Fiona Palmer Barnes' on ethics (Chapter 3). She draws attention to the use by the British Psychological Society and the British Association of Counsellors and Psychotherapists of 'ethical framework' as opposed to 'codes of practice'. It is more demanding to reflect on principles than just to (slavishly) adopt a regulation, but ultimately it is more faithful to reality.

Practice of supervision: the craft of finding coherence in the labyrinth

The setting

Before the supervisee arrives, the supervisor settles themselves, and holds the past history of their relationship in mind, while being aware of being immersed in their own life experience. A ritual for centring, with attention to states of mind and body, is important, both for laying personal material aside (while remaining sensitive to potential projection in mental interpretation), and for sensing anything to do with the arriving supervisee. This matters as it is the beginning in this particular context for orienting into the unknown, being open to the unconscious, to the living symbol which has the potential to be transformative. I focus on a meditating figure I have in my consulting room to help me do this. As in any session with a patient, attention to the first five minutes of supervision can be most informative (see Chapter 7, p. 100). We can be sensitive to how the supervisee is on arrival, and pick up on themes connecting content and style. Sometimes it is possible to settle straight into the work, at other times they need to talk about their practice, or an event in their personal life. Here, there needs to be sensitivity to the personal and professional interface, of particular significance due to potential overlap between analysis and supervision. There is a continuing debate about this (Knight 2003: 41; Stokes, Chapter 2 in this book), especially when the supervisee is not in personal therapy.

How do we respond when they bring a dream about a patient, or when there is a personal reaction while discussing an erotic transference? The consensus is, this being supervision, only material which explicates the pathology of the patient has a place. Maintaining this boundary requires a suitably professional demeanour. Then transference material different from the personal can be picked up and discussed.

This is an example of a necessary boundary. Others would be arriving and leaving on time, paying the bill, no physical violence, respect for the environment and complete confidentiality. By being sensitive to all such appropriate boundaries, the supervisor can demonstrate good practice.

One of the instructive discussions on the course was around a participant's attempt to meet up with a supervisee at a restaurant to celebrate the completion of their work. Twenty minutes after the agreed time to meet he wasn't there. It turned out he was in a restaurant a few doors along. In talking about this, the supervisor could see how the ending hadn't been attended to sufficiently. The hiccup with this meeting could have symbolised this. Martin Stone (Chapter 5) reminds us though that while maintaining personal and professional boundaries, the whole person of patient, supervisor and supervisee needs to be held in mind, lest there be too much emphasis on the technicalities of process.

Re-presentation and attention

Supervision can be seen as an alchemical container, freeing the gold from the *prima materia*, the confusion there at the beginning. The supervisee 'embodies', that is 'en-psyches', the essence of the analysis, out of which communication with the supervisor can occur within the boundaried context.

James Bamber (Chapter 9) writes of 'the essence of supervision, a container for the duo of trainee and patient, a vessel within a vessel, functioning like the chrysalis of an insect which protects psychological development as it is taking place'. With reference to supervision in groups, he describes how this experience and its setting in an organisation 'stretches the *temenos*', bringing into play far more factors than exist in one-to-one supervision in private practice. Alchemical metaphor highlights this complexity of the craft. Richard Wainwright (Chapter 8) takes care to spell out what happens around evocation and witness in this regard. There was a parallel in the course. At the outset, our temptation to assume what was being said was 'true', evident by virtue of the narrative easily being taken for granted. This threw into sharp relief the question of what is being communicated in a supervisory session. For the supervisor receives a re-presentation of something the therapist may have experienced with their patient. An initial filter is already in place. The supervisee brings their version of the narrative, more or less faithful to the precipitating incident. As this is conveyed to the supervisor, another filter operates in its reception, attending and witnessing what is given. By maintaining attention here, an intuitive capacity for registering the key significances in the process can more easily occur (Dale Mathers, Chapter 4). The danger of truth or narrative becoming too relativised is more readily avoided with the right attitude, which in the world of depth psychology presupposes a capacity to recognise. Work with infantilisation and transcendent defences, guilty over-attachment to theory, calls for reverence in the face of complexity from all participants. The informed neutrality I spoke of earlier can be more easily attained, if dogma is recognised, then coherence can appear in the process. This lets interpretative ability develop as a sharply honed, well-timed, sparingly used instrument which make the difference in bringing about change.

When to interpret and when not is a crucial boundary issue picked up by Jean Stokes (Chapter 2) as she addresses the question 'When is a management issue just a management issue?' Here the supervisee has to think about their experience with their supervisor in terms of authority. If the supervisor is too clear in asserting what they think is going on, the supervisee can be overwhelmed. If the process is too obtuse, he loses his bearings. The first, an excess of authority, risks rebellion or subservience; the second, anger and/or panic. Keeping the vessel 'well closed' while achieving one's objective becomes an important feedback indicator of congruence, pointing to an operation of the Self in creating a continuous personal narrative (Covington 1995). Jack Bierschenk (Chapter 6), writes about a training supervision, where students are bathed in theories which can lead to categorisation, from which '-isms' can arise. In these, there is a loss of individuality. He sums up his chapter with: 'wholesome supervision arises from working together rather than from a position of superiority'.

Individuation encompasses a healthy accountability to the collective as against the more narcissistic experience of individualism so evident in much twentieth- and twenty-first-century western culture. The practice of supervision, at its best, is an endeavour of grounded wholesomeness, a seeking to modestly add to the pool of constructive and meaningful energy in the universe.

Discrimination

A solid basis for sorting out 'truth' from 'misconception' is critical in supervision. I am thinking about a supervisee who is unconsciously tetchy with me while complaining of her patient being angry with her, but without being conscious that her anger is displaced. The problem is incarnated but not mentalised. Or when a fantasy figure is not related to a parental figure or other important figure from the patient's life, so an active imagination is split from the transference (Cambray 2006). I use inverted commas around 'truth' and 'misconception' as, in a synthetic enterprise, it is often difficulty to get agreement. Where a concrete matter and directed thinking are concerned there is less of a problem, as sensible use of rationality can be self-authenticating. But with more complex matters a range of variables needs to be used. These might include cross-referencing to preclude contradictions, faithfulness to context, recognising parallel process and a shared sense of an intuitive experience of congruence.

There is debate about the theoretical basis for Jungian supervision. The key areas for me are clear: in the head (meaning conscious psychically), we pick up sense data and intuitions; we use a feeling function to think about this relationally; we stand back and reflect on it in a wider frame, cross-referencing to the body of knowledge and experience held in our field. Where is there projection or identification serving as a compensation? What are the developmental issues? Is this grandiose acting out? Are there a social, political, religious or cultural dimension to be picked up on? What evidence is there of dissociation? What about a transference interpretation? In which way am I picking up countertransference? Where is the split-off 'shadow'? What status do I give to the symbolic value of this part-object? Is there anything archetypal? Is active imagination appropriate here? When enough of this comes together, I experience a congruence evolving out of the safeguards of the triangular relationship (and the quaternity), which can be cross-referenced to a supervisor of supervision, as appropriate.

Reconciliation

I have been describing Jung's understanding of the work of the transcendent function (CW6 para. 828). It may be spirit, or Self, but it is grounded in human operations. When Trickster qualities in the psyche are factored in, a complex, sensitive, 'cunning as serpents and innocent as doves' mentality is required, from which a kind of self-effacing power and authority can distil, self-authenticating the work. Not 'transformation' in a magical or hubristic sense, but a satisfying crafty earthiness which still takes spirit seriously, feels safe and can be respected by others. The struggles in our psyche parallel those in the outer world: the search for kaleidoscopic and synchronistic cohesion of psychic fragments; the courage to let as many symbolically charged healthy part-objects as possible be in good relation to each other as possible, while hoping that what should not get together does not. This is the distillation of the gold of meaning from the *prima materia* in the supervisory vessel. The supervisor helps the therapist facilitate this process, and each is changed. Outer and inner parallel one another.

Finale

My travels to my consulting room at London Bridge often take me to Baker Street, the legendary home of Sherlock Holmes. This 'story' reflects something of what I have been writing about:

> Watson and Holmes went on a camping trip. In the middle of the night Holmes awoke and nudged his faithful friend.
> 'Watson, look up toward the sky and tell me what you see.'
> Watson replied: 'I see millions and millions of stars.'
> 'What does that tell you Watson?'
> 'Well, astronomically, it tells me that there are millions of galaxies and potentially billions of planets. Horologically, I deduce that the time is approximately a quarter past three. Meteorologically, I suspect that we will have a beautiful day tomorrow. Why, what does it tell you?'
> Holmes was silent for a moment, then spoke: 'Watson, someone has stolen our tent.'

References

Cambray, J. (2006) 'Response to Wendy Swan's account of Tina Keller's analyses.' *Journal of Analytical Psychology* 51(4): 521.

Covington, C. (1995) 'No story, no analysis? The role of narrative in Interpretation.' *Journal of Analytical Psychology* 40(3): 405–419.

Fowles, J. (1966) *The Magus*. London: Jonathan Cape.

Hauke, C. (2000) *Jung and the Postmodern*. London: Routledge.

Hillman, J. (1989) 'Therapy: fictions and epiphanies.' In J. Hillman, *A Blue Fire: Selected Writings*. New York: Harper & Row.

Jung, C. G. (1953–1973) *Collected Works*, ed. Sir H. Read, M. Fordham, G. Adler and W. McGuire, 20 vols. London: Routledge & Kegan Paul.

Knight, J. (2003) 'Reflections on the therapist–supervisor relationship.' In J. Wiener, R. Mizen and J. Duckham (eds) *Supervising and Being Supervised*. London: Palgrave Macmillan.

Neruda, P. (1970) 'Lone gentleman.' In P. Neruda, *Selected Poems*. London: Penguin.

Perry, C. (2003) 'Into the labyrinth: a developing approach to supervision.' In J. Wiener, R. Mizen and J. Duckham (eds) *Supervising and Being Supervised*. London: Palgrave Macmillan.

Samuels, A., Shorter, B. and Plaut, A. (1986) *A Critical Dictionary of Jungian Analysis*. London: Routledge & Kegan Paul.

Index

Page numbers in **bold** indicate entire chapters devoted to a subject.

Abramovitch, H. and Kirmayer, L. J. 155
absence 28; intrusive 100; maternal absence in directed and dream thinking 111; parallel processing of maternal 176–7
accountability 133, 188
active imagination 99
Adler, Gerhard 17
aesthetics: of meaning 58–9; of supervision 59; of therapy 60
affective relating 49
agencies: accountability and autonomy 133; confidentiality 34, 44; contracts and 34; setting and disclosure 26–7; and the supervisee's background 25; supervision 22–3, 24
agency 49, 60
aggression: aggressive countertransferences 55; hostile impulses 55; masculine (Animus) 55
alchemy: alchemical metaphor of supervision 5–6; Axiom of Maria Prophetissa 6, 18; *prima materia* 6, 14, 184, 187, 190; *vas bene clausum/vas Hermetis* 5–6, 14, 20, 22, 83, 102–4, 112
amplification, clinical 27–8, 50, 83, 86
analytic conversations 114–29
analytic relationship 84, 91, 167; dreaming of interplay of supervisory relationship with 126; parallel processing with supervisory relationship *see* parallel processes; *see also* therapeutic relationship

analytic setting 16, 89–90, 100; consulting rooms 25, 89–90, 100, 185; 'holding environment' 117; secretaries 100, 101; waiting rooms 89, 100, 101
analytic space 122, 126, 128; *see also* analytic setting; safe space; supervisory space
ancestors: the carrying over of the past 90–2
Anima 14, 55
Animus 14, 55
anti-terrorism legislation 38, 42
Antze, P. and Lambek, M. 154
anxiety 6, 25, 26; about the unpredictable and alien 149; of being discovered as different 152; feeling cut off through 76; of getting things right 113, 116; patients' 38–9; of trainees in organisational settings 136, 139–40; transference 116
appraisal: assessment *see* assessment; reciprocal 121
archetypes 4–5, 18; archetypal patterns 50, 51, 56, 61; collective archetypal issues and supervision 35–6; the difficult patient and 51; the mentor 17; as nodal points of psychic energy 85; the shadow *see* (the) shadow; the Trickster *see* Trickster archetype/ qualities
Arlow, Jacob 177
assessment: evaluation of supervision 78; supervision and 36–7, 81
Association of Jungian Analysts: course for potential supervisors 183, 187, 188
Astor, James 136

attachment: guilty attachments to theory 47, 56, 188; starting sessions and the handling of 100; theory 117
Attenborough, David 171
attention 18, 19, 185, 188; to boundaries 103; focusing of 71; gained through speaking from experience 125; to the Gap 99; to non-verbal communication 177; setting and 22, 185; to what does and does not happen 1; witnessing and 120
authenticity 20–1; self-authentication 189
authority: agencies and 44; conversation with an 'authority' 115; fear of 90; illusion of parental authority in supervision 54; interpretation and 188; and the supervisory setting 185; transference and 91, 127; unquestionable 125
autonomy 44; accountability and 133
awareness 48, 69; body 177; envy as awareness of two-ness 57; *see also* consciousness

Bateman, Anthony and Fonagy, Peter 88
Bauer, Joachim 174–5
Beebe, John 73, 88
'beginner's mind' 2, 6, 7, 62
Bell, Joseph 1
best practice 39; *see also* good practice
Bion, Wilfred 4, 5, 58, 99, 120; Dependent Groups 143–4; group dynamics 141; psychodynamics 136
Boadella, D. 172
body: awareness 177; dissociation from the body 105; embodied character of emotional experience 151–2; embodied selves 152–5; evocation and the body 114, 117; objectifying of the body 128–9; representation and the body 117, 128–9; symbols provided by the body 111
Bollas, Christopher 43
boredom 119, 124, 125
boundaries in supervision 7, **13–29**, 103; analysis and supervision 18, 21, 187; of confidentiality *see* confidentiality; containment; with difficult patients *see* difficult patients; disclosure and 26–9; ego-activity and 14, 18–20; ethical *see* ethics in supervision; framing the task of supervision 16–18; function of the frame 21–5; interpretation and 18, 23, 24, 28, 188; management issues and 25; merger and 14, 19; mutuality and 14, 25, 27, 29; personal boundaries and the learning experience in supervision 20–1; separateness and 14, 16, 19, 29; social acquaintance and 37, 40–1; triangles and fours 25–6 *see also* four/the fourth
Briggs, J. 149
British Association for Counselling and Psychotherapy 43, 45
British Psychological Society 45
Bruch, Hilde 100
Bruno, Giordano 172
Burr, V. 51

Capra, F. 128
Casement, Patrick 107–8, 176–7
categorisation 94, 188
cats 101
centring 186–7
character types 71–3, 74–5; transference and 88
Children Acts 38, 39, 42
Chodorow, N. 149–50
Chomsky, Noam 52
Chopra, Deepak 173
Christensen, P. et al. 151
Chuang Tzu 184
clinical amplification 27–8, 50, 83, 86
clinical responsibility 15, 33–4, 139
coherence 49, 60; in the therapeutic matrix 186–90
collective memory 154
collective non-confrontation 142
collective unconscious 53, 62, 88, 98, 183, 184
Colman, Warren 99
Coltart, Nina 109, 157
communication: indirect/non-verbal *see* non-verbal communication; language *see* language; parallel process 168–9
community networks 160
compensation 106–7
complexes 56

complexity: of countertransference 94, 121; cultural diversity and 160; of ethical rules 44–5; in parallel processes 167, 169; surrendering to 120; of therapeutic relationships 35–7; of transference 121, 169
Conan Doyle, Sir Arthur 1
confidentiality: agencies and 34, 44; and the Data Protection Act 43; ethics and 31–2, 34, 39, 43–4; good practice 42; *see also* containment
congruence 188, 189
coniunctio 29; *mysterium coniunctionis* 173; *oppositorum* 98, 105
consciousness: differentiation of ego-consciousness from the unconscious 19, 20, 70–1; parallel processing interplay with the unconscious 166–70 *see also* parallel processes; as three- and fourfold 47; *see also* awareness
consent 44
consultation 26, 160; supervision and 133 *see also* supervision
consulting rooms 25, 89–90, 100, 185
containment 18, 23, 39, 43, 136, 140; *see also* confidentiality
contextuality 51–2
continuity of self 49, 60, 188
continuous professional development (CPD) 138; *see also* professional development
contracts: of the supervisee and organisation 137; supervisory 13, 32–4, 139
control analysis 17, 24
conversation 114–15; with an authority 115
counter-projections 24; *see also* countertransference
counter-resistance 22
countertransference: addressing with trainee supervisees 70–3, 75–8; and the boundaries between supervision and analysis 18, 27–8; defences 50; definitions and nature of 2, 7, 84–5; and the emergence of supervision 17; engagement in training/professional development 86–94; erotic 110; hostile 54–5; Jung on the bond of 87, 88; *Nachträglichkeit* and 90–2; neurotic 25, 70, 74, 87; parallel processes *see* parallel processes; and relationships within therapeutic organisations 35(Fig.), 36; safe space and 6; supervisee difficulties with 39; in the supervisory space 119, 121–2; symbols and 105; syntonic 25, 87; vulnerability and 16
creation myths 108
Critical Dictionary of Analytical Psychology 84
crowding, in group supervision 142–3
Csordas, T. J. 118
Cultural Psychology Workshop 159
culture: and the academic context of western psychoanalysis 155–7; anxiety and 149; consultation and community networks 160; the crafting of the cultural mind 149–50; cultural concepts of the self 157–8; cultural enactments as embodied rhetoric 154; cultural psychology 159; cultural shadow projections 56; culturally astute supervision **146–62**; empathy and cultural difference 146–7; Eurocentrism 156; exposure to multicultural societies 148–9; group culture 141; 'matching' patient, therapist, supervisor and world-view 159–60; multicultural groups and supervision 158–9; non-verbal communication and 150–2; organisational 138
Cunningham, A. and Tickner, D. 155
Cwik, August 17

Data Protection Act (1998) 42, 43, 44
death fantasies 105
defences: guilt as a defence 56; of infantilisation 50; lack of transference as a defence 88; of mandalisation 50, 55; of notes 116; against strong feelings 76–7
denial 48, 61
Dependent Groups 143–4
Derrida, Jacques 52
despair 6, 119, 127, 146
dialectic process 67–8, 69, 82; in the supervisory triangle 69–79
differentiation 14, 69; of ego-consciousness from the unconscious 19, 20, 70–1; supervision and 19

difficult patients **47–62**; aesthetic challenge of 58–9; for the collective 57–8; for family and friends 59–60; for internal objects and archetypal patterns 61; the meaning of 'difficult' 48–51; specialness and 51; spiritual values and 62; for the supervisor 53–4; for themselves 60–1; for the therapist 54–7
disclosure: mutuality and 26–7; personal 28–9; professional 27–8
discrimination 185, 189
dissociation 61, 105, 189
Doehrmann, M. J. 166
dogs 101
Doyle, Sir Arthur Conan 1
dream thinking 110–11; 'dreaming up' the patient 125–6
dreams: acting-out of unconscious content in parallel processes 177; symbols and 99, 104–9; transformation and 104–9
Dreifuss, Gustav 78–9
Durkheim, Emile 48

ego: auxiliary 103; boundaries and ego-activity 14, 18–20; ego-identity 20–1; ego-loss 20; the Ego–Self axis 19, 20–1, 184; functions 20; Jung and the Ego 18–20; transformation 6
Einstein, Albert 180
Eissler, Kurt 179
Eliot, T. S. 120; *Prufrock* 122, 123
embodiment: collective memory and 154; embodied selves 152–5; of emotional experience 151–2
emotions: of anxiety *see* anxiety; embodied character of emotional experience 151–2; feelings and 71 *see also* feeling
empathy: affective relating and 49; cultural difference and 146–7; empathic practice 14
emptiness 94, 119, 125
enantiodromia (movement between opposites) 54
environment *see* analytic setting
envy 55, 57
ethics in supervision **31–45**; assessment and 36; codes of practice and the law 42–4; the complexity of therapeutic relationships 35–7; confidentiality *see* confidentiality; the contract and relationships 32–4; difficulties between supervisor and supervisee 40–1; finance 40; Jung on 31, 44–5; in organisational settings 137; social relationships and 37, 40–1; 'soul-based ethics' (Sells) 45; supervisee difficulties 39–40; the supervisee's work and 38–9
ethnicity 146–7, 149–55; *see also* culture
Eurocentrism 156
evocation 114–15, 119; evocative speech 121; representation and 116–18; transference/countertransference and 121–2; transformation through emotional evocation 122–5
extraverted function 72, 73, 74–5
extraverts 71

facilitation: in an organisation 136; in supervision 88, 92–3, 136; of the symbolic 108
Fairburn, Ronald 56
family constellation 178–9
family therapy 59
fantasies: fantasy thinking 110–11; of regressive symbols 105; supervisory process as 'shared fantasy' 125–6, 133–4, 141; symbols and 99, 105
feeling: countertransference feelings 25, 71, 76–7; defences against strong feelings 76–7; emotion and 71; envious 57; the feeling type 72; mindful awareness and 48; naming of feelings 48, 50; as one of Jung's 'functions' 7, 71; projected 78; of resentment 90–1; same-feeling (syntonic) countertransference 25; and the supervisory process 2, 4; training and 21; valuing feelings 77–8
fees 22, 100–1, 137
Felder, Gary 172
'Fireside Theatre' 58–9
Fordham, Michael 17, 82
Foulkes, S. H. 141
four/the fourth: Jungian significance of 7, 18; the three and the four 6–7, 18, 25–6, 168–9
Fowles, John: *The Magus* 185–6

frames: framing the task of supervision 16–18; function in supervision 21–5; reframing 59; transference and 89–90; *see also* boundaries in supervision
Franz, Marie-Louise von 5
freedom: analytic 55; to inter-imagine 118; of mind/thought 126; to play 54
Freud, Sigmund 3, 17, 117, 155, 175–6; humour 59; influence of Gross 166; Jung and 52, 143; *Nachträglichkeit* 90–1; signs and symbols 52; transference 83; use of the unconscious as a receiver 173–4, 175
Fuller, Richard Buckminster 47, 53
functions, mental *see* mental functions
fundamentalism 57, 58

Galipeau, Steven 41
'the gap' 99–101
Garvey, Pip 42, 43
Gediman, H. and Wolkenfeld, F. 170
Gee, Hugh 14
gifts 101–2
Gill, Merton M. 89
good practice 39–40, 42, 104, 140, 187
Gordon, Rosemary 2
Gray-Wheelwright Test 73
Gross, Otto 164, 166, 179
group culture 141
group mentality 141, 142
group supervision 140–4; multicultural 158–9; parallel processes in 178–9
group systems 58
Guderian, Claudia 89–90
guilt 77, 92; as a defence 56; guilty attachments to theory 47, 56, 188
Gustin, John 166

Haddon, Mark 1–2
Hauke, Christopher 98, 109–10, 184
healers 157–8
health insurance 34, 40
Hegel, G. W. F. 67
hegemony: of a colonial mind-set 156; hegemonic discourse 154
Heidegger, Martin 115
Heimann, Paula 84
Hermes 7, 13, 14–15, 22

hermetic vessel (*temenos*/*vas bene clausum*) 5–6, 14, 20, 22, 83, 102–4, 112; *see also* temenos
Hesse, H. 54
Heuer, Birgit 172
Highgate Counselling Centre 134
Hillman, J. 94, 183
Hopkins, Linda 161
Hughes, L. and Pengelly, P. 134, 135
Human Rights Act (1998) 42, 44
humour 59
Hurwitz, Emanuel 179
Husserl, Edmund 120

identification 185, 189; over-identification 79, 160; projective 48, 54, 61
images: archetypal 85 *see also* archetypes; energising 85; obsession with 50, 55; supervision and 3; and 'the gap' 99
imaginal capacity/symbolic attitude 98–9, 101
immigration/immigrants 151–5, 159–60
incest fantasies 105
individualism 157
individuality: of the Ego 19; feigning of 143; loss of 94, 188
individuation 47–8, **67–79**, 186, 188; differentiation *see* differentiation; Jung and 47–8, 67, 68, 186; separation and 57; as the therapeutic goal 60, 68–9
infantilisation: as a defence 50; in institutionalised training 81
inferior functions 69, 72, 73, 75, 111, 121
informed consent 44
informed neutrality 160, 161–2, 186, 188
Institute for Group Analysis 140
insurance: medical/health 34, 40; personal indemnity 33
internal objects 50, 51, 61
interpersonal psychoanalysis 164
interpretation, as a boundary issue 18, 23, 24, 28, 188
interpreters 151
introverted function 72, 73, 74–5
introverts 71
intuition 48–9, 50, 56–7, 188; the intuitive type 72; as one of Jung's 'functions' 7, 71; supervisory stories as intuitions 4; symbols and 52–3

irrationality: awakefulness to 94; cultural prohibitions and the resort to 151; formative holding and redemption from 88; irrational functions 71, 72; transcendent function as bridge between rationality and 68
irritation 74, 90, 122, 124

Jacobitti, Edmund 179
Jacobs, D. et al. 16, 24–5
Janus 14
jazz metaphor of therapy 61
Jennings, L. et al. 148
Jensen, P. 148
Jung, Carl Gustav 4, 120, 155; Archetypes 4–5; case discussion 17; complex 56; countertransference and the analytic bond 87, 88; dialectic process 69, 82; dreams 105–7, 111; the Ego 18–20; Ego functions 20; enantiodromia 54; on ethics in therapy 31, 44–5; Freud and 52, 143; function and growth process of supervision 19; 'Gate' diagram 164, 166–7; the Hermetic vessel 102; individuation 47–8, 67, 68, 186; influence of Gross 166; interconnectedness 173; Jungian psychology and the psychoanalytic psychotherapies 184; *Memories, Dreams, Reflections* 17, 45; mental functions 7, 71; mutuality 117, 167; and the need of supervision 17; the number four 7, 18; the number three 18; persona 143; personal analysis in analytic training 16; *prima materia* 14; 'Principles of practical psychotherapy' 82; the psyche 82–3; 'Psychology of the transference' 82, 84, 166; relational/parallel processing 166–70; responsibility in writing psychology 118; the shadow 35, 49; signs and symbols 52–3; 'symbolic attitude' 98–9; symbols 4, 97–8; 'The therapeutic value of abreaction' 69; on theory 7, 51; the therapeutic encounter 82, 88; transcendent function 67–8, 189; transference 84, 85; the Trickster 15; 'Two kinds of thinking' 110; type theory 68, 71–3; *vas bene clausum* 14, 20

Kant, Immanuel 4
Kast, Verena 20
Kernberg, O. F. 36–7, 92
Khan, Masud 161
Kirmayer, L. J. 157
Klauber, J. 54
knowledge: 'implicit relational knowledge' 117; uncertainty tolerance 49, 94; words and knowing 120–1; *see also* not knowing; (the) unknown
Krashen, D. 14

Langs, Robert 103
language: creative relationship to 118; culture and 150–2; of knowing and not knowing 1; metalanguage *see* metalanguage; metaphor *see* metaphor; non-verbal *see* non-verbal communication; in relationship with experience 117–18, 120, 128–9; representationalist theory of 117–18; social position and 152; of symbols and interpretation 51–3, 62 *see also* symbols; words and knowing 120–1
The Language of Psycho-analysis 83
Laplanche, J. and Pontalis, J. B. 83
legislation: codes of practice, ethics and the law 42–4; contracts and 34; and difficulties in supervision 38; disclosure 31
liminal space 4, 5, 14, 23, 99–101
listening: to one's dreams 106; therapeutic 100

McTaggart, Lynne 173
Main, Tom 51
management, boundaries of therapy and 25
mandalisation 50, 55
Martin, Edward 22
massa confusa 14
Masters and Johnson's sex therapy 59
Mattinson, T. 135
Mattoon, Mary Ann 17, 144
Mayman, Martin 179
medical insurance 34, 40
Melville, Herman 165
memory/memories: bombarded facts and memory storage of thoughts 136; collective 154; dream thinking and infantile memory 111; embodiment and 154; evocation of *see* evocation;

meaning and 154; metaphors of memories taken away 87; *Nachträglichkeit* and 91; restructured in the retelling 154; unlocking of 153–4
Menninger, Karl 61
mental functions 7, 71; Animus functions 55; character types and 71–3, 74–5; inferior functions 69, 72, 73, 75, 111, 121
Mental Health Act (1983) 42
mentor archetype 17
Mercury (Hermes) 7, 13, 14–15
merger, boundaries and 14, 19
Merton, Thomas 184
metalanguage 3–4, 52, 57, 58, 59, 60, 62
metanarrative 3–4
metaphor: alchemical metaphor of supervision 5–6; of chewing bus tickets 124–5; metaphysics and 3–5; training metaphor of supervision 6–7; transference and 85
metaphysics 3–5
Miller, Peter 171
mirroring 141; malignant ('mirror reaction') 141–2; in parallel processes 178 *see also* parallel processes
Modell, Arnold 91
motivation, unconscious 135, 141, 143, 149
Mulhern, Alan 92–3
multiculturalism: exposure to multicultural societies 148–9; multicultural group supervision 158–9
mutuality: as analytic organising principle 117; boundaries and 14, 25, 27, 29; mutual choice of partners 167; mutual emotional relating 175; mutual interaction in nature 171; parallel processing *see* parallel processes; in transference 88–9
Myers-Briggs Type Indicator Test (MBTI) 72–3

Nachträglichkeit 90–1
naming 2, 48; and the language of interpretation 51–3; nominalism 121; nominative power 57–8, 59; nominative relations theory 57–8
narrative: metanarrative 3–4; mutuality and 117; postmodernism and 52; transcendent defence 50

Narvaez, R. F. 154
nature, mutual interaction in 171
Neruda, Pablo: 'Lone gentleman' 183–4
Neumann, Erich 98, 108
neurobiology, parallel processing and 173–6
Newtonian physics 170
nominalism 121
nomination *see* naming
nominative power 57–8, 59
nominative relations theory 57–8
non-verbal communication: of the analytic setting 89–90, 100; body awareness and 177; in the caregiver–infant experience 149–50; culture and 150–2
not knowing 1, 7, 50, 94, 98, 123; languages of 1; 'masterly inactivity' in 49; the unknown and the unknowable *see* (the) unknown
note keeping 42–3, 116

Obeyesekere, G. 149
objects: defence against release of bad objects 56; internal 50, 51, 61; objectifying of the body 128–9; positively introjected good objects 94; sense-objects 87; and the symbolic 183, 190; of 'the gap' 100; transferential 101; transformational 127; transitional 100
Ogden, Thomas 118, 120, 126
opposites: *coniunctio oppositorum* 98, 105; enantiodromia (movement between opposites) 54; symbols as synthesis of 98, 105; transcendent function and 67–8
Orange, Donna M. 84
organisational supervision **133–44**; the defining issues 133–7; multiple supervision 140; nodal position of supervision 135, 140; organisational expectations of the supervisee 137–8; organisational expectations of the supervisor 138–9; psychotherapeutic preferences of organisations 139; referrals 139–40; supervising in groups 140–4; taking care of the *temenos* 139–40, 141
Orlans, V. 45

parallel processes 19, 20, 21, 50, 134, **164–80**; amplification and 28; and beginnings of supervision 103; clinical examples 55, 176–9; in context of a 'fourth' 26; contextualisation from nature 170–1; hierarchies and 91; in Jungian analysis and supervision 165–70; neurobiological perspective on 173–6; quantum theory perspective on 172–3; triangular interpretations through 25
patients, difficult *see* difficult patients
peer supervision 22
perception 2, 8, 71; distortion of 84; witness 114, 120, 188
Perry, Christopher 185
persona 14, 17, 143; elements 26, 27; individuation and 68
personal experience, in professional practice 148–50
personal indemnity insurance 33
personal space 90; *see also* safe space
personality disorders 48–9; nominative power and 58
personhood 157
pets 101
Phillips, A. 116, 161–2
play 54
Polden, Jane 44
Popp, F. A. 172
positive connotation 59–60
postmodernism 8, 50, 52–3, 98
potential space 118
predicaments in therapy 47, 123
prima materia 6, 14, 184, 187, 190
a priori environment 3, 47, 53–4, 59, 62; the unconscious as 4, 48, 49, 53
professional development: continuous (CPD) 138; dealing with transference and countertransference in 86–94; in an organsational setting 135, 138; personal development and 17; personal experience and 148–50; supervision and 18, 86–94
Progoff, I. 143
progression: progressive symbols 105; progressive thinking 111
projection 15, 54; countertransference *see* countertransference; objective identification of 24; projected feelings 78; projective identification 48, 54, 61; and relationships within therapeutic organisations 35(Fig.), 36; of the shadow 56; 'spooky' nature of introjection and 170; of the supervisee 104; transference *see* transference
Prophetissa, Maria 6, 18
Proudhon, P. J. and Kropotkin, P. 166
psyche 82–3, 86, 91
Psyche myth 82
psychic space 5–6, 20, 22, 51; *see also* safe space
psychodrama 178
psychodynamics: alpha and beta elements in supervision 136; of parallel processing 165–70
psychological mindedness/symbolic attitude 98–9, 101
Pullman, Philip: *Northern Lights* 85

quantum theory, parallel processing and 172–3
Quenk, A. T. and Quenk, N. L. 79

Rasmussen, S. 154
rationality: rational functions 71, 72; rationalisation 77, 90; transcendent function as bridge between irrationality and 68; western emphasis on rationalism 155; *see also* irrationality
Read, Herbert 17
reconciliation 189–90
record keeping 42–3
Redfearn, Joe 98, 99, 101, 103
referrals 139–40
reflective practice 14
reflective space 45, 48
reframing 59
regression: regressive symbols 105; regressive thinking 111
relational psychoanalysis 164
re-presentation 114, 117–18, 185, 188
representation 114, 128; evocation and 116–18; self-representation and supervision 126–8; and the semiotic and semantic 117; transference/countertransference and 121–2
rescuing urge 49
resentment 90–1
residual transference 109
resistance 108; lack of transference as 88; in training 22

resonance 122, 167, 170, 173–5; attraction and 172
retranscription 91
rivalries: acting out, in group supervision 143; feelings of intrusion and rivalry 90; sibling 57
Rizzolati, Giacomo 174
Rolling Stones 70
Romanyshyn, Robert 179
Rowson, Richard 31

safe space: and intrusion into personal space 90; reflective space 45, 48; *temenos*/hermetic vessel 5–6, 14, 20, 22, 83, 102–4, 112 see also *temenos*; for the three- and fourfold relationship 47
Samuels, A. et al. 68, 183
Samuels, Andrew 176
Saussure, Ferdinand 52
Schaverien, Joy 110
Searles, Harold 166
secrecy 43; *see also* confidentiality
secretaries 100, 101
self: continuity 49, 60, 188; disclosure of 26–9; the Ego–Self axis 19, 20–1, 184; individuation *see* individuation; invarients of 49, 60; primitive defences of 48, 61; and the safe place 14; symbols and 98; in western and non-western therapeutic discourses 157–8
self-authentication 189
self-representation 126–8
self-supervision 107
Sells, B. 45
semiotics 97, 98; representation and the semiotic 117; supervision as a semiotic task 52
sensation: as one of Jung's 'functions' 7, 71; type with strong sensation 71, 72
separateness: boundaries and 14, 16, 19, 29; ending sessions and the handling of separation 100; individuation and separation 57
setting: analytic *see* analytic setting; supervisory *see* supervisory setting
sex therapy 59
sexual abuse 34, 39, 60
the shadow 14, 35, 143; carrying a shadow 50–1; individuation and the acknowledgement of 69; intuition and 49; projections of 56

shamans 157–8
shame 29, 50, 51, 54, 144
Sharp, D. 68
Shearer, Ann 17–18, 24
Shohet, R. and Wilmot, J. 178
shoshin ('beginner's mind) 2, 6, 7, 62
Shweder, Richard 159
sibling rivalry 57
silence 94, 100, 111; indirect communication by 151
Singer-Loomis Inventory of Personality 73
social relationships 37, 40–1
solitude 119
'soul-based ethics' (Sells) 45
space: analytic 122, 126, 128 *see also* analytic setting; safe space; supervisory space; intrusion into personal space 90; liminal 4, 5, 14, 23, 99–101; potential 118; psychic 5–6, 20, 22, 51; reflective 45, 48; relational 45; safe *see* safe space; supervisory *see* supervisory space; the symbolic container 97, 102–4 *see also* hermetic vessel (*temenos*/*vas bene clausum*); 'the gap' 99–101
Spielrein, Sabina 17
spiritual values 62
splitting 48, 61
Spyri, Johanna: *Heidi* 85
Stone, Martin 174, 175
suicide 38, 146–7
supervision: aesthetics of 59; alchemical metaphor of 5–6; as an analytic process 114–29; assessment and 36–7, 81; attention and *see* attention; background to requests for 25, 33–4; beginnings 103–4; boundaries *see* boundaries in supervision; clinical responsibility and 15, 33–4, 139; in the context of individuation **67–79** *see also* individuation; in a cultural context **146–62** *see also* culture; dealing with countertransference 70–3, 75–8; difficulties arising in 38–41 *see also* difficult patients; discrimination and 185, 189; 'dreaming up' the patient in 125–6; ethics *see* ethics in supervision; evaluation of 78; evocation *see* evocation; facilitation 88, 92–3, 108; fantasy and reality of 24–5; finding

coherence 186–90; function and growth process 19; getting the needed supervisee 70; good practice 39, 104, 140, 187; group *see* group supervision; illusion of parental authority 54; intensity 34; interplay of supervisory and analytic relationship *see* parallel processes; keeping alive, well and awake 94; language and vision of 1–2; and the law *see* legislation; as a metanarrative 3–4; naming 48; nature of the craft of 183–4; need to be unhurried 47, 62, 123; in organisations *see* organisational supervision; parallel processes *see* parallel processes; patients as supervisors/critics 107–8; peer 22; poisoned chalice of 135, 140; psychodynamic understanding of alpha and beta elements in 136; re-presentation *see* re-presentation; reflections on clinical scenes and styles of presentation in **113–29**; representation *see* representation; rescuing urge 49; scope of 185–6 *see also* boundaries in supervision; self-representation and 126–8; self-supervision 107; as shared fantasy 125–6, 133–4, 141; social acquaintance and 37, 40–1; stimulating the spirit of enquiry **81–94**; the supervisory alliance 19–20, 24, 118, 126; supervisory contract 13, 32–4, 139; as a symbolic container 97, 102–4 *see also* supervisory space; *temenos*; therapeutic relationships and 17–18, 24, 35–6, 102–4; training metaphor of 6–7; trust and 16, 60, 103; typology and 73–5, 78–9; as working together with the candidate 94, 188

supervisory setting 16, 22, 24, 25, 185, 186–7; disclosure and 26–7; *see also* consulting rooms; supervisory space

supervisory space 5–6, 20, 22, 47, 48, 83, 121–2; evocation in 119, 122–5; in organisational settings 135, 136–7, 140–1; passport into 13–14; potential space 118; as research and rehearsal space 127; as sacred space 135; shared fantasy in 125–6; the symbolic container 97, 102–4; 'the gap' 99–101;

transference/countertransference in 119, 121–2; *see also temenos*

Suzuki, D. T. 7

Suzuki, Shunryu 62

symbolic attitude 98–9, 101

symbolic container 97, 102–4; *see also* hermetic vessel (*temenos/vas bene clausum*)

symbolic transference 108

symbolic transformation 68

symbols 97–9; archetypal *see* archetypes; defences against symbol formulation 61; difficulties and 61; dreams and 99, 104–9; facilitation of the symbolic 108; failure of the symbolic 109–11; and the language of interpretation 51–3, 62; progressive and regressive 105; public symbols and unconscious motivation 149; revelation through live symbols 184–5; signs and 52–3; stories and 4; and 'the gap' 99–101; transference and 105; transformation and 104–9; *see also* semiotics

Symington, N. 55

synchronicity 50

Tarski, Alfred 4, 52

Tarski's theorem 4, 52, 59

Tavistock Clinic, London 148

teaching, therapy and 27–8

temenos 5–6, 22, 135, 139–40; in group format 140–1, 142; as hermetic vessel 5–6, 14, 20, 22, 83, 102–4, 112; Levels I and II 140–2; unconscious motivation in 135, 141; *see also* safe space

theory: guilty attachments to 47, 56, 188; Jung on 7, 51; as a language of interpretation 51–3

therapeutic listening 100

therapeutic organisations: agencies *see* agencies; assessment and supervision in 36–7; complexity of therapeutic relationships in 35–6

therapeutic relationship: as dialectic process 69, 82; ethics and the complexities of 35–6; importance of beginnings 108; supervision and 17–18, 24, 35–6, 102–4; the therapeutic alliance 49, 84; *see also* analytic relationship therapists: boredom 119, 124, 125; countertransference *see* countertransference; getting the needed rather than wanted patient 70, 73–5; health and age 40; irritation 74, 90, 122, 124; personal experience 148–50; understanding, and sense of helplessness from lack of 122–5

therapy: beginnings of sessions 100, 103; endings of sessions 100; fees 22, 100–1, 137; gifts 101–2; importance of beginnings 108; individuation as primary goal of analysis 60, 68–9; jazz metaphor of 61; Jung and the therapeutic encounter 82, 88; and 'the gap' 99–101; therapeutic container *see* hermetic vessel (*temenos/vas bene clausum*)

thought: discursive 120; freedom of 126; mindful awareness and 48; as one of Jung's 'functions' 7, 71; rationality *see* rationality; reality/directive thinking and fantasy/dream thinking 110–11; styles of thinking 143; the thinking type 72

three, number *see* triangles/triads

Throop, C. J. 149

tissues 100

training: areas of tension and potential conflict during 69–73; defacilitation and the production of demons in 92; engagement of transference/countertransference in 70–3, 75–8, 86–94; identity authenticity and 20–1; and the inhibition of creativity 36–7; metaphor of supervision 6–7; multicultural societies and 156; in an organisational setting 135–9 *see also* organisational supervision; personal analysis in analytic training 16; and requests for supervision 33; and the supervisory frame 22

transcendent defence 50

transcendent function 67–8, 189

transference: analytic setting and 89–90; anxiety 116; de-facilitation 90–2, 93; defences 50; definitions and nature of 2, 83–4, 85–6; engagement in training/professional development 86–94; everyday encounters with 85; facilitation 92–3; Freud and 83; informed consent in context of 44; intensity, and character types 88; Jung and 84, 85; lack, as a defence 88; as a mystical experience 176; *Nachträglichkeit* and 90–2; parallel process *see* parallel processes; perversions in the transference relationship 40–1; and relationships within therapeutic organisations 35(Fig.), 36; residual 109; of the supervisee 26, 33, 127; in the supervisory space 119, 121–2; symbolic 108; symbols and 105; transferential objects 101

transformation 104–9; dance of 70, 129; through emotional evocation 122–5

transformational objects 127

transitional objects 100

translation 127–8

triangles/triads: and the 'fourth' 6–7, 18, 25–6, 168–9; individuation and the dialectic process in the supervisory triangle 69–79; parallel processes and 167–8; three as a sacred number 18; triangular interactions between supervision and organisations 135, 137; triangulation and supervision 18, 156

Trickster archetype/qualities 14, 15, 18, 189

trust: and breach of confidentiality 39 *see also* confidentiality; establishment over time 116; safe space for 5–6, 48 *see also* safe space; in supervisory and analytic settings 16, 60, 103; trusting the unconscious 48, 60

truth: contextuality of 8, 51–2; discrimination of 185, 189; finding one's own 186; fundamentalist 58; interpretation and 154–5; metalanguage and 4; 'trivial truths' 56

typology 68, 71–3; misuses of 121; in supervision 73–5, 78–9

Übertragung 83; *see also* transference

Ulanov, Ann 84

uncertainty tolerance 49, 94

the unconscious: archetypes *see* archetypes; collective 53, 62, 88, 98, 183, 184; differentiation of ego-consciousness from 19, 20, 70–1; inquiry into unconscious process 57; as a metaphor 2; parallel processing

interplay with consciousness 166–70 *see also* parallel processes; as the a priori environment 4, 48, 49, 53; psychic space and 5; resonance and 173–5; trusting the unconscious 48, 60
unconscious motivation 135, 141, 143, 149
the unknown: defences against using unknowables as internal objects 61; not knowing *see* not knowing; and the unknowable 48, 50, 52
uroboros 105

vas bene clausum/vas Hermetis 5–6, 14, 20, 22, 83, 102–4, 112; *see also* safe space; *temenos*

Virchow, Rudolf 171
vision: alchemical vision of the *unus mundus* 173; perception *see* perception; a vision of supervision 1–2

waiting rooms 89, 100, 101
Weiner, J. et al. 170
Winnicott, Donald 2, 93–4, 117, 118, 119, 176
witness 114, 120, 188
Wooster, Gerald 100

Young-Eisendrath, P. 49

Zinkin, Louis 24, 125, 133–4, 141–2